ROMAN IMPERIALISM AND LOCAL IDENTITIES

In this book, Louise Revell examines questions of Roman imperialism and Roman ethnic identity and explores Roman imperialism as a lived experience based around the paradox of similarity and difference. Her case studies of public architecture in several urban settings provide an understanding of the ways in which urbanism, the emperor and religion were part of the daily encounters of the peoples in these communities. Revell applies the ideas of agency and practice in her examination of the structures that held the empire together and how they were implicated within repeated daily activities. Rather than offering a homogenized 'ideal type' description of Roman cultural identity, she uses these structures as a way to understand how these encounters differed between communities and within communities, thus producing a more nuanced interpretation of what it was to be Roman. Bringing an innovative approach to the problem of Romanization, Revell breaks from traditional models and cuts across a number of entrenched debates, such as arguments about the imposition of Roman culture or resistance to Roman rule.

A scholar of Roman architecture and Latin epigraphy, Louise Revell is a lecturer in the department of archaeology at the University of Southampton.

ROMAN IMPERIALISM AND LOCAL IDENTITIES

LOUISE REVELL

University of Southampton

CAMBRIDGE
UNIVERSITY PRESS

CAMBRIDGE UNIVERSITY PRESS
Cambridge, New York, Melbourne, Madrid, Cape Town,
Singapore, São Paulo, Delhi, Tokyo, Mexico City

Cambridge University Press
32 Avenue of the Americas, New York, NY 10013-2473, USA

www.cambridge.org
Information on this title: www.cambridge.org/9780521174732

First published 2009
First paperback edition 2010
Reprinted 2011 (twice)

A catalog record for this publication is available from the British Library.

Library of Congress Cataloging in Publication Data
Revell, Louise.
Roman imperialism and local identities / Louise Revell.
    p. cm.
Includes bibliographical references and index.
ISBN 978-0-521-88730-4 (hardback)
1. Rome – History – Empire, 30 B.C.–476 A.D.   2. Rome – Foreign relations –
30 B.C.–476 A.D.   3. Imperialism.   4. Romans – Ethnic identity.
5. Rome – Ethnic relations. I. Title.
DG271.R38   2009
937´.06 – dc22   2008007073

ISBN 978-0-521-88730-4 Hardback
ISBN 978-0-521-17473-2 Paperback

To the memory of my parents

CONTENTS

PREFACE

The book arises out of an interest in how a theorised exploration of social identity might be used to shed new light on Roman imperialism and the unequal power relationships at a local level. Typically, the provinces have been approached through the discourse of Romanization, centred around the idea of cultural change. Consequently, most work has concentrated on the evidence for that transformation, exploring the mechanisms through which such changes occurred, and largely dealing with the initial transitional period. Centred around a Roman-native polarity and the reification of *Romanitas*, this debate has assumed an idealised homogeneity between and within each of the resultant societies after that period of transformation. There has been less work on the variation within communities and the way in which the people of the empire might have experienced Rome after the initial period of annexation. The central question of this book is not 'becoming Roman' but rather 'being Roman': what it was to be Roman, to live and to interact on a daily level within that society. However, I do not want to present this as a homogenous, monolithic experience. There is a danger that we take our archaeological diagnostics of a 'Roman' site, such as glossy red pottery, masonry buildings and coinage, and map them directly onto the people of the past. Instead, by saying that 'Roman' has infinite expressions generated through the varying experiences of the individual peoples of the past, the question I wish to ask is how people lived their lives within the Roman period and how this then constructed a multiplicity of Roman identities.

This book aims to problematize the term 'Roman'. As used to describe an archaeological culture, it has two meanings: one in the present and the other in the past. The majority of Roman archaeologists have concentrated on the problems associated with the former as part of the debate about the term 'Romanization' (e.g., Hingley 2000). However, as we problematize the present meaning of 'Roman', so we come to problematize it in the past. We use the term interchangeably to define a form of material culture, a time span, a geographical location, and a personal ethnicity. These are obviously inter-related, but they are not identical. This leads towards the assumption that there was a paradigm of 'Roman' which was static and unchanging. Instead of a fixed entity, we should think of 'Roman' as a discourse of possibilities, that it could have a myriad of potential interpretations. Yet at the same time, there were certain elements which were common to Roman societies. My aim in this book is to examine these common elements and the aspects of difference within them.

However, when confronting the work of Roman archaeologists, we do not come to the idea of 'Roman' without our own modern, academic preconceptions. The issue of being Roman is tightly bound up within the rhetoric of Romanization; the discourse and the agendas of that debate are so pervasive that they must necessarily provide a contextual framework for this topic. Edward Said has commented that the subject of Oriental studies has been dominated by a single topic: the question of orientalism (Said 1995: 3), and I would argue that in a similar way, Roman archaeology revolves around the subject of Romanization. The question of cultural change, its manifestation and the reasons for it, form a discourse at the heart of the discipline. Even when archaeologists ostensibly deal with an alternative subject, the research frameworks and even the vocabulary they use are already loaded with meanings derived from the Romanization debate. There have been fundamental changes in the theories used to interpret the material evidence, which might be broadly termed as the move from culture history to processualism to post-processualism. Nevertheless, the meta-narrative, or grand theory, of Roman archaeology has remained untouched. The concentration on the topic of Romanization within Roman archaeology has limited the discipline as a whole, leaving little space for the more recent agendas of post-processual archaeology (Laurence 1999a: 388). Thus, the emergence of identity as a research topic within the disciplines of both archaeology and ancient history (and the humanities in general) has been used within Roman archaeology as synonymous with ethnicity. The terminology may be taken on board, but the topics are subsumed within the models for cultural change. Structural properties are considered as part of the process of Romanization, and they are ignored as phenomena within their own right.

This book represents a deconstruction of the term 'Roman'. This term is central to the archaeology of the Roman empire, and yet, paradoxically, it is rarely defined or given meaning. Although both it and the abstraction of *Romanitas* are fundamental, the assumption is that as archaeologists/Romanists, we share a common understanding of the term. Therefore, I shall define how I shall use such terminology throughout this book. I propose to use 'Roman' in its very broadest sense of a person or the material culture of a person who lived within the confines of the Roman empire following the annexation of that area. I shall attempt to reject the concept of 'native', as this term is too value laden in modern studies; instead I prefer 'pre-Roman' or 'non-Roman'. Likewise, the concept of *Romanitas* has a problematic meaning: the use of a Latin term brings with it the aura of authenticity, as though it had meaning in the Roman period (in the same way as *pietas*, *virtus* or *honor*). In fact, it was little used in the Roman period, and absent from works in which Roman authors explored what it was to be a Roman. In spite of this, the term has become pervasive as a term to define Roman culture, suggesting that it has more meaning in the present than the past. For this reason, I shall avoid it and use 'Roman-ness' in its place.

Using these definitions, I explore how the term 'Roman' was made meaningful in the past through some of the structures and ideologies which reproduced a shared understanding of the term. However, at the same time, I explore the tensions or 'give' in the system: how the paradigm breaks down between and within communities. A second theme is that of the relations between the centre and the provinces, and how 'buying into' Roman culture on the part of these provincial communities became one of the ways in which the Roman empire was maintained. My primary evidence is the archaeology of urban public buildings, drawing in the inscriptions and sculpture which adorned them. Consequently, it is not my intention to attempt an overarching narrative of being Roman but instead to concentrate on lives framed through the urban setting. The opening chapter presents a discussion of the background to the research: it expands the ideas presented in this preface, and introduces the material and the case studies. Thereafter, the book falls into two parts. The first examines what might be considered the structures of Roman society. Rather than talking about these as abstract entities, I explore how structures conditioned the activities of communities, and how they were in turn reproduced through the activities of social agents. I focus on ideology, encompassing urban ideology (Chapter 2), the rule of the emperor (Chapter 3) and religion

(Chapter 4). From this I turn to aspects of identity which existed within the overall ethnic Roman identity, and how personal identity was not a given but something negotiated on a daily level through interaction with others of similar or different identities. In Chapter 5, I explore the nature of status, in particular the construction of the elite, adult male. Finally, in Chapter 6, I pull these disparate strands together. I make no claims for reconstructing the truth of any single experience of being Roman, only for how being Roman was always different.

ACKNOWLEDGEMENTS

As ever, this book was produced with the help and support of a large number of people. It is based on my doctoral thesis, which was funded through studentships from the University of Durham, and then from the Arts and Humanities Research Board. An extensive research visit to Spain through the Socrates project was funded by the Rosemary Cramp Fund. Additional funding to turn this into a book was provided by the University of Southampton. The research for this thesis was carried out at the Universities of Durham, Southampton and Complutense, Madrid. My thanks go to all the staff and students: they are too many to mention individually by name, but without their friendship and support, this would have been impossible.

Thanks go to the various people with whom I have discussed (and ranted about) the ideas behind this book, including Tim Champion, John Creighton, Annabel Field, Pam Graves, Pete Guest, Vedia Izzet, Simon James, Matthew Johnson, Ray Laurence, Jason Lucas, John Pearce, Jeremy Taylor and Imogen Wellington. Penny Copeland redrew the images, and Simon Keay generously supplied multiple photographs. I would also like to thank Beatrice Rehl at Cambridge University Press, Peter Katsirubas at Aptara, and the anonymous reviewers for comments and suggestions. Michelle, Alison, Annabel, Julia, Pam, Jackie, Emma and Sue all provided encouragement throughout.

I would also like to thank the examiners of my doctorate, Simon Keay and Greg Woolf, for their suggestions and help in turning this into a book, and my supervisor, Martin Millett, for his support, advice and help throughout, and for making me believe that I could do it.

Finally, I give thanks to my family, the extended Revell clan. But most especially to my parents, for their love and encouragement throughout, but who did not see the final result, this book is dedicated to their memory.

LIST OF ILLUSTRATIONS

ONE

THE CONTEXT OF THE ARGUMENT

1.1 INTRODUCTION

Archaeology is based upon labels: from the artefact in the museum case to the culture we are describing, we provide it with a label. This seemingly small and unproblematic description encompasses much: a geographical area, a time period, or a group of people, often all three. Such labelling activity is rooted in the origins of archaeology as a discipline, and in spite of recent disquiet about their usefulness, it is still central to the way we communicate and practise archaeology. The problem is that a label is more than a neutral shorthand, but forms the fundamental core of the way in which we conceptualise the world, past or present. If we describe a pot as Bronze Age, or Minoan, or Anglo-Saxon, we are assigning it a category which fits into our divisions of cultures in the past, and our understanding of their relationship with others. Therefore, if we describe a pot as Roman, we are grouping it together with a series of other pots and artefacts we recognise as Roman. The problem with this approach is that when we are using such a label to describe Roman material culture, we are using it to describe a set of material which is far spread in time and in space. Yet it has increasingly been recognised that when we examine the material culture in detail, there is similarity, but not homogeneity, both in form and patterns of use. We can account for differences over time through a series of sub-categories, such as republican, early imperial, or late imperial. The differences over space are more difficult: there is no simple equation between the extent of Roman rule, Roman material culture, and by analogy, Roman identity.

Within the traditional teleological paradigm of Romanization, there was an apparent explanation for this problem. As society was conceived as evolutionary, the development from 'pre-Roman' to 'Roman' was underway, but was at various stages incomplete, leaving a blend of the two. With the re-examination of this paradigm in the last two decades, the idea of regionality has become dominant, with a series of works examining the process of Romanization in groups of provinces or smaller areas (for example, Millett 1990b on Britain; Alcock 1993 on Greece; Keay 1995 on Spain; Woolf 1998 on Gaul; also papers in Keay and Terrenato 2001, reviewed by Mattingly 2002). However, these have described the variability more than accounting for it, with the implicit assumption that this variability is a consequence of the starting point, i.e., the indigenous culture. A number of theoretical approaches have been used to explain this (e.g., creolization, post-colonial theory, models of assimilation and resistance), but they are still drawn towards the idea of bounded cultural identities of Roman and pre-Roman, and the ability to label material culture as more one or the other, a hybrid of recognisable constituent parts.

However, until very recently the question which had not been fully thought through is whether we should expect homogeneity within a widespread political or even cultural group. In the case of globalization in the modern world, Hobsbawm has argued that there are some goods which are truly global (such as Coca-Cola), but others which are positional or local (tickets to the opera at La Scala), thereby producing shared global material culture, and regional material culture (Hobsbawm 1999: 62–6, especially 64–6). The paradox which Hobsbawm identified as part of globalization is also a structural part of the Roman empire. There are certain things which we can think of as shared amongst the various groups of peoples (for example, amphora containing oil, wine or fish sauce), but there are also aspects which will remain truly local (regional pottery such as Black Burnished Ware) or restricted to certain social groups (use of silver tableware). Therefore, rather than expecting homogeneity within the archaeology of the provinces of the empire, we need to acknowledge that there is an inherent paradox of similarity and variability, thereby accepting that this is a fundamental part of a Roman ethnic identity.

To be Roman was a discourse rather than an absolute. It was a discourse based upon a shared idea of being Roman (Woolf 1998: 7–16). However, in the absence of the globalising technologies of the modern period, the convergence of this discourse would be less absolute than we might expect today. As an inhabitant of the provinces would likely never see the city of Rome, or even Italy, they did not have the means of comparison available to the modern commentator, who can put together the material remains of the entire empire. Therefore, we should not think of this as a uniform or unified discourse. We need to explore how some structures were shared as part of membership of the Roman cultural group, and other elements remained localised without contradicting such a Roman identity. It is clear that certain aspects were shared, such as political organisation or religious practice, but others were not, such as age and gender structures (Hopkins 1983; Revell 2005). For this reason, this book represents an exploration of what it was to be Roman: which structures were shared between the different groups, how they were enabled through the architectural surroundings, and consequently, how they are manifested within the material remains of the archaeological record.

What it was to be Roman was talked about in the textual sources, but it was also something worked through in the everyday activities of the peoples of the provinces. The archaeological record is the remains of the material which was caught up in such activities: it is the medium and the product of human action. For archaeologists, this means that as we study the material remains, we need to consider the ways in which they were bound up in social practice. This book is primarily concerned with the public architecture of the Roman empire. However, rather than an art-historical approach, I shall consider the ways in which it formed the spatial setting for these activities, and thus became bound up in the discourse of being Roman. This is not to privilege the architectural evidence as being somehow specially representative of Roman identity; rather I have selected one particular form of evidence to provide an in-depth study. It is usual in lengthy discussions of Roman imperialism and Roman identity to consider multiple forms of evidence (e.g., Millett 1990b; Woolf 1998; Mattingly 2006). Whilst this has proved a fruitful approach, the interpretation I shall present rests upon the detailed analysis of public architecture within towns. There is a fundamental connection between identity and everyday activities (or performances) within a communal setting (Goffmann 1965: 28–82): it is through these that we understand both our own and other people's place within any community. The public buildings which form our archaeological evidence are implicated in the maintenance of identity as the settings within which these performances are enacted (ibid. 32–4). With these ideas in mind, we can move from seeing an amphitheatre or a baths as being diagnostic of cultural change, to being bound up in the ongoing maintenance of a Roman identity.

In order to reconstruct the social background and aspects of use of these public spaces, I shall also draw in the epigraphic evidence, in particular religious and political inscriptions. These form a natural adjunct to the public architecture, as they were bound up in the fabric of the public spaces of the towns (Revell in press). These types of inscriptions were spatially located in the public areas, such as temples or fora, and they were an integral part of political processes such as magistracies and munificence (Mackie 1990), and religious worship through dedication (Beard 1991). They provide a means to explore the kinds of activities which were carried out in the public spaces of the towns, and the ways in which certain people strove to highlight or strengthen their social position within these societies.

This study will consider in detail a series of urban sites from three provinces: Baetica, Tarraconensis and Britannia. These have been selected to represent the variability rather than the homogeneity of the urban context within the Roman empire: from the monumental splendour of Italica, to the apparent bareness of Caerwent. Studies of Roman imperialism tend to concentrate on single provinces, or groups of provinces which fall into modern political boundaries; there are fewer extended works which consider more disparate provinces (one exception is Cepas 1989). My aim here is to explore the similarities and differences between towns in the Iberian peninsula and Britain, transcending boundaries constructed by ancient administration and modern academic tradition. The danger is that it would be very easy to slip into a centre-periphery model, perpetuating the split between the (geographically) central Mediterranean provinces and the peripheral north-western provinces. Geography then becomes the only explanation for this variability, rather than a potential factor in questions of social and cultural closeness and distance. This underlying dualism is countered by extending the examination to cover a range of urban centres; thus it will be possible to take the question of variability beyond the issue of regionality.

This study takes an explicitly synchronic perspective. Due to the dominance of the underlying paradigm of cultural change (Romanization) in Roman archaeology, there is a tendency to write the archaeology of the provinces as a historical narrative from the pre-Roman society to either the height of Roman influence or the loss of Roman control during the late imperial period (again, Millett 1990; Richardson 1996; a notable exception is Woolf 1998; see Revell 2002 for a critique of this approach). As this study is concerned with what it was to share in a Roman identity, the exploration of a single time period is more appropriate. Therefore, I shall focus on the first half of the second century AD, after the initial process of conquest in all three provinces, and when the process of cultural change was visible. This is not to claim that by this point Romanization was complete, but rather that the effects of cultural change were visible in all the case studies. Taking such a snap-shot approach is problematic when dealing with the epigraphic evidence, most obviously due to the problems of dating inscriptions. As they provide useful evidence about the ongoing use of the buildings, I apply less rigid chronological criteria.

There are three areas in which I believe we can identify a shared idea of Roman-ness: urbanism, the emperor, and religious practice. These were not the only structures which were tied up in the spread of Roman identity; ideologies of eating and drinking, or economic activity could also be considered in the same way. Nor are these three areas privileged above other possibilities, as somehow being more diagnostically Roman. These ideologies were reproduced in everyday activities, and the daily surroundings of the public buildings were the product of these ideas, but also were bound up in the rituals which perpetuated them. Although these three ideas were shared, they were not identical across space. Therefore the variability in the repeated architectural styles becomes a way to explore the paradox of similarity and difference: which elements of these ideologies were shared, but also where the 'give' or tension existed within the structures.

However, to concentrate solely on the idea of Roman identity and Romanization risks downplaying other aspects of identity and local hierarchies. Such ideologies also allowed for varied experiences within local societies, and so became a new way to understand differences within communities. Thus different groups, whether formed through age, status, gender, profession or legal status, would also be differentiated in part through the same social structures. This leads us to the multivocality and discrepant experience of the architectural setting. Religious or political activity was bound up in the reproduction of Roman identity, but at the same moment, it was part of the maintenance of more local hierarchies. Therefore, in the final part of this book, I shall take the activities and ideas presented within the discussion of these ideologies and use them to explore different experiences of being Roman, and in particular the way in which these Roman structures privileged certain aspects of identity, most especially the adult, free, wealthy male.

1.2 THE MODERN CONTEXT OF ROMAN IDENTITY

Since the late nineteenth century, the dominant theme of Roman provincial archaeology has been the question of cultural change within the context of Roman imperialism. It arose within the particular historical setting of the imperial ethos of the modern nation-states, and as such its leading proponents were embedded within the ideology of empire and civilizing ethos. I do not want to undertake a lengthy deconstruction of the work of the scholars such as Mommsen, Haverfield and Collingwood (see for example, Freeman 1997; Hingley 2000). However, as Richard Hingley has noted, the effect of this on the discipline overall has been a concentration on two particular themes: the incorporation of the provinces into the political system of Rome, and the cultural transformations we term Romanization (Hingley 1991: 91–2). At this early stage, the prevailing paradigm was one of the replacement of one homogenous, static cultural system by another, equally homogenous and static, the language used to denote these two systems was seen as unproblematic and all-encompassing (it should be noted that at this time, it was not a problem unique to Roman archaeology, but was a way of thinking running through the study of all archaeological periods). The narrative was framed around discrete entities labelled 'Roman' and 'native' and these were seen as both describing and explaining the material remains. These were fixed givens with an inherent essentialism, with little questioning of their usefulness or appropriateness. The result for much of the twentieth century has been that the study of the archaeology of the Roman provinces has been based upon a single research agenda with a model of two opposing cultures, each with its own discrete material typologies. Whilst there are a number of problems with this approach to the cultural change visible within the archaeology of the provinces, they can be boiled down to three key assumptions. The first is that it is based upon the fundamental idea of bounded, autonomous groups which can be identified through key diagnostic forms of material culture. The second is that the model of cultural change is teleological, with a defined arrival point of Roman-ness. And thirdly, this was seen within a paradigm of social evolution, where 'native' and 'Roman' were stages on a progression to modernity; as such Roman was somehow better or more civilized than pre-Roman.

In the last 20 years, the question of Romanization has become a contested topic within Roman archaeology, largely as a reaction to Martin Millett's hypothesis of elite-driven cultural change (Millett 1990a, 1990b). Millett argued that, rather than an imposition from the incoming conquerors, the native elite adopted Roman material culture and ways of living as a response to the changing political realities, and these changes then filtered through society as a result of emulation of the elites by the non-elites:

> I have traced the development of Romanization in terms of the aspirations of the tribal elites first becoming Roman and distinguishing themselves from their peoples. Then, as Romanitas permeated the whole of society, its different forms and expansions became key to an understanding of the power structures within the province as the aristocracy indulged in various forms of display through their art, buildings, and manners. (Millett 1990b: 212)

Whilst Millett's work has been influential in producing a more critical debate about the nature of cultural change within the provinces, it has been criticised on two accounts. The first is that it perpetuates many of the problems with the social evolution model, such as the centrality of the Roman/native binary opposition, and the second that it downplays the unequal relationship between the imperial authorities and the conquered peoples (Freeman 1993; Hingley 2005: 40–6; Mattingly 2006: 13–16). This has led to most archaeologists adopting one of two positions with respect to Romanization: those who accept it as valid concept, although in need of some reworking (for example, Keay and Terrenato 2001 argue for weak Romanization), and those who argue that it should be abandoned completely (Barrett 1997; Woolf 1998; Mattingly 2006). It has also produced a fragmentation of approaches to the subject, with a range of theoretical bases, most based within the overarching school of post-processual archaeology, such as discrepant experiences (Mattingly 2006), creolization (Webster 2001, 2003) and agency (Barrett 1997; Revell 1999; Gardner 2002). At the same time, it has led to more explicit approaches to the role of material culture within our interpretations of cultural change through a detailed consideration of the relationship between typology and context (for example, Willis 1997; Eckardt and Crummy 2006).

At the same time, Roman archaeology has been part of wider archaeological (and social) debates about the nature of identity in the past. Rather than constituting a homogenised debate, it has been addressed by archaeologists coming from a range of theoretical schools (compare Barrett 1994; Tilley 1994; Thomas 1996; Fowler 2004). Nevertheless, there are a number of key ideas which are shared by most of these approaches: identity is multiple, fluid and situational; practice forms the point of reproduction of individual identity; material culture is implicated in the internalization and the expression of identity (Jones 1997; Díaz-Andreu and Lucy 2005). This has a number of far-reaching consequences for our models of cultural change (Barrett 1997; Hill 2001): a Roman identity is not a fixed point to be reached, but rather a more fluid concept which needs to be continuously worked at through the routines of everyday life. Consequently, material culture does not represent a particular form of identity, but is brought into the maintenance of that identity through these repeated routines. Furthermore, because we internalize our sense of who we are and how we fit into the world through these routines and the material culture, self-identity is fundamental, and a Roman identity cannot be seen as a superficial veneer, cast off at will. Finally, as any single person's identity is an amalgam of a number of different elements, such as their gender, age, status, occupation, religion and layers of ethnicity, there is a tension between the individual identity and the group identity, with the possibility of variance. So, for example, not all of the women within a single society will have an identical experience of their female identity, but it will be internalized through the same discourse, fragmenting as it overlaps with their age or status. Therefore identity becomes more of a position within a range of possibilities (or discourse) rather than a fixed set of givens.

Such critical approaches have led to a reorientation of research on the subject of identity in the Roman period. Initially much of this work concentrated on the question of ethnicity, leading to the accusation that the topic was being subsumed into models of cultural change, and that other aspects of identity, in particular gender were being ignored (for example, Laurence 1999a: 388). More recently, this has begun to change, and other discrete elements of identity have been looked at, such as military identity (Haynes 1999; James 1999) and age (Gowland 2001; Revell 2005). Others have begun to consider more explicitly the way in which these intersect and break down a paradigm of Roman-ness (Hingley 2005). In this vein, David Mattingly has argued for three major group (or discrepant) identities for Roman Britain: the army, urban communities and rural dwellers (Mattingly 2006, in particular 520–8). Similarly, Andrew Gardner identifies three levels of Roman identity from the global level of ethnicity, or military identity, to a mid-scale of gender or age, down to the micro-level of individual identity (Gardner 2002). He argues that ultimately, as identity is multi-dimensional, any investigation of identity also needs to take place through multiple scales of analysis.

My own work lies within this post-Romanization intellectual climate (if it can be described as such), and as such is not intended to be another book about Romanization. Rather, I am interested in Roman identity as a discourse, and the ways in which it was formulated within a series of social discourses, and how these connected with power relations at both a global and a local level. There is a tendency within many of the studies on Roman identity to concentrate on the relationship between the agent and the material culture, and less attention has been paid to the relationship between the person and the wider social structures. As I shall outline in the next section, these need to be seen in tandem, as two parts of a single process. Certain structures, such as urbanism or religion, were bound up in Roman imperialism, but they were also part of the ongoing maintenance of a shared Roman identity. Someone living within the empire internalized their sense of being Roman through the repetitious actions bounded by such structures. Therefore, through these mundane activities, they actively recreated their own identity, at the same time as they reproduced the social structures which held the empire together. This approach has the effect of transforming Roman imperialism from an abstraction comprising certain social structures to being the product of the decisions and the actions of the people who formed that empire, both those possessing administrative authority (such as the emperor and provincial governors) and those being administered. This is not to deny that these were very unequal relationships, and that there was a power imbalance between them. Therefore when we are dealing with the question of Roman identity, we are also confronting processes of imperialism and the nature of power within the Roman empire.

We also need to move away from thinking of Roman-ness as a homogenous identity. As both John Barrett and Greg Woolf have argued, it is better viewed as a discourse which could encapsulate numerous different experiences (Barrett 1997; Woolf 1997). As each person's identity encompasses a number of variables other than their ethnic identity, and as that identity will change through their lifetime, we lose the fixed point (or indices) at the end of the Romanization process (Mattingly 2004: 10–11 for an example of this fluidity). However, as we cannot disregard the question of what it was to be a Roman within the imperial context, we are left with the challenge of how to approach it. The solution adopted here is to look for the elasticity within these social structures. There is an inherent paradox in that the things which bound the empire together and created a group identity which can be broadly seen as 'Roman', also formed the way in which any homogeneity was fractured. Thus, by incorporating both agent and structure within the interpretation, we can locate this elasticity without trying to force it into a binary opposition of 'Roman' or 'non-Roman'. The forces which created this give within the system occurred at a multitude of levels, and can be seen as enabling different kinds of identity without undermining an overall empire-wide identity.

1.3 STRUCTURATION THEORY AND ITS APPLICATION TO ROMAN ARCHAEOLOGY

The analysis within this book is based upon ideas of agency and structuration, as elaborated by Anthony Giddens (1984). A number of archaeologists have discussed the main principles and its applicability to archaeology (including Barrett 1988; Graves 1989; Johnson 1989; Shanks and Tilley 1992; Dobres and Robb 2000), and to the Roman period in particular (Barrett 1997; Gardner 2002); therefore, rather than repeating this work, I want to explore the ways in which it provides a means of interpreting the spread of Roman imperialism. Structuration theory provides a powerful way of understanding human action and interaction, and how these feed into the reproduction of society. Giddens argues that social structure and individual lives should not be seen as a dichotomy, with one taking precedence over the other. Instead they form a duality, each the precondition and the product of the other (Giddens 1984: 25). In reifying society and social structures as discrete entities, or privileging human action over structural restraints, a false division is set up which obscures this symbiosis. In contrast, within Giddens' argument, they cannot be separated, but instead have a relationship of mutual dependency: social structures constitute the framework for social agents and their actions, providing a range of appropriate behaviours in their daily activities. In turn, these daily activities, routinely carried out, reproduce social structures, and ultimately the social systems themselves.

This idea of the duality of structure and agent allows us to move beyond traditional interpretations for Roman imperialism as either the product of individual intervention, or grand structural systems. We can explore the way in which the people of the empire acquired new ways of acting as the wider social conditions changed; also how their identification with a distant political force was mediated through their daily activities of going about their lives. Conversely, these lives were not lived in a vacuum, and as the socio-political context changed, so their technologies of living necessarily could not remain static. They became constrained by new ways of being and new understandings of their place in the world. The social structures of Roman imperialism bound the various peoples of the empire together. They enabled the reproduction of society on two levels: at a local level of face-to-face interaction, but also at an empire-wide level of shared experience and imagined commonality. The potency of this approach is that it allows us as Roman archaeologists to explore and explain these two levels of social reproduction without a conflict between them. We can analyse aspects of the social structure on both a local and a global level.

This brings us to the question of agents and agency. People in the past should not be seen as mindless automata with their actions dictated by social structures, but rather as possessing the complex skills and knowledge of how to function within their immediate situations (Giddens 1984: 281–5). Agency describes the capacity of a person to act: to make a difference to the situation whether intentional or not. The people of the empire are not victims of the forces of Romanization, but are Roman insofar as they act in a way which can be interpreted as reproducing Roman social systems, a Roman identity, and ultimately, Roman power. The discourse of Romanization has been plagued by issues of conscious intention. Did the peoples of the provinces think of themselves as Roman? Did they deliberately aim to become Romanized? In one sense this question is a red herring. Their adapting to life within the Roman empire, altering their previous ways of living, was a result of their awareness that new customs were necessary to function within a new imperial landscape. And whether intended or not, they lived in a manner which in some way reproduced the Roman system and Roman power. The mundane repetition of their daily lives served to reproduce a political structure and social system over the distances of the empire.

Dealing with agency brings with it the question of knowledge. We are increasingly used to the idea that the literate classes within the empire talked and wrote about their society. The different literary genres share at their core a problematization and a discussion of what was the correct way to live, with an implicit moral tone. Ancient historians have used the remains of these textual sources as a way to reconstruct these concerns, and something of the knowledge held by the elite classes about what it was to be Roman. The problem which faces anyone trying to track the issue of Roman identity within the provinces is how far the people of the provinces were aware of these textual debates: if they had no knowledge of Cicero or Virgil, did they know the meaning of their newly acquired practices, or were they just following what everyone else did? The idea of different forms of knowledge releases us from this dilemma. Giddens argues that there are two forms of knowledge: discursive and practical. In certain situations, people may be unable to describe the reasons for their actions, but at a practical level, they have the knowledge of how to function in their daily existence (Giddens 1984: xxiii). Thus, the textual sources may tell us that the reason for women being banned from officiating over sacrifice is the ancient law of Romulus forbidding them from butchering meat. This may have been debated by the Roman authors, such as Plutarch in the *Roman Questions*, but it is less clear how far this justification was appreciated by the people of the provinces. Instead, they may have been aware of the correct way to sacrifice, and by extension, that it was not appropriate for women to act in an authoritative capacity on such occasions. Their practical knowledge of how to act reproduced a series of Roman social structures: structures of religion, gender and power. This practical knowledge was important for the spread of Roman identity across the vastness of the empire, and it is this which is more easily traced within the archaeological record.

The idea of action has been implicit throughout: the moment of performance is also the moment of reproduction, of both the conditions which govern the action and the agent's understanding of themselves and their world. These routine actions of daily life are founded in encounters and interaction with others, and can be viewed as a form of communication, both in the immediate situation and across time-space. Thus, repetitive routines contain the elements which will reaffirm the structures of society and a person's own identity, grounded in social norms (Giddens 1984: 60; see also Goffmann 1956). These encounters depend upon the spatiality of the body: its positioning, gestures, dress and relationship to others. The awareness and experience of the body lie at the centre of human consciousness, and the familiarity surrounding these encounters leads to a sense of ontological security (Giddens 1984: 64–8). Goffmann (1956) similarly sees social practice as being central to the recreation of personal identity and social structure. Using the extended metaphor of a theatrical performance, Goffmann analyses the techniques a person uses to present a specific image of themselves and to control the impression others have of them according to communally held social rules. He argues that this performance intentionally or unintentionally incorporates the spatial setting and associated material, drawing upon not only their function but also any symbolic meaning (ibid. 34–6). In this way, the architectural remains of the past are part of human action and human experience, and acknowledging this underpins the analysis for my argument.

From this perspective, the inhabitants of the Roman empire are no longer unthinking pawns within an imperial system. Rather, they are Giddens' knowledgeable social agents, using their practical and discursive knowledge to get by within their world. Their interaction, movement and use of specific artefacts, for example, provide the means for negotiating identities within and in opposition to other groups within society:

> [W]e move away from asking 'what kinds of people made these conditions?', to an understanding of what the possibilities were of being human within those material and historical conditions. An archaeological engagement with the past now becomes an attempt to understand how, under given historical and material conditions, it may have been possible to speak and act in certain ways and not in others, and by so doing to have carried certain programmes of knowledge and expectation forward in time. (Barrett 1994: 5)

The public architecture of the Roman past forms the space within which people of the Roman empire lived part of their lives. It becomes a resource bound up in the performance, and the layout and decoration of the buildings are actively used in the reproduction of any individual identity. The analysis of such buildings revolves around the reconstruction of the ways in which they framed such activities: the physical and symbolic markers which are incorporated into their daily use. Such markers include the decoration of the building, issues of visibility (both seeing and being seen), access and ease of access, and the times when areas can be accessed.

One of the key themes running through this book is that of ideology: not in the narrow sense of political ideologies, but in the broader concept of beliefs about how the world should be organized. Ideologies underpinned the shared culture of the empire: ideas of the correct ways of living, hierarchies of social position and political power, all expressed through the shared material culture of provincial societies. At one level, they linked the peoples of the empire through a set of common beliefs. However, they also served to justify one particular view within the wider discourse, and in doing so legitimate the unequal power relations within that society. They upheld the social order through making it seem inevitable and somehow right, even to those who are denied access to power by those very ideologies (Shanks and Tilley 1982; Miller and Tilley 1984). Therefore, we need to examine how particular ideologies formed part of the workings of Roman imperialism, upholding the unequal relations between the imperial authorities and the provinces. Ideology served to represent the world from the perspective of one section of society, promoting their particular interests, be it the imperial authorities in Rome, or the more local-based hierarchical relations. However, it was not merely a superficial image: ideology in its various aspects was a powerful structuring principle of Roman communities. The ideological viewpoint had a moral foundation and presented social discourse as natural and inevitable, often justified through the idea of a past golden age of simplicity and social order. Thus, gender ideologies and the power of the male head of the family were based on a legal discourse which took the laws of Romulus as their validation (Lefkovitz and Fant 1992: 94–7 for the relevant excerpts from the Laws of the Kings and the Twelve Tables). The use of the iconic founder of Rome provided a justification for the established order, and as gender relations shifted during the late Republic and first centuries of the principate, provided a moral authority based on the weight of tradition.

Within the duality of agent and structure, ideology forms a discourse through which social conditions and social experiences were reproduced (Shanks and Tilley 1982: 130–2). Ideological representations of the world are embedded in the social system through the daily activities or rituals, and in turn are the conditions which frame these activities. Thus, ideology and power are bound up with the idea of practice (or praxis), reproduced by action and existing in the practical knowledge of how to act within a particular social context. They may become part of the discourse of that society, and its members may be able to elaborate on why it should be so. To return to the prohibition on women sacrificing, this ideology was acted out in the frequent religious rituals both within the house and in public festivals, and on each occasion the relative positions of men and women were worked through and reproduced through the performance of such rituals, and the implicit acknowledgement that this was appropriate. We can trace from the textual evidence how this discourse is formulated and debated (for example, Feeney 1998). However, this is not to place the primacy of text over archaeology: the material products of the archaeological record were an integral part these daily activities, and as such are bound up within the same discourse (Shanks and Tilley 1982: 132; Miller and Tilley 1984: 14). Archaeological evidence such as temple architecture, altars and priestly paraphernalia were imbued with gendered meaning, and were implicated in the moment of performance. However, this particular ideology contained certain tensions and ambiguities, and did not form a coherent and unproblematic discourse (Asad 1979: 620). There were occasions when women might take a more prominent role within religious festivals, threatening the established positions, and creating a tension within the structure which needed careful policing (Scheid 1992 for details of such occurrences). We should not assume that ideology was either an accurate reflection of reality or true experience, or a system of false beliefs (Asad 1979: 621–2; similarly, Barrett 1994: 77): as a discourse, its position within social knowledge was more subtle.

In applying this theoretical approach to the Roman empire, I aim to move beyond the sterile dichotomies inherent within the Romanization debate: of non-Roman/Roman, imposition/adoption, acceptance/resistance. My concern is with the way in which Roman power and Roman culture were actively reproduced at a local level through the agency of those incorporated within its sphere of influence. The peoples of the empire were constrained by a structure, or structuring principles, which increasingly became part of the discourse of Roman culture. However, by their actions and their practical knowledge of how to act in new situations, they reproduced those structures at a local level. The day-to-day encounters within the provincial town formed the point of reproduction, when the power of Rome was recreated in the lives of its subjects.

1.4 APPROACHES TO BUILDINGS AND INSCRIPTIONS

My argument lies in a detailed analysis of the public architecture within provincial towns. Roman architecture and architectural decoration have long been seen as an emblematic or diagnostic feature of Roman culture and Roman identity. Moreover, architecture is seen as one of the aesthetic contributions of the period, and because of this, its study has largely been seen as the preserve of the art historian. Even when discussed within an explicitly archaeological context, until recently archaeologists have adhered to this conventional discourse, perpetuating these restricted agenda. This approach is not restricted to Roman archaeology, but it has profoundly influenced the way Roman archaeologists have approached buildings and architectural space. However, if we are to explore the way in which the use of such buildings is part of the construction of Roman identities, we need to question whether the traditional approach is in fact the most useful. In this section, I wish to provide a critique of some aspects of traditional scholarship on Roman buildings, before moving on to consider recent developments within the discipline, focusing on their impact on public architecture in particular.

As stated above, until recently the study of Roman buildings has tended to be carried out within paradigms of art history. This can be seen within two distinct areas: firstly, the way in which the physical remains of the architecture are studied and written about, and secondly, the underlying discourse (or meta-narrative) through which the buildings are interpreted. Whilst these constraints can most clearly be observed in synthetic books on Roman architecture, which deal with broad themes, historical trends and large numbers of buildings, they also provide the dominant discourse for the way archaeological reports deal with individual buildings. The subjective description and evaluation of the archaeologist in the report reproduces the language and agenda of the art historian. To write about buildings is essentially to describe the constituent parts in a pseudo-objective manner, concentrating upon the minutiae of the decoration at the expense of the whole. Thus, a typical example of this approach is the following description of the entablature of the Temple of Vespasian:

> The frieze with relief bucrania and sacrificial vessels and implements is capped by enriched egg and acanthus leaf mouldings, dentils with 'spectacles' between and a prominent egg and dart. The modillions have heavy acanthus cladding and there is a rosette in each coffer between. The corona has a tongue moulding and is separated from the sima by a cyma reversa decorated with linked palmettes.   (Sear 1982: 147)

Individual elements are removed from their context and then used to construct typologies such as Strong's study of column bases in Hadrianic Rome (1953). These might then be used to study the distribution of particular styles (for example Wilson Jones 1989 on the distribution of Corinthian capitals), or the relationship between them (Blagg 2002 on the military and civilian architecture). However, as with all typologies, there is the danger that we lose the social context which made them significant in the past. For buildings in particular, we lose the temporal dimension: there is no sense of a past construction, present use or future modifications. Similarly it divorces the building from the activities carried out within it (the separation of the aesthetic from the functional) and the people who used it. Hidden within this image of objective description is a careful selection of examples and an unstated aesthetic ideal against which all Roman buildings are measured. The ideal is taken as the form which appears in Rome or central Italy. Provincial architecture, rather than being considered on its own merits, is treated in relation to this ideal (for example, Wilson Jones 2000: 153).

These problems are further compounded by the underlying academic discourse which has been used in the past. Although this meta-narrative has mainly been applied to the representational art forms, such as sculpture or painting, the assumptions behind it have influenced the way in which architecture is viewed. This is essentially the discourse of advancement, climax and decline, and operates on two levels with respect to Roman architecture. The first story is that of the advancement of art from the archaic *kouros* to the flowering of realistic representation in fifth- and fourth-century Greece (specifically Athens), with a gradual decline during the Roman period. This narrative has a long pedigree, dating from Vasari's writings in the sixteenth century, justifying the Renaissance movement away from the Medieval style (Elsner 1995: 13), but its most influential advocate in the twentieth century has been Ernst Gombrich (1995, first edition published in 1950). Gombrich advocates the idea of a 'Greek revolution' during the classical period, with the creation of naturalistic art form. From then, there is a gradual decline, until its disappearance in the Late Empire to be replaced by the less naturalistic forms of Christian art (ibid. 65–93 for the Greek/Roman 'story'). Thus, fifth-century BC Athens is the ideal, and Roman art is merely an imitative copy. This view of the inferiority of Roman to Greek is long standing, as illustrated in the assumption that the best Roman art is merely a copy of Greek, or the result of the migration of Greek artists to Rome (this narrative is explicit throughout Toynbee 1965 and more recently Grant 1995; see MacDonald 1982: 192–4 and Gazda 1991a: 2–3 and f/n 5 for a fuller critique). There was an undeniable influence of Greek art and architecture on the Romans, specifically during the Augustan and Hadrianic periods, which included the movement of artists and architects from Greece to Rome, but we need to remove this from a discourse of artistic evolution, and examine it as a phenomenon in its own right (for example, Gazda 2002 on the changing approaches to *aemulatio* and copying).

The second trend is within Roman art itself, and follows a similar evolutionary narrative from the primitive art of the Early Republic, through to the apogee during the period from Augustus to Hadrian, with the gradual decline until the transition to 'Late Antique'. Thus, the dominant presentational form for Roman architecture is a chronological narrative of gradual development and improvement, with a concentration on the early imperial period. In contrast to the narrative of post-medieval architecture which is structured by the biography of the architect, in Roman architecture the framework is the biography of the emperors, historical events and political change (Sear 1982; Stamper 2004). However, any connection between political power and architectural building is implicit, the possible relationship between them is not always fully explored (notable exceptions being Hannestad 1986; Zanker 1988). There are a number of possible reasons for this, such as the lack of named architects making it difficult to understand development through a biography of their work (Wilson Jones 2000: 19–21), the emphasis on Rome as the paradigm for Roman architecture, and the most iconic architecture of the Roman period dating to the early imperial period, for which we can document the political activities of the emperors. Whilst this does not necessarily invalidate constructing a narrative in this way, it has had the effect of dominating the ways in which we approach the material remains.

However, in a post-modern climate, such narratives have now been found unsatisfactory, challenged both within the discipline of the history of art and architecture (Elsner 1995; Beard and Henderson 2001 on classical art; Arnold 2002 on architectural history), and within the field of archaeology. For archaeologists, this is bound up within wider post-processual ideas which explore the way in which meaning is generated through inhabiting built space (Parker Pearson and Richards 1994a). Matthew Johnson has called for a repositioning in the interpretation of architecture in his article *Vernacular architecture: the loss of innocence* (1997), where he argues that we have collected the data in all its minutiae, but have yet to come to terms with their meaning. He establishes 10 principles which should underlie an informed analysis of architecture, as applied to vernacular buildings. Whilst all are appropriate for the study of Roman buildings, I want to concentrate on five themes which underlie Johnson's arguments, and expand on how they are applicable to Roman architecture.

Johnson's principles explore the nature of meanings associated with buildings and building styles. The first of these themes stresses the cultural meaning of buildings: they are the product of cultural attitudes or mindsets, and these are not necessarily self-evident or ahistorical. Rural villas were a product of the mentality of urban living and *otium* (Purcell 1995), whilst the changing plans of baths and *thermae* responded to changing ideas of bathing and luxury (DeLaine 1992). These ideas were not necessarily articulated outside Rome, and certainly were not part of the written discourse within the provinces, but they were part of the knowledge of how to act in a Roman way. The second aspect is that they had an active meaning: they were bound up in the way people understood the world around them, and their relationships with others in the same society. The actions of living within these spaces communicated positions within local hierarchies (e.g., free as opposed to slave, male as opposed to female), but also were involved in the broader idea of a shared Roman-ness. Thirdly, that meaning is multi-vocal: again, the reading of the buildings and social space would differ for a magistrate and for his public slave, or one of his female relatives. It is not that one reading is prefer-able to others, but that the multiple experiences and meanings were an inalienable feature of the use of material culture. Fourthly, the discourse surrounding the meaning of public buildings is not separate from other aspects of life. They need to be studied contextually, both in terms of the physical context (urban setting, region, province, etc.) but also in terms of the broader discursive context. For the historic periods, this means that textual sources and epigraphy can be used to complement and sup-plement the evidence of the buildings themselves. Fifth, and finally, the reinterpreted meanings of these buildings do not cease with the end of the Roman period. The classical artistic tradition has had a continued potency through the ages (see for example, Haskell and Penny 1981; Beard and Henderson 2001), and this is also true for classical architec-ture. Similarly, for three centuries, attitudes to western imperialism have been interwoven with attitudes to Roman imperialism (e.g., Hingley 2000, 2001). We do not come to Roman buildings as neutral observers, but as active readers already embedded in a discourse concerning Rome and its architecture.

For the archaeologist, this idea of multi-layered meaning poses the question of how we study the structural remains of the past. The approach advocated in this book entails a shift in the way buildings are viewed: from the building as architectural aesthetic to the building as social space. This revolves around a reflexive relationship between building, people, and activities: each influences and is influenced by the other two factors. A building is given meaning through the people who use it and the activities they carry out in it; people make sense of their lives and who they are through their daily activities, as carried out within the built envi-ronment; and practice becomes meaningful according to the who and the where. This concept of architecture as lived experience fundamen-tally shifts the way we approach the study of a building: the architectural structure becomes a place inhabited by people and the focus for their activities. Furthermore, the layout of the building and the hierarchies of decoration will be dictated or constrained by these factors. The archi-tecture is not neutral, without value or meaning; rather it has a meaning generated by the people using it, through their expectations and use of the building (Parker Pearson and Richards 1994b: 40). This meaning is not divorced from the ideologies of the rest of their lives, but related to the broader experiences of the society as a whole, and consequently cannot be studied in isolation from it. Furthermore, in turn, buildings and their use become key in social reproduction: the perpetuation of the individual identities, communal identities and power relationships central to any society. Each person's interaction with a building forms part of the process of how they make sense of the world: their own identities, their relationship to each other, and their environment. Thus, more recent approaches to architecture have centred around the idea of regionalization (for example, Gilchrist 1994; Graves 2000; Johnson 2002). By looking at issues such as movement, orientation, access and appropriate behaviour, and how varying social groups might experience architecture differently, archaeologists have begun to explore how social reproduction might occur.

The study of Roman architecture has not been immune to these new theoretical concerns, and these can be traced through two related strands of study. The first has been the exploration of buildings, and in particular urban space, as the product of the lived experience, movement and activity. This found early expression in Frank Brown's argument that Roman urban space was shaped through ritual, whether political or religious (Brown 1961). Others have looked at the town as a unit of analysis rather than individual buildings, exploring the way in which even the most apparently insignificant element, such as the arch or the position of the doorway, formed part of the way in which urban space was made to be meaningful (MacDonald 1986; Laurence 2007). Through these and similar forms of analysis, focus has moved away from the individual building studied in isolation, to a contemplation of the building within its context, both spatial and temporal. The second element has been the move from the study of architecture to the study of the building. Although I have used the two terms interchangeably so far, in fact they might be seen as encompassing separate areas of study: the former referring to the architectural stonework and the plan, and the latter to all the material which make up the building including stonework, decoration and moveable furniture. Academic practice has been to study integral stone decoration as part of the general description of the building, whilst other items of decoration such as wall-painting, mosaics and *opus sectile* are torn from their context (often literally as well as metaphorically) and analysed in isolation (Toynbee 1965: 13; Krautheimer 1986: 14). Toynbee's handbook *The Art of the Romans*, for example, covers architectural sculpture (Toynbee 1965: 85–8) and mosaics and *opus sectile* (ibid. 146–59), but not the buildings themselves. As Andrew Wallace-Hadrill succinctly argues:

> The constant danger is that the house, the social unit, merely acts as a repository for items of evidence. The objects studied are divorced, whether physically, as in the museum collections of the previous century, or conceptually, as in the publications of this century, from their social context. (Wallace-Hadrill 1994: 7)

In order to understand its spatial logic, the building needs to be considered in its entirety, integrating the architecture with other forms of decoration and furnishing, and interpreting it as a single unit. The analysis of social space as a whole, rather than merely the architectural components, has led to a variety of works considering the relationship between decoration, context and use (papers in Gazda 1991b; also Wallace-Hadrill 1994; Scott, S. 1995, 2000), or the relationship between furnishings or paraphernalia and the interpretation of spatial meaning (Berry 1997).

Part of the associated material decorating the public spaces of the towns are inscriptions. The study of epigraphy tends to focus on the text itself as a means of constructing a historical and social narrative for a local area. They become evidence *for* various political and social structures, rather than being seen as material culture bound up in the structures themselves. Increasingly, this approach is being contested, and in particular three theoretical concepts have formed part of new approaches to the subject. The first of these is the idea of an 'epigraphic habit'. There are noticeable differences within the number of inscriptions set up, varying across time and space, which are attributable to the differing use of inscriptions within any society (MacMullen 1982; Mann 1985; Meyer 1990; Prag 2002). Ramsey MacMullen stresses the interaction between the dedicator and the reader (or viewer) as a crucial factor in this:

> ... what was written on stone almost always addresses nobody in particular – rather the whole community ... Apparently the rise and fall of the epigraphic habit was controlled by what we can only call the sense of audience. (MacMullen 1982: 246)

The second influence has been the connection between epigraphy and power, arising from work on how power relations were located in and reproduced through inscriptions (Bowman and Woolf 1994). This has included work on the relationship between inscriptions in Latin and Roman imperialism (Woolf 1994; Cooley 2002), or they way in which tombstones are used by gladiators or *liberti* to contest the dominant hierarchies (Hope 2001). The third concept is that of context or location: that these inscriptions possessed a spatial location, often a public area, and this formed part of their significance (Cooley 2000; Lefebvre 2004; Salway forthcoming).

All three approaches force us to acknowledge that inscriptions are embedded within a particular context. They are produced to satisfy a specific need, and reflect social relations, power structures and ideologies of that society. Furthermore, the nature of these public inscriptions means that they need to be considered as involved in two distinct processes: one of commissioning, and the other of viewing. As John Barrett has argued, they not only mark specific events, but they also form a long-lasting memory of specific allegiances and obligations (Barrett 1993). This brings to the fore two ideas, which are the product of the act of reading inscriptions. The first is that they have a life beyond the moment of their installation: that the act of reading continues their use and their role in social reproduction. The second is that to be interpreted, the reader was not only required to be conversant with the Latin, but also with the social structures which made the limited activities commemorated meaningful: that is they had to be read on two different levels. This implication of the reader decentres the person commissioning them, giving them a wider role in social reproduction. The non-funerary inscriptions actually convey a limited number of messages, such as euergetism, political office and honorific dedication (for the significance of these, Revell in press). To understand their message did not require full literacy, and the repeated magisterial titles and phrases such as *decurionum decreto* (and its common abbreviation as DD), can almost be treated as symbols. As the wider population came to recognise their significance as material culture, and in particular their connection with a new form of social and political organisation, they internalised the messages they contained and their own position within these systems. Recent archaeological evidence suggests that, at least in Britain, literacy was more widely spread than previously might have been hypothesised (Hanson and Conolly 2002; Tomlin 2002), and so it is likely that a sizeable proportion of the viewers could recognise the meaning of inscriptions. It is likely that public inscriptions played a much wider role in reproducing social institutions than has perhaps been allowed for in approaches which concentrate on the person who paid for them.

To pull these various strands together, the public buildings of the empire form the cornerstone of this study, with the inscriptional evidence as a supplementary addition. For the architecture, I propose a narrative of use in place of a narrative of historical sequence. Construction is important, but a building's biography continues as it forms part of an inhabited townscape. The elites had an important role in the construction of the public buildings through commissioning and paying for them, but thereafter the urban community as a whole was involved in the generation of meaning through their ongoing use of these spaces. Although the buildings form the primary evidence, they are not my primary research interest; rather it is the people who inhabited them, who moved through them and occupied them on a daily or routine basis. Thus, at the centre of the analysis is the issue of how the people interacted with the physical environment: who was allowed in, on which occasions, what they could see, where they could go. Inscriptions support this enquiry in that they formed part of the lived experience of the town. They allow us to reconstruct activities carried out in the space, and to investigate acts people thought worthy of commemoration and the social structures which gave them meaning. Both the buildings and the inscriptions allow us to glimpse the lives of the people in the Roman past, and the society within which they operated.

1.5 THE TEMPO OF ROMAN IMPERIALISM

It is not my intention in this book to present a historical narrative of the origins and progression of Roman imperialism, the story of how Rome begins as an unremarkable Mediterranean city-state and becomes the centre of a large empire. There are multiple works on the subject in general, and the provinces of Iberia and Britain in particular (for example, Frere 1987; Richardson 1996). Nevertheless, in examining the nature of Roman power in the provinces, it is necessary to make some comments about how we arrive at the circumstances of the second century AD and the implications for dealing with two groups of provinces usually considered as possessing different relations to the centre. These comments focus on the tempo or periodization of Roman society and relations between the parts: that Roman imperialism was not a linear progression, and that how when we think of the variability in what it was to be Roman, we are not only dealing with the where, or the spatial context, but also the when, or the temporal context. Whilst the division of the Roman period into sub-periods (early, mid and late republic, high empire and late empire) and the main characteristics of these are long established, the impact these changes might have on Roman imperialism can be overlooked when dealing with the question of Roman rule from the perspective of the provinces.

The first theme to address is that of the pace of conquest. When studying the history of any single province or area, it is easy to forget that the acquisition of the empire took over 600 years, and arguably was a project which the Romans never quite thought of as complete (Whittaker 1994). Although there is some debate whether the conquests were a deliberate policy, or an accidental by-product of internal and external conflicts (Hopkins 1978; Harris 1979; North 1981; Rich 1993), they occurred in a series of stages, as the political context within the Mediterranean basin changed. As the territory controlled by Rome expanded, there were consequences in terms of both relations with neighbouring political entities, and social organization in Rome. For example, some Iberian tribes were initially brought under Rome's control as a result of conflict with Carthage, whereas later conquests were bound up with the increasingly bitter elite competition for political and military power in the city. The first incursions into Britain by Caesar were also part of this internal civil conflict, although at a later stage, and the more substantial conquests by Claudius were the product of the (relatively) new principate, and the need for a new emperor, perceived as weak and feeble, to make his mark. At the same time, there were changes in the way in which the conquered territories were ruled (Lintott 1993). The earliest oversees territories were loosely governed through the consular system of political office at Rome, with few requirements other than taxation, and this was contracted out to tax farmers. It is only really with Augustus and Agrippa that we begin to see the imposition of what we think of as the "imperial structure" when the systems of governors, census and taxation become more formalised (Nicolet 1991).

These changes in tempo are not only evident within the political structures of the city of Rome, but also the changing relations between the provinces and Rome. It is clear that the process of cultural change is not dependent upon time from conquest, but rather time of conquest. Thus, even in areas conquered by Rome centuries earlier, the process of 'Romanization' is only evident from the time of Augustus onwards, and in areas brought into Roman control from then on, we can see a rapid integration with the rest of the empire (Whittaker 1995; Woolf 1995). In the established provinces of Baetica, Tarraconensis and Narbonnensis, very little urban architecture and political inscriptions date to the initial

period after incorporation into the empire; instead the vast majority date
to the time from Augustus onwards (Ward-Perkins 1970; Keay 1995).
In contrast, in provinces conquered much later, such as Gallia Belgica
and Britain, there is a more rapid (although not necessarily immediate)
construction of Roman buildings in the decade or so following conquest (Woolf 1998: 29–40 for the differences between Narbonnensis and
Tres Galliae). Alongside this, there was growing integration of personnel within both politics and the military, with those of Italian origin
increasingly being replaced by those of provincial stock. By the time of
Antoninus Pius in the mid-second century AD, only 57.5% of senators
and 53% of consuls of known origin were actually from Italy (respectively Hammond 1957: 77; Alföldy 1976: 281–91). There was a similar
decreasing percentage of Italians in the legions from the first century AD
onwards, with replacement by troops from local sources and a high proportion of them then settling in the area where they had served (Mann
1983). Whilst a somewhat unsatisfactory term, there is an increasing
maturity in the governance and integration of the provinces, with the
greatest stability in the system during the first and second centuries AD.
There is obviously a danger of seeing this as some form of 'high point' in
a rise and fall narrative, but nevertheless, it should be recognised that the
processes of incorporation and assimilation, of both people and territory,
are more complex than a linear trajectory.

This syncopated process of change is increasingly being recognised, and
should be seen as a backdrop to the period under consideration within
this book. Although there are a number of centuries between the incorporation of Spain and Britain, by the early second century both areas
had a fairly well-developed series of provincial structures. The provinces
existed as physical and legal entities. Towns formed the cornerstone of
imperial government and local elite identity. The economic threads were
spread across the provinces through taxation, coinage and the movement
of goods. Although there was still some idea of expansion, army activity was more about policing and consolidation. Thus, it is possible to
move beyond the process of incorporation, and examine these imperial
structures and the way they were bound up into the articulation of a
Roman identity. The first half of the second century, and in particular
the reign of the emperor Hadrian provides a fruitful temporal context
for such a study. Hadrian has been called "the restless emperor" due to
his peregrinations through the provinces of the empire (Birley, A. 1997),
and his extensive building programme (Boatwright 2000: 108–71). With
a *patria* outside of Italy (Syme 1964, although he does seem to have been

born in Rome), his rule is emblematic of the broader social and political processes linking together the provinces. It is at this period that we can see the workings of the relations between the imperial authorities and the provinces, and the way in which the wider view of the people of the provinces had altered to encompass the broader power of Rome. Therefore, at this point we can begin to explore the structures which reproduced the authority of Rome in daily life, and the resultant forms of local identity.

1.6 THE CASE STUDIES

In undertaking a study of this kind into an empire of such a scale, it is necessary to tread a fine line between the general and the particular. In the case of the former, the temptation is to provide an overview based on evidence from the empire as a whole, or selected areas. This then becomes an exercise in cherry-picking either the most well-known or noteworthy examples, thus losing the sense of the detailed context. In the latter, concentrating on a single town or province, questions are asked about the applicability of any conclusions to a broader scale. As this study focuses on ideas of similarity and diversity, a selection of case studies have been chosen, but taken from a range of provinces in the western empire. The advantage of this approach is that it allows the detail of a close contextual study of various themes investigated in a limited number of areas, and, at the same time, it transcends the familiar categories or blocks of evidence grouped through ancient provinces or modern political boundaries.

The criteria for selection within this study were determined by the requirements of the methodology. In order to reconstruct the daily use of the buildings, it is necessary to select well-excavated sites. These were well developed by the beginning of the second century, with a range of public buildings. They have all been subject to a substantial period of excavation and publication, and for some, there is additional information from various survey techniques. The case studies cover a variety of urban types: provincial capitals, major towns, and minor towns which might seem underwhelming to the modern (and ancient) visitor. The objection might be raised that these are not necessarily the best examples and that various sites might be better, due to either quality of fieldwork or perceived typicality. In searching for the perfect or most 'typical', we run the risk of endlessly using the same case studies (the Pompeii scenario) or imposing our own preconceptions.

Here, I must draw attention to two problems with the evidence used. Firstly, there is the incomplete nature of the data themselves. Obviously, the most basic problem is that of partial preservation; but, in addition, not all the buildings I shall discuss have been the subjects of large-scale, total excavation. Some lie under modern cities (most notably London and Bath), and research has been carried out as areas become available, with the interpretation based upon a number of excavations separated by time and distance. Other sites were excavated before the acceptance of more rigorous scientific methods, and the data are not always of the quality we might expect today. Some of the sites have yet to be fully published and for these, the evidence has been pieced together from a selection of accounts, with less detail available than might be desirable. However, it is the nature of archaeology that the evidence is always less than complete, and it is a limitation we must deal with. Secondly, there is the danger of circularity. In all cases, due to the problems I have outlined above, the whole has been reconstructed from a part, usually with the implicit assumption that it will adhere to what we might expect if it were Roman, based on evidence from other parts of the empire. Furthermore, in using the textual sources to reconstruct the activities carried out in these buildings, there is the inherent supposition that they are being used in a Roman manner. Both assumptions are problematic if we then argue that it is a part of the reproduction of Roman social institutions. However, throughout the descriptions which follow, I will explicitly differentiate between what is in the archaeological record, and what is assumed; in addition, I shall also present the direct and circumstantial evidence which might suggest the adoption of new practices as well as new building types.

In the following sections, I shall provide a brief snapshot of each of the towns as they existed at the beginning of the second century AD, with some details about the level of the epigraphic record. This is a brief summary of the archaeological evidence; further detail will be presented within the subsequent chapters as relevant.

COLONIA AELIA AUGUSTA ITALICA

The town of Italica in the province of Baetica lies on the River Huelva and was originally a Turdetanian settlement dating from the fourth century BC (Rodríguez Hidalgo and Keay 1995: 397; see Figure 1.1). Scipio Africanus settled a contingent of wounded soldiers on the site in 205 BC (Appian *Iberica* 38), although little is known about the development and

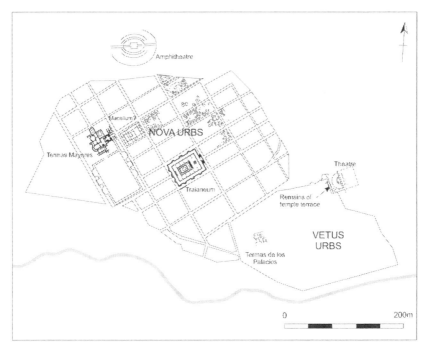

Figure 1.1. Italica: plan of the town.

layout of the Republican town as it lies underneath the modern village of Santiponce (see Keay 1997a for a critical survey of the evidence). The town appears to have acquired municipal status under Augustus, and colonial status under Hadrian. The latter change coincided with the construction of the 38 ha extension to the town, possibly funded by the emperor himself. Termed the Nova Urbs by modern commentators, in contrast to the earlier Vetus Urbs (García y Bellido 1960), this produced a sizeable town with a range of public buildings enclosed within town walls. Much of this area has been excavated, and more recently has been the subject of an extensive geophysical survey (Corzo Sánchez 1982: 305–6; Rodríguez Hidalgo et al. 1999). Thus Italica potentially forms the closest example to the ancient (and modern) idea of an imperial town, with a particular significance due to its association with Hadrian.

Municipium Flavium Muniguense

Munigua was also in the province of Baetica, some 40 km from Italica. Its layout exploited the natural terrain, with the public buildings occupying

28

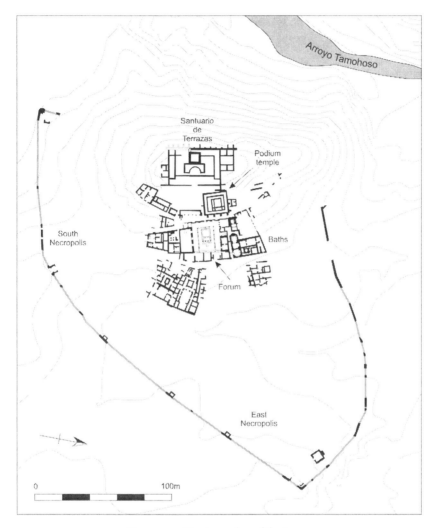

Figure 1.2. Munigua: plan of the town.

the summit and east side of the hill on which it was built, and the plan based around a series of processional routes rather than a grid system (see Figure 1.2). There is evidence of occupation from the third century BC onwards, but the earliest public buildings date to the first half of the first century AD (Hauschild 1991a). The main period of construction seems to have been during the Flavian period, when the town presumably acquired the status of *municipium*. It has been the subject of an extensive excavation programme by the Instituto Arqueológico Alemán in Madrid

29

since 1956, which has revealed a series of public buildings, houses and cemeteries. The religious architecture of sanctuary and associated temples dominates the town, in contrast to the centrality of the forum in many Roman towns.

Colonia Clunia Sulpicia

Clunia was a *conventus* capital in the province of Hispania Tarraconensis. The settlement seems to have been spread out across the whole of a 130ha plateau near a tributary of the river Duro (see Figure 1.3). It is unclear whether there was a pre-Roman settlement on the site, and the date of foundation is unknown, although it is attested in historical sources in the first century BC. It has been suggested from the magisterial titles that the town had municipal status by the time of Tiberius, and it later acquired colonial status, possibly due to its role in events surrounding the accession of Galba (for a summary of the evidence, Palol 1991c: 15–17). The monumentalisation of the town has been dated to between approximately AD 30 and AD 65–70, with the construction of the central public area (Palol and Guitart 2000: 234–5). The public buildings have been extensively excavated since 1958 by what is now the Servicio de Investogaciones Arqueológicas under the direction of Pere de Palol, providing a good picture of their layout and organisation. The town's judicial status as head of a *conventus* capital suggests that it had an important role in the area.

Municipium Augusta Bilbilis

Bilbilis is also in the province of Hispania Tarraconensis, and was constructed on a mountain-side, utilising two peaks to provide the topography of the town (Martín-Bueno 1975). There is some suggestion that there was a pre-Roman settlement, but little evidence for the construction of Roman-style buildings before the late first century BC, at about which time the town gained the status of *municipium* (Martín-Bueno 1982a). The site is dominated by the monumental forum-temple complex exploiting the topography of the Santa Barbara hill (Martín-Bueno 1987), with other public buildings and houses spread along and down the sites of the two hills. The public areas have been excavated by Martín-Bueno since 1970 producing a reasonably clear plan of their layout (Martín Bueno et al. 1985: 256–7), although less is known about

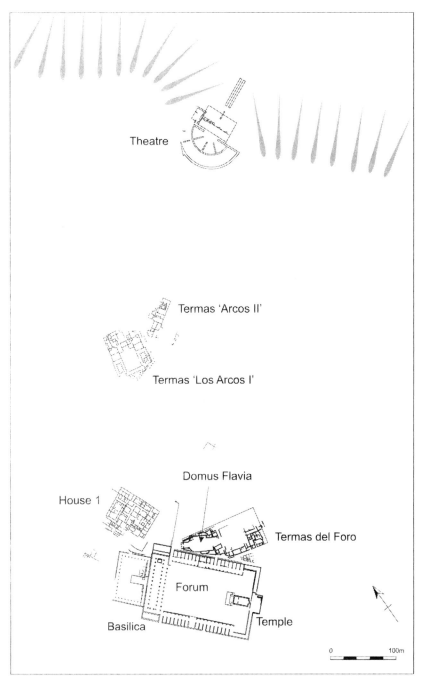

Figure 1.3. Clunia: plan of the town showing the known public buildings.

the domestic buildings. Bilbilis is possibly one of the more unremarkable Roman towns in Spain, with a limited range of public buildings and very few inscriptions, providing a counterpoint to the perceived typicality of other Spanish examples.

Londinium

London seems to have been a new Roman foundation; whilst there is some evidence of Iron Age farmsteads, these do not seem to have formed a substantial settlement (see Figure 1.4). The Roman town was founded very early after the conquest of south-east Britain, although it is unclear whether its initial function was military or commercial, or what its constitutional status was. By the second century, London was an important town, with both an administrative and a commercial role, and with evidence for a planned expansion during the second half of the first century AD and the enlargement of existing buildings in the first half of the second century (Bateman 1998). Excavation has been piecemeal since the nineteenth century, but in the last 30 years, our knowledge of the town has increased substantially due to the Museum of London Archaeology Service (which replaced the Department of Urban Archaeology) working within the commercial redevelopment of the City of London since the 1980s. The Roman town provides an interesting case study due to its role as a provincial capital, with the administrative role that entailed, the blend of military and civilian, and the apparent cosmopolitan nature of the inhabitants.

Venta Silurum

The compact town of Venta Silurum was situated near the coast of the Severn Estuary, on the road from Gloucester to Caerleon (Brewer 1993). The Silures seem to have been conquered in the 50s AD, and the town seems to have been dated in the late first century AD, when the first public buildings were constructed. For much of the second century, the town seems to have consisted of the forum and the baths, and a few domestic structures. At a later date, it was formalised through a regular gridded plan, with the public buildings at the centre, but the archaeology evidence suggests that the town remained relatively small until the fourth century AD, and that certain areas were never built upon. The plan of the town was mainly reconstructed through a thorough programme of

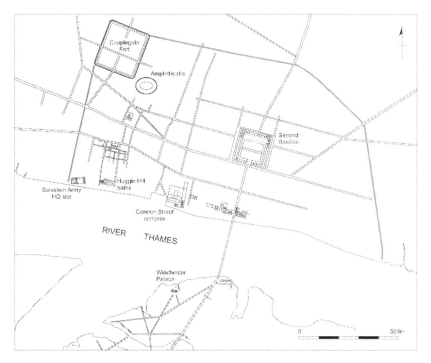

Figure 1.4. London: plan of the town showing the public buildings and road layout, second century AD.

excavation by Hudd and Ashby between 1899 and 1913 which uncovered nearly two-thirds of the town (Brewer 1993:56). More recent work by Brewer has been aimed at answering stratigraphic questions concerning the development of the town. As the smallest town in Roman Britain, with a very limited number of public buildings and inscriptions, Caerwent can be seen as fulfilling the modern stereotype of underdeveloped urbanism (see Figure 1.5).

Viroconium Cornoviorum

The town of Wroxeter is situated at a major crossing point of the River Severn and on the road joining Chester and Gloucester (see Figure 1.6). The site was a fortress for legions XIV and XX until it was demolished around AD 90 and used for the new *civitas* capital for the Cornovii tribe (Webster 1993). There seems to have been an early stage when domestic strip buildings were constructed, and a forum and baths laid out but

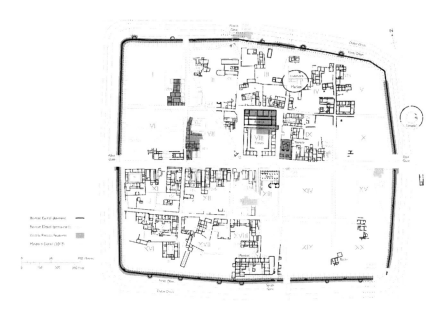

Figure 1.5. Caerwent: plan of the town.

never built. These were abandoned, and in the early second century the area of the town was extended, with the positions of the forum and baths reversed. The public buildings of the town are reasonably well known, thanks to excavations from the nineteenth century onwards, and a complete town plan has been produced through geophysical survey by Birmingham University. With its military origins, Wroxeter could be seen as an example of imposed urbanism, and the suggestion by both Swan and Creighton that legionary veterans were settled there might indicate a disruption of pre-Roman social relations (Swan 1997 f/n 2; Creighton 2006: 119).

Aquae Sulis

In spite of being one of most famous Roman sites in Britain, we actually know comparatively little about Bath as a town, outside of the temple and baths complex (see Figure 1.7). The extent of the Iron Age activity on the site is unclear, and although there is some suggestion of early Roman military activity at the site, no structures have been found dating to the period. The monumentalisation of the site dates to the Flavian period, with the construction of a temple and a series of thermal structures, and there is some evidence of a restructuring of the public areas of the

34

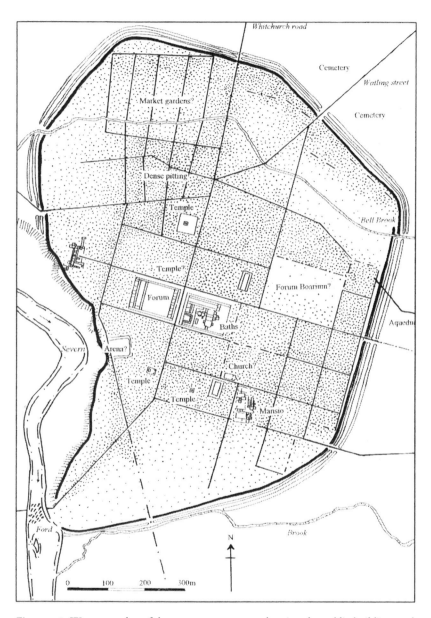

Figure 1.6. Wroxeter: plan of the town, 150–500 AD, showing the public buildings and areas of occupation.

town during the middle of the second century AD (Davenport 2007). Excavation has concentrated on the complex centred around the King's Spring, although less is known about the character of the rest of the town due to the continued occupation of the site. The town has many of the characteristics we would expect in a Roman town, with the public architecture and the city walls, but it lacks the political architecture associated with a chartered town.

1.7 IMPERIALISM, IDENTITIES AND ROMAN URBANISM

A Roman town was more than the sum of its bricks and marble. It was bound up with the idea of how to live: how to live a series of Roman lives. Within it resided the conditions for understanding what it was to be part of the Roman empire. And through a life lived within the town, the people of the provinces re-enacted over and over again the structures of politics, social organisation, religion and ideology which formed the shared cultural discourse holding the empire together. At the same time, through the differences in their roles within the towns, this urban life also fragmented a common experience, undermining the uniformity of identity. As the brief descriptions of the case studies provided above demonstrate, the towns and public buildings of the empire were subject to different trajectories, which were reflected within the physical appearance of the towns. These differences provide the distinctiveness in the present within the archaeological record, but also distinctiveness in the past, in understanding what it was to be Roman. A detailed description of the urban record allows us an insight into two separate but complementary processes. Firstly, the structures which were bound up in Roman power, and which were reproduced through the daily activities of those using the towns; but also the slippages which lead to the fragmentation of this perceived cultural commonality.

Roman culture and power are not ephemeral concepts, entities with an autonomous existence which somehow influenced all those that came into contact with them. They were embedded in the everyday lives of the peoples of the empire and reproduced through their daily activities. Consequently, the Roman empire had no existence outside the people of that empire: it was the product of their interactions (Barrett 1997). Conversely, it provided the conditions for their actions and the way in which they understood their world. In many theories of Romanization,

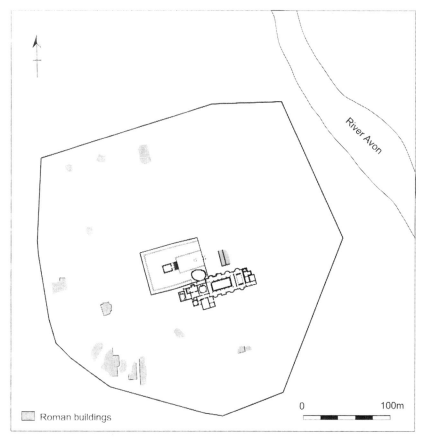

Figure 1.7. Bath: plan of the known remains of the town.

the terms 'Roman' and 'native' have been taken as unproblematic, polar oppositions, and the pre-Roman communities have been seen as passive recipients of the dominant, and active Roman culture, their societies transformed through military intervention and acculturation (Barrett 1989: 236). The concept of agency shifts the balance within this equation: as power is a dialectic, the people of the subject communities actively reproduced Rome within their own societies. They used Roman structures to make sense of their world, and in so doing replicated these structures over the physical space of the empire. In this way, Rome (in the sense of a cultural discourse) was grounded in the daily activities of the peoples of the empire.

We should not begin with a pre-conceived blueprint of what 'Roman' was. We need to problematize the concept, and accept that it is not constant, whether between communities, within communities, or over time. Nothing is diagnostically Roman, yet at the same time, everything is part of this reproduction of Roman power. Similarly, we should not argue that any one society had a more 'authentic' experience of being Roman (or non-Roman). Each person would re-enact the meaning depending upon their previous experiences. A contextualized meaning should not only encompass their pre-Roman experiences (as advocated by Woolf 1998: ix–x), but also the personal histories of participants. As each person approached a particular encounter, they brought with them the memory of their experiences of previous encounters. It is through these differing trajectories that the discrepant experiences of being Roman were built up. These do not only encompass levels of ethnicity, but other factors such as gender, age or rank. The combination of all these factors will determine the way in which each person used the Roman social structures to negotiate their way through daily life. However, as individual experience is a very personal thing, built up through each person's life history, and furthermore as the search for the individual in the archaeological evidence is in theory contentious and in practice impossible, we should not expect to build up a single picture of how it was for any one person. Instead, we should look for the point of rupture: that place where the idea of a unified experience breaks down and different meanings emerge.

I shall take these ideas as a way of exploring how routinized daily activity was a reproductive institution of Roman society. My argument is that public buildings in the urban context formed the setting for these encounters, and that epigraphy not only provides evidence of their use, but also formed one of the resources constitutive of the structure. My approach is to reconstruct these encounters as far as possible using a variety of evidence: literary sources, inscriptions, artefacts which might have been used during its enactment, and iconographic images. These are then recontextualized into the buildings and the society to explore how the building was used. I shall go beyond a description of the buildings, examining how they were used: what kinds of activities were carried out and how different sections of a society might have had different roles to play within them. This side-steps the issue of whether Roman style buildings were a 'Roman imposition' or a 'native adoption'; each building had an ongoing history after its initial construction, and that history included its role as a bearer of specific cultural values. My approach consists of examining that history, exploring the situations of daily use as far as is possible. In the following chapters, I shall use these reconstructions to build up a picture of the shared experiences of Roman identity, and the way Roman power was grounded in the re-enactment of these ideologies.

TWO

LIVING THE URBAN IDEAL

1.1 URBANISM AS IDEOLOGY

At Wroxeter, sometime around AD 160, a fire broke out damaging the forum and surrounding buildings. Excavation of the destruction layers revealed stacks of *mortaria*, nests of *terra sigillata* and a substantial pile of whetstones, all in the deep drain running along the front portico of the forum (Atkinson 1942: 63–4; see Figure 2.1). Grooves in the bases of some of the columns suggest that wooden stalls were set up here, and that the material in the drain represents the wares on sale at these stalls. Within the basilica, debris from the fire was also found in room 1 in the rear range, including lock plates, padlocks, bolts, keys and a *sigillata* inkpot, which, when taken together, suggest a number of lockable wooden chests or cupboards. This room may have been a *tabularium* or archive, and the people using this room may have been involved in keeping the town records and accounts (Hassall 2003); this would also account for the military diploma found in the same room (RIB 2.2401.8). This archive, taken with the census and payment of taxes, would have given the basilica a central role in the administration of the area. Here we can see how the ideal of Roman urbanism was more than an ephemeral concept for the people of the empire, but a fundamental part of their everyday existence. Each time someone visited one of the stalls in the front portico and bought a *mortarium* or a *sigillata* bowl, or paid their taxes in the basilica, they reproduced the idea that a town was the most appropriate place for such daily routines, thus actively reproducing the importance of the urban setting.

In contrast to this picture of mundane everyday living in the town, the more usual approach to urbanism is one of grand narrative. The starting point is the construction of an account of major episodes in the

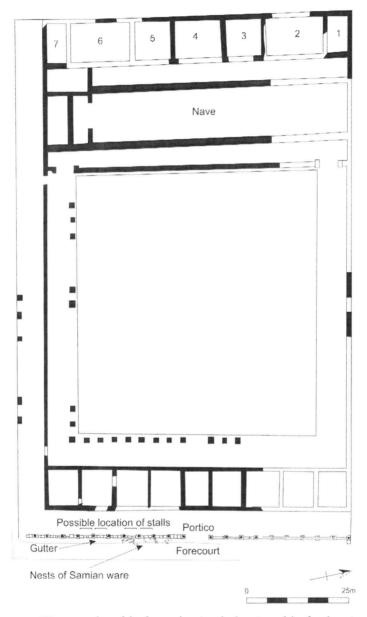

Figure 2.1. Wroxeter: plan of the forum showing the location of the fire deposits and the probable stalls.

development of a town, based upon historical sources, epigraphy, and dated major building phases. Where possible, this is tied into known wider historical events, such as the visits of Hadrian to Italica or Britain. At Wroxeter, for example, the forum dedication to Hadrian (RIB 228) has led various authors to assume that it was funded through his patronage, possibly at the time of his visit to Britain in AD 122 (for example Potter and Johns 1992: 82), and hypothesize that it was part of a grand plan for the stabilization of the frontier areas of the empire (Webster 1988: 140–3). These individual narratives then feed into wider discussions of long-term processes. The most influential of these has been the relationship between towns and Roman imperialism. Whether applied to Italy during the mid-Republic (Salmon 1969; Laurence 1999b: 11–26), or Dacia in the second century AD (Hayes and Hanson 2004: 15–18), the founding of towns has been seen (not incorrectly) in terms of an imperial strategy for the assimilation of conquered territories. This has been linked to the relationship between the towns and cultural change: the creation of towns where none had previously existed, or the reconfiguration of existing towns, is seen as signifying the process of Romanization. In the case of the tribal capitals of Roman Britain, this debate has concentrated on whether urbanism was a result of military imposition or local adoption (summarised in Creighton 2006: 71–4). This places an emphasis on the moment of, and the motivation for, their construction. One important proponent of the imposition view has been Frere, who argues that the appearance of towns was the result of a deliberate, pacifying policy begun by Frontinus and Agricola, which depended upon the use of military manpower and expertise (Frere 1987: 99–100, 229–30; Hanson 1997). The logical conclusion to this argument is that urbanism was only a superficial and minor part of Romano-British life, and soon died out in the third century to be replaced by small towns or villas (for example, Hingley 1997: 89–93). The counter argument is that towns were adopted by the peoples of Britain themselves, part of the indigenous elites' desire to participate in different lifestyles (e.g., Millett 1990b: 69–78, 99–101; Creighton 2006: chapters 4–7). Urbanization arose out of the pre-Roman social organization, as it adapted to the new imperial context.

A second area of debate has revolved around the function of Roman towns. Moses Finley developed the argument of the primacy of the economic role of the town, through his model of the consumer city, a parasite on the productivity of the countryside (Finley 1973; see also Morley 1996). More recent approaches to Roman towns have questioned the idea that Roman urbanism was primarily economic in character, and instead concentrated more on a human engagement with the town using ideas of the experience of living and moving within a town (Favro 1994, 1996; Laurence 2007; Bayliss 1999). Similarly, following the work of Paul Zanker (1988) on Rome, the idea of the town as embedded in the negotiation and expression of political power has similarly offered new ways of thinking about urbanism (papers in Trillmich and Zanker 1990). The argument I shall present here fits within these approaches, but specifically I want to think about how the idea of the town formed a shared discourse or ideology. As Paul Zanker argues, "[a townscape] not only shapes the inhabitants but is shaped by them, for the buildings and spaces, having been constructed to embody certain messages and values, continue to communicate these same messages to succeeding generations" (Zanker 1998: 3; see also Zanker 2000). The archaeological evidence from the Wroxeter forum provides an insight into some of the ways in which it was used by the people of the area in their everyday lives, how they encountered these 'messages and values'. Their reproduction of Roman urban ideology lies not only in them building the forum, but in their continuing practice of visiting it and using it, making it part of their mental maps. This illustrates the shift in approach advocated in Chapter 1, to the idea of Roman society as reproduced by the people of the empire, their daily activities, and their understanding of how to function effectively in a Roman context.

From this standpoint, questions of imposition or voluntary adoption form only one part of a more complex narrative which, for such buildings, includes their extended histories of use and alteration throughout the Roman period. As the people of Wroxeter began to use the town on a repeated (although not necessarily frequent) basis, they began to participate in the shared culture which held the empire together (Hingley 2005: 51–4). Urbanism was an ideology about the correct way of living a life, and that ideology involved more than just building a town, but also locating daily activities within it, making it part of the unquestioned mental map of the people dwelling there (Keay 1997b: 203–4). It also moves us beyond the elite role in paying for the construction and refurbishment of the public architecture, and brings in the active participation of the wider community. Their level of engagement will have been different to that of the elite: they may have lacked the same level of discursive knowledge and the textual discourse of urbanism. Instead, their practical knowledge of what a Roman town should be like and how to act in the various buildings provided the conditions for their role in the reproduction of urbanism. Whether that town was adorned with marble, reflecting the wealth of the empire, or its poor relation of stucco walls and *opus signinum* floors is less important than the way in which the architecture enabled certain activities to be located within the town and emphasized the relative importance of certain buildings.

In the remainder of this chapter, I shall explore the ideology of urbanism as a preferred form of dwelling. In this, I shall demonstrate how it was both the frame for and the product of the lived experiences of members of the Roman empire, carried in their knowledge of how to act on an everyday level within that social context. However, if we are to view the ideology of urbanism as an embedded structure, we require a framework through which to investigate it. If it operated as a dialectic, conditioning the actions of both imperial authorities at Rome and the people in the provinces, then we must examine both sides of the coin. We need to define urbanism within Roman discourse, then explore how it formed part of the conceptual framework through which the empire was ruled and the response of those who were being ruled.

2.2 THE IDEOLOGY OF URBANISM

Just as ideology must be seen as specific to any society, so urbanism as an ideology took differing forms within different societies. The ideology of Roman urbanism is somewhat problematic. That of the Greek πόλις was explicitly explored at length by the ancient writers and philosophers; however for the Roman period, such attitudes are at best implicit in the texts, and are more complex and ambiguous. From this has arisen the assumption that Roman urban ideology was a pale imitation of its Greek predecessor and that, rather than a statement of ideology, the increase in the number of towns under the empire was merely a response to the administrative imperative of ruling an empire (for example, Garnsey and Saller 1987: 26). This view is coloured by modern attitudes about the inevitability of urbanism and the evolutionary connection between civilization and urban dwelling, itself ironically the result of the influence of Graeco-Roman culture on western thought. Such assumptions reduce Roman urbanism to a pragmatic solution rather than an embedded ideological statement. That the Roman town was the setting for the reproduction of other forms of ideology has been demonstrated beyond question (for example, Zanker 1988), but we should go further and ask whether the Roman commitment to urbanism was itself a form of ideology. Whilst as an ideology it lacked the apparent unity of the Greek discourse of the πόλις, the discourse of urbanism and its changing nature demonstrates how the city became a subject of contention and debate, bound up within wider debates of social immorality and perceived decline (Juvenal *Satires* 3, Tacitus *Agricola* 21; see also Braund 1989). It became a discursive location for the expression of dissent to imperial society, but rather than undermining the importance of the town as an idea to the Romans, it actually reinforced its potency as a symbol of social and political idealism.

In his work on oratory, *de Inventione Rhetorica*, Cicero describes the role oratory played in the way Romans conducted their lives, and recounts a story of cultural evolution from savagery to civilization, of how at one time humans lived their lives in the fields, with no ordered communal institutions:

> For there was a time when men wandered at large in the fields like animals and lived on wild fare; they did nothing by the guidance of reason, but relied chiefly on physical strength; there was as yet no ordered system of religious worship nor of social duties; no one had seen legitimate marriage nor had anyone looked upon children whom he knew to be his own; nor had they learnt the advantages of an fair code of law. (Cicero, *de Inventione Rhetorica*. 2.1)

In time, a single man gathered them together and introduced them to the advantages of urban living (2.1–2). Cicero continues with the point that once the people had been brought together in cities, oratory was the means through which they lived harmoniously together and justice was administered (2.3). Whilst the main aim of this morality tale is to demonstrate the role of oratory on civilized life, the underlying narrative is that of country dwellers as rough savages, lacking the necessary social institutions (law, religion and marriage) for civilized life; these only arrive with the introduction of towns and communal living. The *Aeneid* is based on the same mindset: when driven out of Troy, Aeneas does not seek a secluded spot where his followers might live a rural life. His goal is to found a city in which to pursue an urban lifestyle, and the reader is seduced by the inevitability and the correctness of that ideal.

This ideology of urbanism as the civilized form of living can most clearly be seen in the way Roman authors viewed other peoples, and how they used towns as a way to define themselves. It is possible to see Roman identity being explored in geographical and historical works through the description of so-called barbarous peoples (Stewart 1995). The ideology of dwelling plays an important part in this: the more barbarous (non-Roman) a people, the fewer trappings of an urban lifestyle they display.

In Strabo's account of the Britons, the description of their culture is set against the ideal of Roman civilization (Strabo 4.5.1; Braund 1996: 83–4): the Britons' barbarism rested in their inability to live in an urban settlement. Similarly, in the *Germania*, Tacitus portrays the Germans as the anti-Romans. Throughout the first half of the work, his account of their culture and society must be set against the Roman ideal of living; without this knowledge, his description is meaningless. Thus the Germans practise human sacrifice (ch. 9), reckon time by night (ch. 10), carry out public business armed (ch. 10 and 13), and follow different patterns of slave labour (ch. 25). Predictably, part of their lack of civilization was their inability to live in the proper way:

> It is well known that none of the German tribes live in cities, that even individually they do not permit houses to touch each other: they live separated and scattered, according as spring-water, meadow or grove appeals to each man: they lay out their villages not, after our fashion, with buildings contiguous and connected . . . They have not even learned to use quarry-stone or tiles: the timber they use for all purposes is unshaped and stops short of all ornament or attraction.
>
> (Tacitus *Germania* 16)

The otherness of the Germans goes beyond the fact that they do not live in cities, but includes the idea that they dwell apart, as opposed to the ideal of living as a communal group. Furthermore, they choose a site according to their own desires, rather than consulting the gods through elaborate rites to ascertain which is the most propitious. The settlement is not organised, nor are the buildings constructed from the correct materials. The Roman way of living is here presented as the normal expectation through the counterpoint of the barbarian lifestyle. But it is more than where they dwell: it incorporates ideas of how to dwell, how to structure both the settlement and the surrounding area. The Germans not only live in the wrong type of settlement, they also fail to organise it according to Roman ideas of civilization.

As with all ideologies, urbanism in the Roman world was a means of legitimating one particular form of discourse, obscuring the validity of other forms of dwelling. This was in part achieved by the projection of the image of Rome (and by extension other towns) as having a moral or religious right-ness. In addition, the rituals required to found a town reinforced the ideology of urbanism through the idea of divine sanction for the town. Rykwert (1988: 41–71) has reconstructed the elaborate rituals involved in the founding of a town. The site was revealed through augury, observing the flight of birds and other omens, and the day and site of the actual foundation were deemed favourable by taking the auspices, consulting the entrails, primarily the liver and intestines, of a sacrificial victim. Once the site was cleared, a ritual offering of the first fruits was deposited in a pit, the *mundus*. The town boundary was sanctified through the ploughing of the *pomerium*, cutting the first furrow with a plough yoked to an ox and cow, with the plough carried across the line of the gates, making these the only points where the boundary could be crossed. In legend, as Romulus ploughed the *pomerium* of Rome, his head was covered by his toga, in the manner of a priest officiating at a sacrifice, thus reinforcing the religious significance of the boundary. These ceremonies (taking the auspices and ploughing the *pomerium*) were enhanced through the authority of tradition: they were tied into the foundation of Rome and the Romulus and Remus stories, thus legitimating the ideology through their connection to the most significant figures in Roman mythology. The potency of the rituals can be seen in the iconographic representations of the ploughing of the *pomerium*, on coinage and on relief sculpture, and there is evidence for *mundus*-style foundation deposits on the Arx at Cosa, and at a number of towns in Britain including Dorchester and Silchester (Brown 1980: 16–7; Woodward and Woodward 2004). Such rituals reinforced the sanctity of the town and reified it as an independent entity, conceptually divorced from and elevated above the rest of its landscape.

Even the language of urbanism subtly negated the validity of competing ideologies as it was not value-free, but bound up in a series of associations. The concepts of *urbanus* and *rusticus* each had implications beyond their simplest meanings of dwelling. *Urbanus*, on the one hand, incorporated the positive qualities of elegance, refinement and intelligence; on the other hand, *rusticus* included the negative qualities of roughness, simpleness and boorishness (Lomas 1997: 22–3). Similarly, in order to be *urbanus* it was not enough to live in a city: it was necessary to adopt the correct manner of living (Richardson 1995). The polarity of *urbs* and *rus* was highly complex, forming the extremes of possibility within a single discourse, with neither possessing a meaning independent of the other. As Purcell (1995) has argued, the villa needs to be understood as an extension of the city: it formed part of the discourse of elite power, with political status dependant upon a particular ideology of production (see also Wallace-Hadrill 1998). The ideological relationship between *urbs* and *rus* existed on a number of different planes, at times contradictory, but always dependent upon their juxtaposition. The meaning of each was located in the meaning of the other, and thus, the ideology of urbanism incorporated the idea of dwelling within the Roman style town, but at the same time, extended far beyond it. This ambiguity is problematic for the Roman archaeologist. For the urban form to be truly reproductive of Roman society and ideology, the presence or absence of towns with Roman architecture is not enough in itself (Richardson 1995: 348). This poses the challenge of what we mean by a Roman ideology of urbanism, and how we recognise its existence archaeologically. The approach used must go beyond the unquestioned correlation between the towns and urban ideology; a more careful investigation is needed, examining how the town came to define and be defined by its inhabitants' real and metaphorical conceptions of their worlds.

It is clear that the Romans did possess an ideology of the town and urban living. This encompassed the physicality of the town: a nucleated settlement with a range of public buildings which would form its showpiece, and into which a considerable amount of energy would be expended (Pausanias 10.4.1; Tacitus *Agricola* 21; Lomas 1997; Ortiz de Urbina 2000: 72–3). From the time of Augustus onwards, there was the assumption that the town would reflect the wealth of the community (Ovid *Ars Amatoria* 3.11.3–4; this also underlies Augustus *Res Gestae* 19–21). The political and religious structures would be interconnected, with an overlap between the space and the personnel for the two activities (Zanker 1998: 6–7). Furthermore, the town was not merely a physical reality, but possessed a metaphysical identity: as a personified deity (Roma as the personification of Rome) or as a genius, a quasi-divine entity. This was reinforced by the ritual sanctions surrounding its siting, construction and maintenance (Rykwert 1988). However, as demonstrated above, urbanism encompassed more than the idea of a place to dwell: it also incorporated the ideology of the correct way of living a life. For a Roman, that involved an independent political existence, albeit within a broader network of provincial and empire-wide structures (Fear 1996: 6–7). Politics relied upon the active participation of the citizens of that town, with power acquired and expressed through public display and acts of munificence towards the community (Lomas 1997; Zanker 1998: 7; Ortiz de Urbina 2000: 59–60). This structure should be seen as broader than the narrow political field of the modern world, conceptually divorced from other areas of life: instead, urban participation incorporated activities such as religion and public spectacles (Fear 1996: 6–7). The citizens of the town (whether *coloni*, *municipes*, or *cives*) formed a communal body at a basic level, whose group interests were synonymous with those of the town, and this urban community was a fundamental part of self-identification through that citizenship.

Taking this as a broad definition of Roman ideology of urbanism, I shall now discuss how it was reproduced as a dialectic between the rulers at Rome and the inhabitants of the provincial towns. It is designed to counteract the idea of an imposed urbanism: the ideology was reproduced on two levels, as the framing conditions and as a lived experience. My purpose here is to explore some of the ways in which these might be detected archaeologically.

2.3 AN EMPIRE OF TOWNS

From the earliest period of conquest, towns were seen as an essential part of imperial and military strategy. The Roman authorities used urban centres, ranging in size from *fora* to *coloniae*, as a means of holding and controlling territory, transforming the political landscape of an area (Cicero *Orationes de lege Agraria* 2.73; Salmon 1969: 13–28; Laurence 1999b: 27–38). By the imperial era, the institutions through which the empire was administrated were primarily located in the towns, reinforcing their importance. It has often been remarked that the Roman empire involved government without bureaucracy: handing power and responsibility back to the local elites through the urban system. It was through the towns that taxes were collected, the law administered and soldiers recruited (Garnsey and Saller 1987: 32). Its efficiency relied upon the liturgical system, with the wealthy elite donating time and money for the benefit of the community as part of their service as local magistrates (ibid. 33). The administrative measures formalised by Augustus set in place a system for the control of the empire as a single entity, with towns a necessary part of its conceptualization (Nicolet 1991). The underlying assumption of these reforms was that an urban community, whatever its size, would form the basic unit through which these measures operated. To take the census as an example, this was used as a regular method of ordering the resources of the empire, and was organized through the urban network: people registered in their own towns and the urban magistrates were ultimately responsible for its success (ibid. 126–33, f/n 22; *Tab. Her.* 1.142ff). Similarly, the physical space of the empire was controlled through surveying, measuring and laying out the landscape in relation to the towns, with the urban magistrates responsible for the maintenance of records for taxation purposes (Nicolet 1991: 149–63). In all such measures, the authorities at Rome held the assumption that the people of the empire would be grouped in towns, and devised administrative procedures accordingly. In this, their decisions were influenced by their own ideological beliefs, and in turn, promoted a distinctly Roman form of urbanism within the provinces.

We can trace the way this Roman urban ideology dictated the legal and social formation of the towns through the charters of the *coloniae* and *municipia*. With such legal evidence, there is always the problem of how far these laws were followed in reality. However, they were enacted in accordance with the views and mores of those in power at Rome. Consequently, rather than using them as proof of how people lived their lives within provincial towns, deconstructing these documents provides an insight into how the ruling administration thought the peoples within the empire should organise their communities, and the political and social institutions considered necessary for orderly living. Some of the best evidence we have is from Spain, with the partial remains of one colonial charter, the *lex coloniae Genetivae* and the Flavian municipal charter. The former was the charter of a Caesarean *colonia* in Baetica, founded on the site of an earlier Roman town. The extant copy has been dated to the Flavian era on the style of the writing, with certain additions made after its original composition. The extant remains consist of five bronze tablets and 12 fragments found in 1870–71 and 1925 (Crawford 1996: 393–4). The text and translation used here is that prepared by Michael Crawford in collaboration with Armin Stylow (ibid. 393–454). In contrast, the *lex Flavia* appears to have been a single master charter following the grant of *ius Latini* to the Spanish by Vespasian, later confirmed as law by Domitian (Fear 1996: 131–50). Over 20 fragments have been discovered, ranging in size from large sections to small fragments which add more to our knowledge of its distribution than its actual wording. The most substantial versions are the Irnitana, Malacitana and Salpensana, and together these provide the most complete reconstruction, although there are still considerable lacunae. The text used here is the version published in the *Journal of Roman Studies* (González 1986; for the sake of simplicity, the *lex coloniae Genetivae* is cited as *lex col.* and the municipal charter as *lex Flav*).

It is clear from these charters that for both a *colonia* and a *municipium*, the town acted as the centre for judicial and financial organization, forming the setting for communal institutions. The *duoviri* and their prefects were responsible for the administration of justice (*lex col.* 94), with provisions for appointing further judges (*lex Flav.* 86). Similarly, the town had its own funds which were administered by the elected magistrates and the decurions within the guidelines of the statute. Whilst these handed the administration of the empire back to the local elites and removed the need for an extensive bureaucratic system, they also reflected an ideology of each semi-autonomous community responsible for its own affairs. Furthermore, this ethos of the town having its own interests separate from those of its neighbours can be seen in the adoption of ambassadors and patrons. The municipal law states that ambassadors might be sent out to represent the common business of the *municipium* (*lex Flav.* G; see also *lex col.* 92). Similarly, the decurions could vote to co-opt a patron to act on behalf of the town (*lex Flav.* 61; *lex col.* 97). However, whilst the town was independent in some matters, it also operated as part of a broader network of political relationships. The patron is assumed to be from outside it, and to act in dealings with Rome itself or other communities, tying the town into the wider social and political system.

The ideal of public participation within political life, encompassing a sense of duty towards the community, formed an underlying theme throughout both charters, reinforcing the ideology of a publicly lived life. The election of the magistracies was organised in such a way that, whatever the reality, the underlying assumption was that of political power and activity shared amongst an extended section of the community, with no explicit reference to an automatic, inherited position (which was most likely the de facto situation). Nor was supreme authority granted for an extended period of time: the tenure of office was short lived, and authority was then passed on to the next man. The system of annual elections and the role of the *ordo* of decurions in theory distributed power throughout a number of eligible people. The municipal charter set out the procedure for the election and swearing in of magistrates. González argues that eligibility to stand was confined to the members of the decurion class (González 1986: 215), and it is clear that there was some form of wealth qualification (*lex Flav.* 60; this was also the case for judges, *lex Flav.* 86). Nevertheless, the citizen body as a whole had the right to vote, extending political activity beyond the elite (*lex Flav.* 55), and elaborate measures were laid down to ensure a fair election. Prior to the election, the names of the candidates were to be published with the stipulation that they should be readable from ground level (*lex Flav.* 51). The election was supervised by the elder of the two serving *duoviri* (*lex Flav.* 52), who first administered an oath to the three *municipes* who supervised each voting enclosure. He then summoned all the voting groups (the *curiae*) to cast their votes, each in a separate enclosure (*lex Flav.* 55). As each magistrate was elected, that person immediately swore an oath in the name of Jupiter, the members of the imperial family and the Penates that he would carry out his duties as laid down in the charter, and that he had never done anything contrary to it (*lex Flav.* 59). Within these precepts, there is the underlying ideology of the election of the magistrates as a highly public event, located within the public spaces of the town, involving the active participation of the *municipes* as a group, and with the new official being placed under a moral constraint to act for the good of the urban community.

Once elected, the magistrates had a continuing responsibility towards the citizen body in the form of magisterial *munera*. In the *colonia*, the *duoviri* were charged with holding a show or dramatic spectacle lasting four days. Each man was to spend no less than two thousand sesterces, to be supplemented by an equal amount of public money (*lex col.* 70). Similarly, the aediles were to organize three days of shows, again using a combination of private and public funds (*lex col.* 71). The idea of public service extended further down the social scale, although without the same opportunities for public renown. Each adult man (over 14 and under 60 years of age) could be called upon to work for up to five days, and to provide a pair of draught animals for up to three days of construction work (*lex col.* 98). We have already seen that the charters contained the idea of public events involving a large part of the community in the elections and shows and spectacles, and this also applied to religious festivals. One of the clauses of the *lex coloniae* states that at the foundation of the colony, the *duoviri* and decurions were to agree which days were to be religious festivals, and on which days public sacrifices would be held (*lex col.* 64). Public money was to be set aside for sacrifices performed in the town and also for those undertaken at other locations in the name of the whole community (*lex col.* 65; see also 69). These clauses all reflect the ideology of an urban lifestyle involving shared activities, specific occasions when the people gathered together as a community, and acted together.

This idea of the community as the basic unit underlies many of the more mundane clauses of the charters. Certain activities were carried out on behalf of the citizen body, and goods could be held in their collective name. Lands, woods and buildings are described as assigned or attributed to the colonists of Colonia Genetiva (*lex col.* 82). In the same way, slaves were owned by the *municipium*, and their manumission required the authorisation of the decurions; significantly, on manumission, the slave became a *municeps* of the *municipium* (*lex Flav.* 72; see also 78 for allotting of tasks to public slaves). Public servants were required to swear an oath in public that they would act for the good of the town. The scribes of the *colonia* swore that they would guard its finances and keep accurate accounts (*lex col.* 81), whilst the municipal scribes swore the oath that they would write the common records of the *municipes* (*lex Flav.* 73). In both of these instances, to carry out the task incorrectly or in bad faith was to harm the community as a whole, and these oaths carried with them a sense of responsibility towards it. This idea is also found in the repetitious phrasing which continually grouped together the town and its inhabitants as two halves of a single entity. In the *lex Coloniae Genetivae*, the community is repeatedly described as the *coloni coloniae Genetivae Iuliae*, that is the colonists of the *colonia*; for example, the public land around the *colonia* was assigned to the colonists of the *colonia* (*lex col.* 82). Similarly, in the municipal law, financial and judicial matters were carried out in the name of the people: for example, the quaestors were charged with looking after the common funds of the *municipes* of the *municipium* (*lex Flav.* 20). Thus, the town was perceived to be the free citizens as a collective social body, with, conversely, citizenship defined through membership of the urban centre. Moreover, it was not enough to live within the confines of the town to qualify as a member, and throughout there was a distinction between those included within the body politic, and those who merely dwelt there. A person's allegiance was defined by the place in which they were born (their *origo*), and if they moved, they became an *incola*: subject to the laws of, and with certain responsibilities towards, their adopted town, but with few privileges and only limited political rights (Mackie 1983: 44–6). In both charters, there is a dichotomy between the *coloni* or *municipes* and the *incolae* as mutually exclusive groups (*lex col.* 126). In the municipal law, a chapter with the rubric *de incolis* specifies that *incolae* were subject to the laws of the *municipium* in the same way as the *municipes* (*lex Flav.* 94). However, they could be elected as decurions (Curchin 1990: 24–5), suggesting that there was a certain amount of inconsistency.

It is clear that writing played a crucial part in the smooth running of the town, with the duties of the town scribes set out as keeping the records, books and accounts of each town (*lex col.* 81; *lex Flav.* 73). Furthermore, there was an emphasis on the public display of written records concerned with the political processes. As we have already seen, the names of the candidates in magisterial elections were to be prominently displayed prior to the election, and similarly, the names and details of the judges were to be displayed in the vicinity of the tribunal, at the political centre of the town (*lex Flav.* 86: *cognomina in tabulis scripta aput tribunal suum*). The municipal charter stipulates that its text was to be inscribed on bronze and affixed in the most prominent position, so that it could be read from ground level (*lex Flav.* 95). The physical remains of the *lex Irnitana* suggest that it would have comprised 10 tablets, and that when displayed, would have occupied a stretch of wall approximately nine metres long (González 1986: 145–6). Furthermore, Williamson has argued that such charters also had a symbolic role, 'witnessing' the enacting of these laws (Williamson 1987). They were considered sacred objects: belonging to and therefore protected by the gods, and at Rome they were displayed in public spaces ritually consecrated. The public and permanent display of these charters and other similar legal documents demonstrates how the materiality of the written script formed part of the ideology of urbanism, which considered the public display of writing as necessary for the smooth running of the social and political institutions.

Perhaps not surprisingly, the idea of the town as a physical and metaphysical structure is less well represented in the statutes; nevertheless, there are some indications. There is an underlying idea of the sanctity of the *pomerium*, with a prohibition on building a tomb or funeral pyre within it or bringing a corpse inside it (*lex col.* 73). No one was to build a place for the cremation of corpses (an *ustrinum*) within 500 paces of the town, or a tile works within the town (*lex col.* 74, 76). It also required decurions, augurs and pontiffs to dwell within a mile radius of the town for five years before taking office (*lex col.* 91). There is little explicit provision for the public buildings themselves, although in some places their presence is assumed. The chapter of the colonial law dealing with offerings brought to temples presupposes that there would be such buildings within the town (*lex col.* 72), and similarly, in the municipal charter, it is set down that the full name of the judge should be displayed by the tribunal (*lex Flav.* 86), again assuming that such an area existed and that it was a public area.

In both examples, we see how these urban charters reflected a particular ideology of urbanism. Whoever drafted them was influenced by this view of urbanism: that it was the natural way to live, and that it was morally superior to other options. The charters also demonstrate how Roman urbanism involved more than living in a town, but presupposed that certain social and political practices would be located there. However, within the provinces the reproduction of urbanism should be seen as a dialectic: these charters provided a frame through which certain social and political activities might be conducted, but the other side of the duality was the active reproduction of this ideology through the daily lives of the inhabitants of provincial towns.

2.4 LOOKING AT TOWNS: THE BUILT EVIDENCE

We have seen that the ideology of urbanism formed an important factor in how the ruling authorities at Rome dealt with the administration of their subject communities. However, to understand its role in Roman imperialism, we also need to explore how it was recreated through the daily activities of the inhabitants of those communities. Urbanism should not be regarded as a single event: a town is built and an urban ideology unproblematically adopted, but rather as a continuous and repetitive process, reproduced by people as they situate the town at the heart of their daily routines. If the urban charters provide one side of the dialogue, we need to examine the reproduction of urbanism in the everyday lives of the town-dwellers. In this instance, Roman power was recreated through their acceptance of an urban lifestyle and the ways in which they situated the town within their routines. However, we are also looking for the elements of a specially Roman ideology which adheres to similar principles as we saw in the case of the town charters in the previous section.

In essence, I am looking for two factors. The first is how far we can detect an investment in the elaboration of the public buildings. By the imperial era a certain level of opulence was expected in the political and religious buildings, and so we should expect to see this reflected in the form and the style of the buildings themselves. Secondly, the public buildings provided the setting for an urban lifestyle, with an emphasis on politics and communal activities, and the inter-twining of politics and religion. However, we should bear in mind MacDonald's caveat about looking past the ostentatious display and the duplication of buildings:

> ... neither quantity nor quality is the issue. In addition to the forum with its temple and basilica, a simple arch over the main street, a decent, up-to-date bath building, and a theatre, perhaps of wood and built to double as a small amphitheatre, would do. Such towns may have been poor relations architecturally, but schematically and symbolically they were in close touch with grander places. (MacDonald 1986: 272)

Too often, the extent of urbanization (and by extension, Romanization) has been seen as directly proportionate to the number or the decoration of the public buildings, without considering whether their use fulfilled the essential requirements of an urban lifestyle. We know, for example, that it was not necessary to have a permanent amphitheatre in order to hold gladiatorial shows (Wiedemann 1992: 18–23). Nevertheless, public architecture was bound up with Roman urbanism, and from the time of Augustus, this was a relationship which was evident within the western provinces (Ward-Perkins 1970). Therefore, the monumentality of the towns formed part of the reproduction of an urban ideology, and without it, the people of the provinces were recreating different styles of living, and interacting with Roman power in a different way. In the same way, it is easy to adopt a quantitative approach to the epigraphic record, with the number related to the degree of urbanization. Yet ultimately it tells us little more than whether a particular community has adopted the practice of inscribing on stone, particularly when comparing numbers of inscriptions between case-studies. In contrast, a close reading of the texts can indicate whether certain aspects of urban ideology were adopted, such as public participation, the personification of the town and the wider links between towns. Many of the inscriptions record elite activity, but they were also read by a non-elite audience who would understand the significance of these actions and their commemoration.

There is a certain temptation, when analysing Roman towns, to focus on the activities of the elites as a result of their visible impact upon the physical fabric of the town. In general, they were more likely to be responsible for paying for the construction of the public buildings and their upkeep, or to have either commissioned or been the subject of the inscriptions and statues which adorned them. Thus, it becomes very easy to reconstruct their roles as active agents in an ideology of urbanism. The roles of the rest of the townspeople are less obvious: the people who were involved in the mundane activities of living and working in a town. Even less obvious is the role of someone living in the countryside, who might only come into the town occasionally to sell goods at market or to pay taxes. Nevertheless, all these groups were involved in the project of urbanism, although at different levels. As the non-elites moved through the town, internalising the symbolic messages of the physical setting through their ability 'read' the buildings, the inscriptions and the statues, they took an equal role in the maintenance of Roman urbanism through their practical knowledge of how to incorporate the town and its routines into their conceptual landscapes.

The four case studies presented here represent the commonality and variability within the urban experience. They are from different provinces (Baetica, Tarraconensis and Britannia), they played different roles in the administrative system, and they display different physical characteristics in terms of size, numbers of public buildings, elaboration, and so on. In doing so, this crosses categories or boundaries imposed upon the data, both in the past and the present. For instance, during the Roman period there was some debate over the significance of the constitutional status of a town. Aulus Gellius wrote of Hadrian expressing surprise when the townspeople of Italica and other *municipia* including Utica petitioned to have the rights of *coloniae* (Aulus Gellius *Noct. Att.* 16.13). Clearly there was some disagreement between the emperor and his subjects over the meaning of the constitutional categories of towns, and their relative merits. It demonstrates the problems for the modern viewer in trying to understand how constitutional status impacted on the lives of the people living within these towns (Millett 1999). We know something of their significance to ancient authors, but can we be sure of their meaning to the people of these communities? Similar difficulties occur when we try to categorise towns by other variables: by size, by quantity of buildings, by province. Instead, we need to interrogate such categories and the boundaries between them, and begin with a fundamental questioning of what urbanism meant to the people of the provinces, those who inhabited these towns. Which elements of urban experience were shared? Which differed? And how far did they impact upon the integration of the inhabitants into the structures of imperialism and a perceived Roman identity?

2.5 ITALICA: AN IMPERIAL SHOWPIECE

The Baetican town of Italica probably reflects most people's assumptions about the physical form of Roman urbanism. Its owes its significance to its association with the family of Hadrian, having previously been a rather unremarkable *municipium* without an apparent major administrative role. The transformation of the city in the early second century was almost certainly due to the favour and patronage of the emperor, with the substantial construction of public buildings and domestic residences, and the change in legal status to *colonia* (Boatwright 2000: 162–7). Within this building programme, whether instigated by Hadrian himself or not, there was a deliberate investment in the public buildings: both in their quantity and in the quality of their decoration. The imperial character of Italica has resulted in a somewhat atypical town, with the building of the Nova Urbs transforming it from a small Baetican town to one with an unexpected quantity (and quality) of public architecture.

It is likely that the forum lay under modern Santiponce, and so it is impossible to reconstruct the relationship between the political centre and the rest of the town. Pilar León has argued that it was located in the Los Palacios area, and this was the area where antiquarian excavations revealed a series of structures consistent with a public space, and finds including imperial inscriptions and sculpture (León 1995: 18–20). In spite of this lack of information concerning the forum, it is clear that other aspects of public participation were well catered for. Temples occupied prominent locations within the town; the Traianeum lay at the centre of the Nova Urbs, at the highest point in the city, with a possible *quadrifons* or monumental arch further accentuating this area (León 1988: 19–22). There was a clear investment of wealth in the complex as a whole: it was elaborately decorated with extensive use of marble throughout, including polychrome columns with green cipollino shafts and white bases, floors of *opus sectile* and a rich decorative scheme of acanthus leaves, volutes, flutings and mouldings in white Luni marble (ibid.). The courtyard, within which the temple was set, offered the opportunity for large communal religious festivals, as well as the possibility that the space, with its shady porticoes, might be used on a more informal basis. This was not the only temple, and there is evidence for other religious structures located within the town. The Republican temple at Cerro de los Palacios seems to have been enlarged during the imperial era, and there was probably another temple on the hillside above the theatre dating to the early second century AD (Bendala Galán 1982; Rodríguez Hidalgo and Keay 1995: 412).

We can also see the importance of public gatherings in the provision of buildings for spectacles and shows. The theatre complex was constructed during the Tiberian era incorporating the theatre itself, a rear portico and an upper portico (see Figure 2.2); this scheme was then frequently modified and rebuilt (Rodríguez Gutiérrez 2004). Again, the theatre shows substantial investment, decorated with marble and painted stucco from a very early date (Roldán Gómez 1993: 81–2; Rodríguez Hidalgo and Keay 1995: 402). By the Hadrianic era, it was an elaborate structure, with marble decorating the *orchestra* floor, the *balteus* and the seating in the lowest part of the *media cavea* and the *ima cavea*. The original *scaenae frons* was replaced by a more elaborate one of polychrome marble, probably with a second order of columns (Rodríguez Gutiérrez 2004: 190–219, figures 60–3). The seating capacity has been estimated at almost 3,000, so the theatrical *ludi* would have been large, communal events (ibid. 83, table 3). The rear portico was also extended to form a four-sided portico, with a shallow pool at the centre, and the number of inscriptions and statue bases in this area suggests that it was an important part of the overall complex (Corzo Sánchez 1993: 168). The five *tabulae lusoriae* or gaming squares discovered in the area of the theatre (Bendala Galán 1973), point

Figure 2.2. Italica: the theatre.

to these areas being used on a more informal basis, outside of the festival days.

As part of the construction of the Nova Urbs, a monumental amphitheatre was built on the outskirts of the town, extending the opportunities for public gatherings (Corzo Sánchez 1994). More *tabulae lusoriae* have been found in the entrance area, again suggesting more frequent use of the building. Resistivity survey carried out in the Nova Urbs has located another probable public building to the south west of the Traianeum, tentatively identified as an odeion due to its elliptical shape (Rodríguez Hidalgo and Keay 1995: 409). Thus, we can see that from the early imperial era, the townspeople of Italica met for public gatherings, with the facilities substantially extended during the Hadrianic period. Whilst to a modern eye these theatrical and gladiatorial entertainments may seem frivolous, the evidence from the urban charters warns against such assumptions. Within Roman culture, such public spectacles played an important role within the political calendar: the political elite were responsible for putting on these entertainments as part of their magisterial duties, occupying privileged positions in the rituals surrounding them (Revell 2000). Furthermore, the interlinking of the theatres and the imperial cult would have reinforced the political overtones of these spectacles, again locating imperial political power at the heart of the urban experience (Gros 1990).

The final group of public buildings from Italica are the two bathing establishments: Termas de los Palacios in the Vetus Urbs and Termas Mayores in the Nova Urbs. The larger of the two was the Termas Mayores. The complex was divided into a main bath block, with a *palaestra* and a possible school to the south (Rodríguez Hidalgo 1997: 106). The entrance lay on a main thoroughfare, near the focal area of the Traianeum. Again, the importance of the building is indicated through the building materials, with more columns of cipollino marble, and slabs of polychrome marble lining the walls and floor, and the *piscina* (Roldán Gómez 1993: 120; Rodá 1997: 169). The monumental size of these baths (over 32,400m^2), the large areas suitable for congregation (such as the *palaestra*), as well as the reduplication of the earlier bathing complex all point to the importance of public areas. Whilst Termas de los Palacios were less spectacular, their remains nevertheless show that they were an important part of the urban fabric, with some of the decorative elements carved from marble (García y Bellido 1960: 107). Here again, an urban life was one lived in public spaces; not just in terms of formal political and religious events, but in more mundane daily activities.

This architectural evidence is reinforced by the epigraphic record. Perhaps the most obvious point is that there is a substantial corpus of inscriptions from Italica, many from the public buildings, demonstrating that writing was an important and visible component of urbanism. Bronze plaques such as the gladiatorial edict and the probable municipal *lex* would presumably have been prominently displayed in the town (CILA 2.339–40), and inscriptions found in the Traianeum (CILA 2.342–4 and 348) and the theatre (CILA 2.397, 2.383 and 2.392) point to the relationship between public space and the display of inscriptions. Publicly written texts became one way in which the inhabitants of the town ordered their place within the world, with their fellow townspeople and with the wider Roman world. The inscriptions also demonstrate how for the townspeople of Italica, the colony was more than a physical structure: it was also a semi-religious entity encompassed within the idea of a Genius and to whom it was appropriate to dedicate offerings. Two dedications were set up to the Genius Coloniae Splendidissimae Italicensis, one recording the dedication of four statues in its honour (CILA 2.343–4). At the same time, the town was seen as the uniting principle for the inhabitants: the structure forming the basis of their social and political grouping. During the third century, a series of inscriptions was set up to a succession of emperors in the name of the *res publica Italicensium* (CILA 2. 370–3), and the *res publica* also set up inscriptions to prominent imperial officials (CILA 2.378–9, see below for details). Finally, Marcus Cocceius Iulianus, his wife Iunia Africa and son Quirinus, set up a hexagonal altar in the theatre to the *res publica Italicensium* itself (CILA 2.392). In all these cases, we see the Roman concept of the *res publica* forming the core of the group identity of the townspeople.

As in all constituted towns, the political system of Italica was run according to the Roman ideology of communal participation: popular election, elite magistracies and euergetism towards the community as a whole. The participation of the non-elite in the political structures is the most difficult to trace, with no epigraphic evidence for elections and the only hint of collective organization being a reference to a funerary *collegium* (CILA 2. 455). However, this is not atypical due to the role of inscriptions in maintaining distinctions in social rank (Revell in press). Over a dozen inscriptions mention magistracies, such as Lucius Herius who served as *duovir* at least three times, as well as being one of the first *pontifices* in the town (CILA 2.382). With these offices came the responsibility of providing *munera* for the community, and Herius set up this inscription in the theatre to commemorate the dedication of an arch and portico. Similarly, Lucius Caelius Saturninus, to celebrate becoming *sevir*, provided games for the community (CILA 2.345), and Lucius Blattius Traianus Pollio and Gaius Traius Pollio jointly refurbished the theatre with work on the orchaestra, proscaenicum and itinera, as well as the dedication of altars and statues (CILA 2.383). For men of their rank, part of urban living was holding magisterial office: their social power within the community was derived and expressed through the political offices of the town. Furthermore, this power was re-enacted on the urban stage with gifts of largesse to the community, permanently commemorated through these inscriptions.

We can reconstruct something of the way in which the town inter-acted with the wider structures of the imperial system. There was a certain level of autonomy in terms of day-to-day decisions. The *ordo* authorised the sites for the tomb of Aelia Licinia Valeriana (CILA 2.389) and for the dedication of statues (CILA 2.358). The townspeople also formed relationships with prominent officials, placing them in wider net-works of influence and obligation, cementing these relationships through honorific dedication. Dedications of this type have been found to Gaius Vallius Maximianus, Procurator of the provinces of Macedonia, Lusitania and Mauritania Tingitana in the late second century (CILA 2.378), and to Marcus Lucretius Iulianus, the Procurator of Baetica, in the early third century (CILA 2.379). Further afield, the townspople were responsible

for a dedication set up at Vienne in Narbonensis to C. Iulius Paca-
tianus, an imperial procurator (ILN V.1.65). These demonstrate how the
quasi-independent urban community relied upon broader networks of
influence and obligation, and the mechanisms through which such relationships were reproduced and situated within the localised daily activities of the people through their commemoration in stone. In contrast,
a group of four imperial dedications were set up by the *curator rei publicae*
(CILA 2.370–1, 378–9) showing how their autonomy was tempered by
the authority of officials appointed by the emperor, and how the community reacted to these more powerful individuals (Garnsey and Saller
1987: 22, 34).

Overall, the evidence of the public architecture and the inscriptions
suggests that in going about their daily routines, the inhabitants of Italica
recreated an ideology which placed the town at the centre of their
religious and social activities. The monumental scale of these buildings
and the liberal use of imported marble indicate a massive investment in
the physical appearance of the town and its public buildings, and their size
demonstrates the expectation that they would be used by large groups of
the population. The inscriptions point to the political workings of the
town, and its relationship with the wider networks of imperial power.
Regardless of who was responsible for this expansion, these structures
framed the daily activities of the inhabitants of Italica, forming part of
how they joined in the discourse of urbanism.

2.6 CLUNIA: A *CONVENTUS* CAPITAL

Whilst it is tempting to take Italica as a paradigm for urbanism in the
provinces of the Iberian peninsula, if we turn to the evidence from Clunia
we can immediately see the subtle variability between case studies. Clunia
had a different historical trajectory, gaining municipal status by the time
of Tiberius, and colonial status possibly during the second half of the first
century (Palol 1991c). It also had a different role in the administrative
system as a consequence of its status as *conventus* capital (Pliny *Historia
Naturalis* 3.18; RIT 27). Moreover, the form of dispersed urbanism seen
here is very different from the nucleated settlement at Italica: the town
appears to have occupied the whole of a 130 ha platform, with remains of
buildings and ceramics found throughout the area (Palol 1991c: 361–2).
The layout and density of the settlement are uncertain, but the forum
area seems to have provided a focus. The provision of public areas is

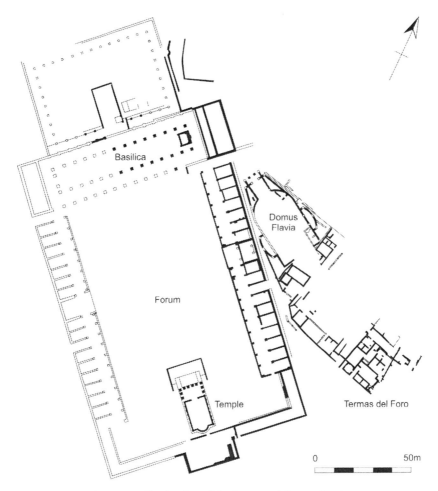

Figure 2.3. Clunia: plan of the forum and Domus Flavia.

somewhat similar to Italica, but the difference is that here at Clunia we have definite architectural evidence for the town as a political centre.

The construction of the forum (see Figure 2.3), now dated to the later Julio-Claudian period, required the demolition of parts of the surrounding houses (Palol 1991c: 362, Palol and Guitart 2000: 234), demonstrating how public architecture within the town took preference over the domestic. It took the typical form of a large piazza, with *tabernae* and possibly shrines along the two long sides, and a basilica and podium temple facing each other on the shorter sides. The rich decoration enhanced its importance, with copious use of marble (Palol and Guitart 2000: 26–35). The basilica façade was decorated with pilasters and a succession of large door jambs of polychrome marble (Palol 1991d: 387–9). The triple-naved interior was marked by Corinthian columns and at the eastern end stood the tribunal, decorated with *opus sectile* in geometric or floral forms (Palol 1991f: 170). In addition to the tribunal, a probable *curia* spanned the complete width of the basilica (Palol 1991d: 389). Within this complex, the religious and the political structures existed side by side: a podium temple lay at the south end of the piazza, and there appears to have been a triple-roomed shrine in the east portico (rooms 7–9). This shrine was richly decorated with pilasters, a paved floor and marble skirting; pedestal bases and marble bases for the columns were added later (Palol 1991c: 366, 1991d: 388, 1991g: 287). A second courtyard adjoins the site, and although only partially excavated, the layout and location suggest that it was a public area, possibly a temple set within a precinct. Here we can see that there was no distinction in space allocated for politics and religion: the buildings for both were located in the same complex. Furthermore, these activities occurred in very open, public areas, reinforcing the ideology of wider participation, its central position, monumentality and rich decoration emphasising its importance. The various alterations over its history, such as the construction of additional rooms, demonstrate its ongoing adaptation to meet changing requirements (Palol and Guitart 2000: 35).

The town provided the setting for other public events. A theatre lay just outside the city walls, built into the slope of the plateau (see Figure 2.4). The *scaena* was decorated with two superimposed tiers of columns, traces of which survive in situ, and excavation has produced fragments of grooved shafts and Corinthian capitals of limestone (Palol 1991e). Three sets of baths have been uncovered, Los Arcos I and II, and the forum baths, all dating to the first century AD. Los Arcos I consisted of a rectangular precinct with a façade approximately 50 m long. This split into a double complex grouped around a central area which may have been a piscina or garden, each wing comprising a basilica or porticoed courtyard, apodyterium, frigidarium and tepidarium, and culminating in a single, shared caldarium (Palol 1991c: 371–2). The complex was richly decorated: the floors of the apodyteria were covered with polychrome, geometric mosaics whilst those in the frigidaria were of marble opus sectile. The smaller Los Arcos II had a linear arrangement with a palaestra or patio leading into an octagonal apodyterium and so into the suite of hot and cold rooms (ibid.). As at Italica, they adhere to the ideology of

Figure 2.4. Clunia: the theatre.

elaborate decoration, multiple facilities and public areas, the duplication of facilities emphasizing the importance of these activities in the lives of the inhabitants of Clunia.

Again, the epigraphic evidence can be used to flesh out this picture. Whilst many of the surviving inscriptions are too fragmentary to read fully, enough have been found to demonstrate that the epigraphic habit, and the public display of such texts, formed a visible part of the urban landscape. Fragments from two inscriptions on bronze plaques were found in the north-eastern part of the forum (Palol and Arias Bonet 1991; Clunia II 113, 115). These are just two of the numerous inscriptions found within the forum complex: one almost complete inscription and ten fragments were found in the temple; one partial example and 30 fragments in the basilica; thirteen fragments in the shrine; one complete example and six fragments in the tabernae; and finally six fragments in the north-east entrance (all locations taken from Clunia II). Others were clearly meant for public display, such as the *tabula hospitalis*, whose context is unknown, but which has holes in the corners, presumably to attach it to a wall (Clunia II 116).

As at Italica, there is evidence for the personification of the *colonia*: a marble plaque was dedicated to the Tutela Coloniae Cluniensium, or guardian deity of the town (Clunia II 22). This extended to the personification of specific parts of the town, with dedications to the Lares Viales (Clunia II 11), and the divine spirit of the theatre, the Numen Theatri (Clunia II 21). The latter possibly supports Wiedemann's argument that at least some theatres were consecrated as *templa*, sacred places belonging to the gods (Wiedemann 1992: 3). The town also became a way of defining communal identity: the dedication to the Numen Theatri was set up by a *servus rei publicae Cluniensium*, a communally owned slave (Clunia II 21). However, the evidence for the way in which individuals identified themselves is more ambiguous. There are no inscriptions in which anyone identifies themselves as a Clunian, although this was typical practice: usually only those from outside the community ever explicitly state their origin. But here, we see self-identification by urban community; for instance, Tulleia Araucia describes herself as from Caesaraugusta (Clunia II 35), and Marcus Aemilius Murrianus describes himself as from Uxama (Clunia II 37). There are references to elite participation within the local political organization, although these are limited. The *flamen Romae et Augusti* is attested twice (Clunia II 18 and 28), and also a possible aedile, although the inscription is corrupted at this point (Clunia II 30). One of the priests was also a *magister*, suggesting the presence of a *collegium* within the town (Clunia II 28), and the dedication to him acknowledged his donation of corn to the people, the kind of euergetism expected from someone of his rank. The inscriptions on stone are supported by the coin evidence, where the legends bear the names of the Clunian *quattuorviri* and aediles (Palol 1991c: 15).

Again, there is some indication of the autonomy of the town, and for its wider social links. The *tabula hospitalis* shows the *colonia* acting as an independent unit, but within the context of a wider network of political influence and obligation (Clunia II 116). Such relationships of hospitality, like relationships of patronage, provided a means of connecting local towns into the broader networks of empire (Nicols 2001; Beltrán Lloris 2003). This was a formal relationship, initiated through the political institutions of the town, established by official ambassadors, and enshrined through religious sanction. They were typically commemorated through a formulaic text on some form of written marker, or *tessera*, of which a number survive. This example from Clunia is typical, with consular dates and the name of those sent to establish the link; the holes in the corners indicate how it would have been affixed to a wall, often in a public place (Cicero refers to one example displayed "*in curia*", *In Verr.* 2.12.112). These relationships of *hospitium* seem to have been predominantly between unequal parties (Badian 1958: 154–5, although Nicols argues that the evidence is more ambiguous, Nicols 2001: 99–100), and involved the provision of hospitality and influence on both sides. The agreement commemorated here was between an individual equestrian and the town as a whole, demonstrating that these networks operated at least nominally on behalf of the community as a whole. The *conventus* system imposed an intermediate layer of political networks, but many of these features were repeated: as *conventus* capital, Clunia would have been the setting for the *concilium conventus Cluniensis*, and when in AD 222 it adopted as patron the legionary legate Gaius Marius Pudens Cornelianus, the envoy negotiating the agreement was an inhabitant of Clunia, and the *conventus* set up a bronze tablet at Clunia to commemorate the event (Clunia II 117).

At first glance, Clunia appears a somewhat unusual urban form given the dispersed nature of the settlement and the lack of a formal urban plan. However, the inhabitants of the town were reproducing a recognisable form of Roman urban ideology through their daily activities. Their use of the public buildings firmly located the urban centre in their understanding of how go about their daily lives, with a clear connection between religion and politics seen in the layout of the forum. The numerous inscriptions and the details of the texts demonstrate the working of the political institutions and how, through setting them up and viewing them, the members of the community internalized these political structures.

2.7 LONDINIUM: A PROVINCIAL CENTRE

Although there were some differences, the people of Italica and Clunia clearly shared a broadly similar experience of urban living. However, when we turn to Britain, the picture becomes more complicated. The Mediterranean area was in general more urbanised than the northwestern provinces, with a higher density of towns which in turn contained more public buildings. From this it is easy to see towns in Britain as the poor relation of their Iberian counterparts, and to conclude that the province was less 'Roman'. Towns in Britain were more widely dispersed than in Italy or Baetica, with each controlling a larger territory. The question of density impacts upon how often people were able to visit the town, how much effort it required, and what kinds of activities were shared by the whole community. The so-called 'small towns' may have featured more prominently than the constituted towns for those who lived within the countryside, fulfilling requirements for markets or religious centres (Millett 1990b: 143–51; Hingley 1997: 91–3 for an alternative reading). However, with the exception of temples and associated ritual structures, these lacked the monumental public buildings which formed a key element of the urban experience, and most significantly the political architecture deemed such a necessary part of urban life. Although, their constitutional status is unclear, it is unlikely that they fulfilled the same judicial and administrative role (Mann 1965). Nevertheless, whilst comparisons of distribution, size and decoration between provinces are not meaningless, I have argued that this was not the only aspect of Roman urbanism, and we need to explore whether these towns enabled certain ways of acting and internalising wider meanings of urbanism.

Although London was the largest Roman town in Britain, defining its relationship with Rome and its place in the Roman administrative system is somewhat problematic. The most immediate question is the legal status of the town: the textual evidence suggests that it was not a *civitas* capital, but a town of the Cantiaci (Ptolemy *Geog.* 3.2.12, Millett 1996: 35; for the opposing argument, Perring 1991: 44–8). During the early second century it may not have been formally chartered as a *colonia* or *municipium*, with strong arguments for it being a *conventus civium Romanorum* (Wilkes 1996; Millett 1998: 8). It has long been assumed that it replaced Colchester as provincial capital following the Boudiccan revolt, even if the provincial cult and possibly the provincial council remained at Colchester. One consequence of London's administrative role has been the assumption that the governor had a permanent residence within the town. In the 1970s, Peter Marsden argued that this was the monumental complex at Cannon Street, which apparently incorporated an audience chamber and courtyard with substantial water feature (Marsden 1975). However, based in part upon recent excavations, Milne has suggested that rather than a single complex, this was in fact a series of buildings, which may not all have had a public function (Milne 1996). Furthermore, given that the governor was necessarily peripatetic, spending much of his time either with the military forces in Wales and northern England, or in other towns of the province, it is not clear whether we should expect an identifiable palace (Birley, A. 2005: 11–2). Other officials are more likely to have been permanently installed in a single location. The tombstone of Classicianus (RIB 12; Birley, A. 2005: 303–4) found within the town suggests that the procurator and his staff were located there, and there is epigraphic evidence for imperial slaves, presumably connected with the provincial administration (Tomlin 2003).

The presence of military personnel at London is well attested, with a permanent contingent of troops within the city (Hassall 1973). The fort at Cripplegate points to their presence (Howe and Lakin 2004; see also Grimes 1968), and a military detachment is attested epigraphically at the Winchester Palace site (Brit. 16.1; Yule and Rankov 1998; Yule 2005: 75–6). Other troops may have been seconded to London temporarily from other garrisons, such as the centurion from Vindolanda (Bowman and Thomas 1994 number 154). Although the dating is difficult to pin down, it seems to have been extended throughout the second half of the second century AD (Yule 2005), raising the possibility that it assumed the function previously fulfilled by the Cripplegate fort, which the most recent excavations suggest went out of use in the second half of the second century AD (Howe and Lakin 2004, although firm conclusions await the republication of Grimes' excavations). In the absence of an official staff, governors of the imperial provinces relied upon officials from the army, the so-called *officium consularis* (Rankov 1999; Birley, A. 2005: 11), and epigraphic evidence for *spectatores* from legio II Augusta Antoniniana (RIB 19) suggests that more specialised military personnel were stationed within the town. Cumulatively, this evidence points to London as a centre for the administration of the province, incorporating a permanent personnel and infrastructure, whether or not that included the physical presence of the governor on anything more than an occasional basis.

Turning to the physical fabric of the city, the earliest structures date to the AD 50s, with two major phases of public buildings dating to the Flavian period and the early second century AD (see Creighton 2006 for a discussion of the development of the town incorporating the most recent publications). The town was spread across the north and south banks of the Thames, but it is possible that each had a different function or status: there was a more formal street grid to the north, and the third century town wall seems to have excluded the area to the south of the river. Both sides of the river appear to have been used for the very visible placement of monumental buildings, with both the possible temple complex on the Salvation Army site to the north and the Winchester Palace site to the south occupying waterfront locations (Williams 1993 fig. 6; Yule and Rankov 1998 fig. 15). Lying at the intersection of the road from the Roman bridge across the Thames and one of the main east-west through-routes, the forum-basilica placed communal political activity at the centre of the town. It was rebuilt in the early second century, making it the largest forum in Britain, and this construction work was phased, with the new structure built around the existing complex to allow the building to continue in use (Brigham 1992: 81–3, fig. 31). It consisted of a large open courtyard with central walkway, surrounded by wings on three sides with internal ranges of rooms. Statues may have been displayed in the inner portico of the southern range: it is wider than the others, with remains of the foundations for their bases. The basilica was on the northern side and comprised a central nave with side aisles and an apsidal chamber at the east end, presumably the tribunal (Marsden 1987: 43–52). The building's decoration accentuated this area, with multi-coloured wall painting, and possibly marble plaques (Brigham 1992 and Crowley 1992: 101–4, figs. 37 and 38). The northern end of the basilica consisted of a range of rooms, presumably connected with its political function, and an external row of shops indicating more everyday uses. Compared to the forum at Clunia, there is a notable lack of religious space: during the first phase, there was a small classical temple alongside it, but this was demolished as part of the rebuilding process and there is no evidence for its reconstruction. Nor is there any evidence for a shrine within the basilica, suggesting a separation of political and religious activity at the site.

Other public buildings in London include the amphitheatre and the Huggin Hill baths. The former was initially a timber structure, and appears to have been at least partially reconstructed in masonry at about AD 125: the arena wall and the entrances were constructed of brick and ragstone, whilst the seating remained a timber superstructure (Bateman 1997: 56–9). The excavated remains consist of the eastern entranceway leading to the arena, with two rooms on either side, both with doorways onto the entrance and the arena itself (ibid. 56–8). The southern one was probably used for holding animals; the function of the northern one is unclear. Unlike the amphitheatre at Italica, there is no suggestion that the public were able to use to these rooms, thus reducing the available areas for social display. Whilst the plan is incomplete, the minimum and maximum possible sizes give a seating capacity of between 6,800 and 11,000 spectators, suggesting it could hold a substantial proportion of the local population during a single spectacle (ibid. 73). This undermines suggestions that the amphitheatre was mainly for the use of the soldiers from the Cripplegate fort. A substantial part of the Huggin Hill baths has been excavated, and it is clear that it was a monumental complex, with the addition of a second bathing suite in the early second century increasing the available facilities (see Figure 2.5). There was considerable investment in the decoration of the building, with mosaic floors in the

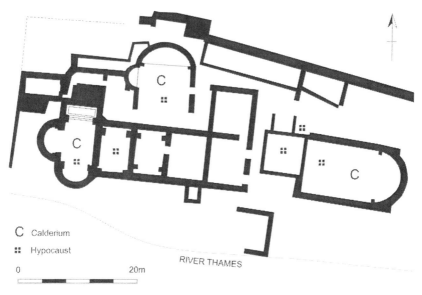

Figure 2.5. London: plan of the Huggin Hill baths, period 2 dating to second century.

original *caldarium* and the *frigidarium* (Orton 1989), and fragments of Purbeck and Italian marbles in other rooms (Marsden 1976: 59, nos. 35–41).

There is some suggestion for a large temple on the north bank of the Thames, although the evidence from the excavations is not completely conclusive. At the Salvation Army Headquarters site, monumental foundations have been uncovered which seem to have formed a portico and some form of podium (Williams 1993: 7–12 and figure 9). Re-used building material in the area includes *tesserae* and marble veneers, as well as decorative sculpture with religious themes, for which this complex is the most likely source. The most plausible interpretation is that this was some form of monumental religious area, probably consisting of a podium temple surrounded by porticos and richly decorated with imported marbles. It occupied a prominent waterfront location, and was subject to continued elaboration, for example with the Screen of the Gods and Monumental Arch. Further religious structures have been more securely identified through recent excavations south of the river at Southwark, which have produced a series of Romano-Celtic temples (Burnham et al. 2003: 345; 2004: 301). Taking the city as a whole, we can see an investment in the public spaces of the town, in their monumentality and their decoration. Whatever the origins or constitutional

71

status of Roman London, the townspeople through their daily routines were creating a form of urban ideology not dissimilar to the people in Italica and Clunia.

It is in the epigraphic evidence that we see the suggestion that the urban experience in Britain differed to other parts of the empire. I shall deal with the question of the inscriptions in Roman Britain as a whole in more detail in Chapter 5. Here it is sufficient to mention that outside of the military areas, there are fewer inscriptions than in other provinces. The small number from urban contexts suggests that the inhabitants rejected the idea that public inscriptions were a necessary requirement for the smooth running of a town. However, it is important not to overstate this rejection, as a careful examination shows that the fora at least were decorated with inscriptions and sculpture (Revell 2007; also Isserlin 1998 figure 9.1). Whether the rejection of the epigraphic habit can be taken as a rejection of urban ideology is problematic and the evidence from London is ambiguous. There are no urban magistracies attested, and the two inscriptions mentioning acts of munificence are from people from outside of the province: an imperial freedman (presumably engaged in an administrative role) and a governor of one of the third-century British provinces (Brit. 7.1–2). Instead, more refer to the role of London as the administrative centre of the province: in addition to the two imperial officials, an inscription was set up to the Numen of the emperor in the name of the province of Britannia (RIB 5) and a second inscription mentions the *legatus Augusti iuridicus provinciae Britanniae* (RIB 8; Birley, A. 2005: 206, 336 for an alternative reading). The only evidence for the local political organisation is in the form of a religious dedication in the name of a district (*vicinia*; RIB 2) which might mean that there was some internal political organization, with townspeople acting through these. Overall the epigraphic evidence suggests that London became a place for the negotiation of the province's role within the imperial structures, reflecting its role as provincial capital.

The public buildings from London suggest that, whilst at first appearance they are not as opulent as those in Italica or Clunia, their role in the reproduction of urban ideology is very similar. The range and the investment in the public buildings points to the town becoming the centre for a range of activities: politics, entertainment, religion and bathing. This points to the ways in which the inhabitants of the town came to adopt the urban setting as part of the everyday environment. However, the evidence from the inscriptions must make us question the level at which political activity in particular took place: the emphasis on the provincial rather than local personnel and links suggests a different level of political participation. Furthermore, the divorce of religion and politics suggests that a different understanding of urbanism as an ideology. Overall, the evidence from London demonstrates the reproduction of an urban ideology which incorporated some elements which have been seen in the previous two case studies, but which differed in other areas.

2.8 VENTA SILURUM: SCARCELY URBAN AT ALL?

This picture of different experiences of urbanism is reinforced at Caerwent, the smallest of the British *civitas* capitals. During the early second century, this was a small nucleated site, the stone forum-basilica and baths contrasting with the timber built domestic structures, such as the workshop and living quarters in insula IX (Brewer 1993: 58–9). The town was not walled until the late second century, and it seems that the even then, the area enclosed was not completely built upon (Guest 2002). The forum dominated the town, fronting onto the *decumanus maximus* and occupying the central insula in the urban grid. It had the typical structure of a basilica and courtyard with porticoes and shops. Fragments of a cornice, consoles and Corinthian capitals, all found in or around the basilica, show some investment in the decoration of the building (CSIR 1.5.82, 85–6); whilst these may appear rudimentary and of poor quality compared to the decoration from Italica or Clunia, it suggests that the people of the town would have internalised the idea that public buildings should be more elaborately decorated than domestic ones. Within the basilica, the areas associated with political and administrative activities were highlighted architecturally: the tribunal at the eastern end of the nave was raised and decorated with columns and wall paintings, making it the focus of the nave (Ashby et al 1909: 574; Frere 1991: 225). Within the rear range of rooms, room 3, which seems to have been the council chamber, had restricted access via an antechamber, and the walls were painted with an architectural scheme of pink dado, yellow columns and coloured panelling (Ashby 1906: 128, plate 19; Ashby et al. 1909: 570–7). The room behind the antechamber was probably an *aerarium* or strong room, as indicated by the thicker walls, again providing for the administrative needs of the town. The central room, room 4, also decorated with wall paintings, had a wide-arched entrance, possibly with a removable wooden screen, and seems to have served as a shrine. Thus, as at London, the forum situated political activity at the heart of the urban experience, emphasizing architecturally the areas connected with these activities. However, it lacks the inscriptions and political statues which adorned the fora of other towns in Britain and further afield (P. Guest pers. comm.; Revell 2007). As in the forum at London, there is little emphasis on the religious role of the building, and it is difficult to see how the small shrine in the centre of the rear range of rooms could have been used for large-scale, ritual activities in the same way as a freestanding temple in a forum courtyard such as that at Clunia.

The only other public building in Caerwent at this time was the baths complex, which was demolished and rebuilt during the Hadrianic era. It lay opposite the forum, also fronting onto the *decumanus maximus*. The façade consisted of nine massive engaged columns and led to a triple-naved hall, either a *palaestra* or basilica (Nash-Williams 1930: 232–3). The architectural decoration may seem poor, but the half-domed apse in the plunge pool and the remains of a masonry frieze with floral decoration point to the resources being invested in the building. Again, we can see the urban experience extending beyond the political sphere, with a visit to these baths reproducing the ideology of the town, and with the provision of additional communal areas beyond the rooms of the bathing suite indicating that such a visit was seen as part of public life. However, these two buildings were the extent of public space within the town in the early second century. The circular feature which has been sometimes been described as an amphitheatre was probably some form of market, and the temple in the central area of town was not constructed until the fourth century. The lack of buildings for religious activities and public spectacles point to a very limited form of urban experience. Although these activities could take place within a temporary structure, they would have had less impact in framing the ongoing experience of urban living.

Overall, the public buildings from Caerwent indicate a different form of urban ideology being reproduced. The town was adopted as the polit-ical centre of the community, with the decoration of the basilica privileg-ing the areas used for political activity. This impression of predominantly political activity is reinforced by the epigraphic evidence. Whilst there are very few inscriptions from Caerwent, there are suggestions of political organisation and alliances in the form of the dedication set up by the *res publica civitatis Silurum* to Tiberius Claudius Paulinus (RIB 311; see Figure 2.6). This was enacted by the decree of the *ordo* or town coun-cil, and so we see the community was expressing its identity through Roman forms, centred around its urban allegiance. The mention of the decree of the *ordo* reinforces the evidence from the forum for the town

Figure 2.6. Caerwent: dedication to Tiberius Claudius Paulinus (RIB 311).

as the setting for specifically Roman political institutions, with some form of communal participation. Paulinus was the former legate of the Second Legion at Caerleon, later a provincial official at Narbonne and Lugdunensis and governor of Britannia Inferior (Birley, A. 2005: 342–4), and it is possible that this inscription is a product of the sort of links of patronage and hospitality we have seen elsewhere. It demonstrates some knowledge of political structures and awareness that on certain occasions (here, to the audience of an imperial official) it was the correct form of self-expression, as well as the political knowledge of how to exploit the political links with imperial officials. Further evidence for political organisation in the town is provided through an inscription referring to immunity from the obligations of a *collegium*, usually a formal group with its own constitutions (RIB 309).

At Caerwent, there seems to be an acknowledgement of the town as the political centre of the community, with the emphasis on activities carried out in the basilica supported by the meagre epigraphic record. In addition to the political role of the town, the *tabernae* in the forum and the baths complex suggest other ways in which the local people incorporated the town into their daily activities, with the idea that these were buildings whose importance should be expressed through the investment in their decoration. However, as at London and elsewhere in the province, there is clearly a rejection of the connection between politics and religion, and that the urban setting was the natural place for religious buildings. The town formed part of the mental landscape of the local population as the appropriate place to carry out political activity, to bathe or to shop. However, the limited numbers of town houses suggests that the majority of the people forming the urban community actually lived outside of its walls. This raises the possibility that the town functioned as a focus for the organization of their lives, but in a different way to towns with a high density of elite and non-elite housing. Therefore, whilst still working within the same discourse of public architecture and political activity, Caerwent tests the limits of the ideology of urbanism.

2.9 URBAN IDEOLOGIES – SOME CONCLUSIONS

The physical remains of the Roman towns, their size and their perceived opulence, lead us to associate Roman urbanism with the architecture itself. This is not an erroneous association, as it was one the Romans themselves made. However, it can lead us to overlook the other aspects of urbanism, manifested within both literary texts and the archaeological record. Urbanism was more than the buildings: it was (and still is) an ideology about how to live, privileging one form of dwelling above any other, with a series of values attached to lessen the appeal of other alternatives. It was a discourse or debate through which the world was judged: levels of civilization were measured by how urban a people were, and for writers of the imperial period, the decadence of the city of Rome became a metaphor for the moral and political decline of the society as a whole. Urbanism as a concept encompassed not only dwelling, but also the correct way of inhabiting a town: political participation and responsibility, communal events in religion and public spectacles, and the wealth of the community being reflected in the magnificence of the physical structures. A town was a physical entity, a metaphysical personification, and the necessary condition for the correct way to live.

This particular idea of urbanism formed one of the structures which reproduced Roman power and imperial authority. Instead of approaching urbanism through an imposition/adoption dichotomy, we need to think of it as a two-way process. Urbanism as a social institution formed part of the mentality through which the imperial authorities ruled the empire: more immediate processes of political power and taxation rested on the assumption that the subjects lived in towns, and specifically towns within a particular model, as can be seen in the urban charters from Spain. The other side of this imperial ideology was the way in which the people of the empire came to participate in this discourse of urbanism. The town formed a backdrop for the repeated daily activities which constituted Roman life. Less frequent activities such as markets or the census also served to reinforce the idea of the town as the obvious and inevitable place for such occasions. These provincial towns can be seen as responding to a specific form of urbanism, with investment in public buildings, the importance of political activity and the provision of public space for communal events. The buildings framed the daily routines of the people of these communities: as they incorporated these buildings within their everyday experiences, they were both constrained by and reproduced this specific discourse, accepting a Roman urban ideology, thereby perpetuating the power of the imperial authorities.

It is clear from the examples discussed in this chapter that there are certain similarities between the towns in architecture and in praxis. There is investment in the public buildings, and political and communal activities are central to the daily activities carried out within these towns. However, there are also differences between them: obvious differences such as the limited role of writing in Britain, and the divorce of religion and politics within the urban setting, as well as more subtle differences, such as the apparent lack of political participation at a local level in London, and the apparent lack of a formal layout at Clunia. It is tempting to explain this by the stereotype of the Iberian examples being 'more Roman' due to their proximity to the centre of the empire, or their greater degree of 'Romanization'. Yet, the case studies demonstrate that even within single regions or provinces there were different urban experiences, and if we were to cast the net further, we would find that these differences would merely increase. Bilbilis, for example, contained some of the features usually regarded as typical of towns in the outer areas of the empire, such as no reduplication of public buildings, and a lack of inscriptions. An alternative to the centre-periphery model might be the chartered status of the town and its legal position in respect to Rome. Although much has been written about these, it is still poorly understood what, if any, the relationship was between juridical status and urban morphology (Millett 1999). Towns could change status (Italica, Clunia and probably London), but again, it is unclear what effect this might have on the physical form of the town (Italica should here be taken as an exceptional oddity due to the patronage of Hadrian). Further explanations could rest on the presence of the army or the social organisation prior to conquest, that urbanism did not flourish in areas with a stronger and more warlike tribal organization. However, for all of these, there are counter arguments which rule out a simplistic monocausal explanation for the variability in urbanism throughout the empire.

Consequently, we should accept that the social structures which held the empire together allowed for regional variability. There were shared ideals within town life, but not a fixed paradigm; rather urbanism was a flexible discourse into which the people of the empire entered. If we were to transpose a person from each of Caerwent and Clunia, how much would be similar and how much different? Each would find certain elements familiar, other elements strange, but they would share the idea that a town was important for certain things: politics, imperial authority, possibly religion. However, Bath points to the limits of urbanism, and if our travellers visited it, they might have questioned its status. Again, it shared some features, such as the investment in public architecture, but in this case, a limited range confined mainly to its role as a thermal sanctuary. The lack of evidence for political activity, or even that it was a legally constituted town with a defined role in the administrative system, all point to a significant difference. On the other hand, the people living in or visiting Bath would have understood it though their wider experience of Roman monumental architecture, raising the possibility that, as in the case with Phocis (Pausanias 10.4.1), it proved an awkward place to classify.

This paradox of similarity and difference runs counter to the assumption that 'Roman' was a fixed entity, but accepting this paradox as inherent within the imperial system allows us to move beyond rigid dichotomies of acceptance and resistance, or judging whether a town possessed enough features to be described as Roman. The people of these communities were actively engaged in a discourse which encompassed variability between communities, and further produced different experiences at a local level as global and local identities intersected. Nevertheless, here we can see the townspeople as a whole engaged in the routines of urban living, making a town part of their practical knowledge of how their world was organised. The differences within the towns meant that this knowledge differed in detail, as their experiences of urban living differed. However, this shared commitment to the idea of a town formed one part of a common Roman identity, and a communal experience of Roman power.

THREE

THE ROMAN EMPEROR

3.1 INTRODUCTION

The museums of Roman art and archaeology are filled with statues of the emperors and their families, almost anonymous in their similarity. Alongside them are inscriptions reiterating the same dedication to Imperator Caesar whomsoever. Decontextualised in this way, we might lose the experience of how they would have been encountered in the past. Yet at the same time this formulaic repetition can still provide an insight into one of the things which held the empire together: the power and ideology of the Roman emperor, and the tension between the institution and the individual holding that power at any moment. When Augustus gained supreme power as *princeps*, he set the Roman political system on a track from which it was not to deviate for the duration of the empire: whilst the rhetoric of a return to Republican democracy might appear in elite texts, the events of history demonstrate that it was never again seen as a viable alternative. The ability of specific individuals might be challenged, but not the figure of the emperor as the holder of political authority. His rule stretched over the vast distances of the Roman Empire, at the centre of a system of shared cultural values, but for the majority of his subjects he was a remote and distant figure. Some towns enjoyed a privileged relationship: he might reside there for a time, or act as benefactor, but these were exceptions. For most, his authority was presenced through a series of mechanisms which permeated their everyday existences and constructed their understanding of the world.

The relationship between emperor and subject was necessarily ideological: the structures binding this relationship also served to mystify the power of the emperor and to make the unequal relationship between them seem natural and unchallengeable. The emperor stood at the centre of a complex series of power relations within the empire, but any attempt to classify them under a single heading, whether social, political, ideological or religious, risks obscuring this complexity. This is not to downplay the importance of previous studies which have explored in detail specific elements of his power, whether socio-political structures (Millar 1977; Boatwright 2000), the imperial cult (Etienne 1958; Price 1984; Fishwick 1987–2005) or ideology (Zanker 1988). However, they have separated the various elements at the expense of the paradoxes inherent in the system. As Hopkins argues, the emperor was one of the lynch-pins holding together the Roman political system (1978: 197), and an alternative approach is to address the multiple aspects together and explore how the relationship between the emperor and the provinces encompassed religion, politics, ideology and social relations.

As an illustration, in AD 132 the people of Munigua set up one (or possibly two) inscriptions to Hadrian. Now incomplete, the surviving portion reads:

IMP CAES DIVI TRAIANI PARTHICI F DIVI
 NERVAE NEPOTI TRAIANO HADRIANO AVG
P P PONTIFICI MAXIMO [T]RIB POTEST XVI
COS III IMP XVI OPTVMO MAXVMO
QVE PRINCIPI RES [P] MVNIGV[EN]
[SIVM]

To the emperor Caesar Trajan Hadrian Augustus, son of the deified Trajan Parthicus, grandson of the deified Nerva, Pater Patriae, Pontifex Maximus, holding the power of tribune for the 16th time, consul for the third time, imperator for the 16th time, Optimus, Maximus and Princeps, the people of the Res Publica of the Muniguans . . .

(CILA 2.1068; also 2.1069)

In this we can see how the elements of imperial authority interconnected. Constitutionally, Hadrian's power rested upon him holding the political magistracies of the Republic; consequently the reiteration of these political titles reinforces his political authority. Trajan's title of Parthicus, celebrating his annexation of territory in Mesopotamia, serves as a reminder that military success was still seen as a part of political authority (even when it included a certain level of diplomacy). In contrast, Hadrian is the son and grandson of the deified Trajan and Nerva, with the expectation that he will become a god himself at his death. Combined, these elements legitimized his position, recreating the image of the emperor as the worthy recipient of supreme power. At the same time, this dedication also demonstrates the other side of this relationship. Whilst the partial survival of the text means that we do not know the reason for its dedication, it is clear that the people of Munigua claimed enough of a relationship with the emperor to consider it appropriate to set up the inscription in his name. As we saw in the case of urbanism, power and ideology were both a dialectic, and not a one-way imposition. The emperor's authority relied upon the local residents situating him within their daily experiences. By the very act of setting up these inscriptions, the inhabitants of Munigua acknowledged and reproduced the ideological power of the emperor.

For the Romans, the emperor was both political leader and god, whom they might approach through letters and embassies, or prayers and sacrifices, and their understanding of the emperor and their own position within this system was constructed through all of these elements. The ideology of the emperor was an unstable phenomenon which relied in part upon the superior political and military might of the emperor himself, but also on the his subjects recognising his position of authority over them (Elsner 1998: 53). In this chapter, I will explore these power relations and the ways in which they were reproduced within the lived experience of the inhabitants of the urban communities. Adopting a thematic approach, I will look at the particular structures which made the distant power of the emperor a real part of their everyday lives, before concluding with an examination of a single example leading to a discussion of the ways in which this experience might differ in varying contexts.

3.2 THE EMPEROR'S IMAGE

As we have already noted, the vast majority of the people of the empire would never see the emperor in person, but the iconography of imperial power and symbols of the emperor permeated their daily lives, making his portrait a recognisable image. The particular form these portraits took served to express and reinforce the ideology of the emperor. There is a remarkable level of standardization throughout the empire, reinforced by a uniformity between the statuary and the portraits on coinage (Price 1984: 172). The limited number of portrait types all recall the sources of authority used by the emperor to justify his position: as a magistrate, and as sacrificing magistrate with his head veiled by his toga; as a military commander in uniform, often with the breastplate depicting images of victorious campaigns; or as a heroic nude, anticipating his apotheosis. These types served to reinforce the ambiguity of the emperor, presenting him both as a member of the elite, but also as distinct from his subjects. We can also see this blurring of mortal/divine symbolism in the images of the emperors' wives and daughters, which incorporated elements of matronly virtue, but also attributes of specific goddesses (Wood 1999). We shall never know how many people in the provinces could fully read the messages and symbolism of these statues and inscriptions, but the repetitive accumulation of the images and titles on a range of media would have reinforced their association with the emperor's power.

The portrait was not necessarily an accurate representation of the physical appearance of the emperor. It was more important that the viewer recognised the statue as emperor than as an individual, and in this the visual characteristics were less important than the attributes relating to the imperial 'type', such as the military armour (see also Reece 1999: 30-1). As Elsner has noted, the emperor would model his official image within the tradition of other imperial types, either appropriating the style and attributes of popular predecessors or changing his style to distance himself from them (Elsner 1998: 58-63; Wood 1999: 14-15 for female statues). The question of how these images were propagated is one which will probably never be fully resolved. Simon Price has argued for a combination of official sanction of certain images on statues and coins, with official images sent out centrally, but that these were then copied locally and erected with inscriptions by the townspeople themselves (Price 1984: 173-6). Given the uniformity and restricted types found throughout the empire, it is clear that they were based upon identifiable prototypes, and that there was a certain level of official promotion.

However, to take the story further, if the reproduction of ideology is an active dialectic, then arguably viewing an image is as important as creating it. Recent trends within art history have explored the role of the viewer as a participant in the process: a statue in itself is only one half of the story, and the image of the emperor is only effective if the viewer accepts the status quo which it represents, and the message it is intended to convey (for example Elsner 1995: 167-9; also Elsner 2007: xi-xvii). In a letter to his pupil, the future emperor Marcus Aurelius, Fronto writes of the proofs of his affection, one of which was the effect the prince's image had on him as he moved through the city:

> You know that in all the banks, booths, stalls, shops, eaves, entrance-ways and windows, anywhere and everywhere, there are portraits of you set before the eyes of the world...
>
> (Fronto *Epistulae ad M. Caes.* 4.12)

Such images were cloaked in the majesty of the emperor himself, and were accorded an authority in Roman law which distinguished them from those of the less powerful. To harm one was tantamount to harming the emperor himself, as is apparent from the often quoted story of the martyrdom of Thecla (Price 1984: 170; Elsner 1998: 58). During her rejection of the unwanted advances of a local magistrate, she threw to the ground his official crown, which contained the image of the emperor. This constituted the act of sacrilege for which she was sentenced to be thrown to the beasts (Hennecke and Schneemelcher 1965: 360). Similarly, the emperor's statue acted as a place of asylum: in Roman law, if a slave complained at an imperial statue of cruel treatment, being starved, or forced into prostitution, then the emperor was bound to adjudicate on the matter (Ulpian *Digest* 1.12.18; Hopkins 1978: 221–3). The ambiguity between the emperor as man and god was also reflected through ritual: his image received sacrifice and supplication, and could be carried through the streets in religious processions (Price 1984: 188-9). Through such rituals, these statues were privileged above those of other mortals, and treated in a way more appropriate to those of the gods. To make a strict distinction between the images associated with the imperial cult and other statues of the emperor and the imperial family which may not have received the same level of veneration, is to produce an overly rigid dichotomy. Each would be recalled in viewing the other, and together they imbued all imperial statues with a divine mystique, reinforcing the emperor's power and authority.

Of the eight towns included in this study, the greatest number of imperial statues has been found at Italica, which is perhaps not surprising in view of its connections to the families of Trajan and Hadrian. A high proportion of these are from excavated contexts, and this allows us to build up a picture of how the public areas of the town reinforced the position of the emperor. Pilar León has identified four areas as the major sources of sculpture: the forum area, the theatre, the terrace above the theatre, and the area of Los Palacios (León 1995, especially 18–24; see Figure 3.1). Thus to pass through the public areas of the town was to

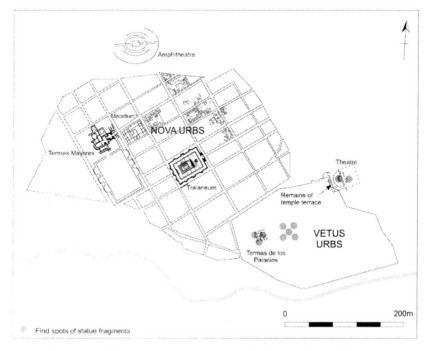

Figure 3.1. Italica: approximate locations of find-spots of imperial statues.

walk past multiple representations of the emperor, his family and his predecessors. If we reconstruct the experience of a visitor to the town during the Hadrianic period or shortly after, we can begin to understand how such images became part of daily life. Starting from the theatre, they would see a 'Hüftmantel' statue from the Hadrianic period, that is a heroic nude with a cloak draped around his hips, as well as a larger-than-life-size head of a Julio-Claudian prince (León 1995 nos. 7 and 20). Walking further into the Vetus Urbs, they would then reach the probable forum area, which Cortina's excavations suggest was an open area with traces of monumental architecture (ibid. 18–20; fig. 2). The majority of statues on display here seem to be imperial portraits, and include another 'Hüftmantel' statue, this time of colossal size, which is thought to represent the deified Caesar or Augustus (ibid. no. 1), as well as a colossal head with a corona civica from the Flavian period, possibly of Galba or Vespasian (ibid. no. 21). This honorific wreath had originally been a military decoration, but had formed part of the imperial iconography from the time of Augustus. Also from this area are fragments of two colossal male torsos, one a heroic nude, the other cuirassed, as well as a headless togatus (ibid. nos. 2, 4 and 15 respectively), all of which could be representations of the imperial family.

From here, our traveller would approach the Los Palacios area, where they would have seen three colossal statues: a heroic nude of Trajan, a second nude which might represent Hadrian, and a third in military garb, of which only the leg remains (ibid. nos. 5, 6 and 10). These are usually thought to be from the Trajanic baths (for example, García y Bellido 1960: 142–55, nos. 8, 20 and 23), although León has argued that it is equally possible that they came from the Traianeum. Moving on from here to the Traianeum itself, excavators have found fragments from the hands of two colossal statues (León 1988: 82). If, as the evidence suggests, this temple was dedicated to Trajan, then at a minimum, there would have been a cult statue to the deified emperor, and there may have been a dynastic series of other imperial statues. Further examples of imperial statues from Italica which lack find spots include two heads of Augustus (León 1995: nos. 18 and 19), a bust of Hadrian (ibid. no. 22), a later head of Marcus Aurelius (ibid. no. 23) and possibly the torso of a cuirassed statue, the lower part of a colossal torso, and the right leg of a statue (ibid. nos. 3, 9 and 11).

Therefore, to walk through the public areas of Italica was to be confronted with images of the imperial family. The act of viewing and recognising these images as those of present and past emperors served to manifest their authority within the daily lives of the inhabitants of the empire, reaffirming the empire-wide networks of political power. Certain themes have been repeated within this collection: the colossal size, the military garb, the heroic nude. Whilst there has been much discussion about how each emperor was depicted (concentrating on the identification of specific originals, or particular characteristics such as the hair style), in this case it is the homogeneity which is important: the repeated themes and characteristics which made a statue identifiable as an emperor or member of the imperial family. In her discussion of the imperial statues from Italica, León acknowledges the difficulty of distinguishing particular Julio-Claudian princes, as their portraits were realised through a combination of individuality and idealization (ibid. 76). Similarly, there is some debate over the identity of an imperial head from Bilbilis, as to whether it depicted Tiberius himself, or Claudius modelled on earlier styles of Tiberius (Balil 1982; Beltran Lloris 1981 respectively). However, this misses the cumulative effect of these portraits. The repetitive and limited nature of many of the themes seen at Italica and elsewhere served to create a recognizable imperial type, and thus communicated the ideological themes underpinning imperial power. The heroic nude reinforced the emperor's super-human nature, as prior to Augustus this form had been considered appropriate only for gods and heroes; likewise, the depiction of the emperor in the costume of a general reaffirmed his claim to power through military ability. The recognition that these characteristics represented a statue of the emperor reconfirmed the viewer's knowledge of the power of the emperor, recreating the ideology through which his power was exercised. Although Italica is exceptional, we can see the use of public space for the display of political power repeated in the other towns (Garriguet 2004 argues for 22 groups in Baetica; see also Boschung 1990; Whittaker 1997: 146–7). At Clunia, for example, images of the imperial family adorned the forum, including a statue of Julia, the daughter of Titus, which was found in the forum piazza, and the heads of Augustus and a youthful Nero in the triple shrine (Palol 1991a, 1991c: 366). Similarly, remains of a bronze statue depicting the emperor in military garb were found in the forum at Wroxeter, which may have been one of a pair flanking the entrance to the basilica (CSIR 1.9.184; Atkinson 1942: 83).

This deliberate positioning was mirrored with inscriptions, which also clustered in the public spaces of the town and the forum in particular. At Pompeii, for example, the forum was visually dominated by buildings and inscriptions relating to the emperor and the imperial cult (Laurence 2007: 26–34 and fig. 2.3; Zanker 1998, fig. 37). Such inscriptions could take a variety of forms. Honorific dedications were a common way of articulating this unequal relationship: for example a group of four marble pedestals from Italica were dedicated to a series of third-century emperors (CILA 2.370–3). Two of these altars were set up by the same man, Aurelius Julius, in successive years to Florianus (who was only emperor for a few months) and Probus (CILA 2.370–1). Such dedications might be on statue bases, the statue reinforcing the visual display of power. A second form of inscription was the dedication of completed building projects, as in the case of the inscription above the entrance to the Wroxeter forum (RIB 288). Likewise, the forum at Bilbilis was dedicated to Tiberius, and the plaque was presumably displayed in a prominent location (Martín-Bueno 1981:249–50). Analysis of the inscriptions from Britain suggests that the emperor was the most frequent recipient of building dedications, pointing to one form of dedication which we might expect within the urban landscape (Raybould 1999: 258–66 for catalogue, although the data are somewhat distorted by the greater adoption of the epigraphic habit in the military zone). Along with these more formal dedications, we should not forget other forms of inscriptions, such as letters from the emperor, inscribed on bronze plaques and set up in public locations (CILA 2.1052 from Munigua). Similarly the more mundane and ubiquitous milestones, engraved with the name of the emperor, also formed part of this visual repetition (for example from Clunia, Clunia II 229; Italica, CILA 2.367).

The ideological importance of these images and inscriptions can be seen in the practice of *damnatio memoriae*: the sanctioned erasure of the memory of a person, and for an emperor, the conceptual opposite of deification (Taylor 1931: 236). The clearest evidence for this is not related to the *damnatio* of an emperor, but of Cn. Calpurnius Piso: the *senatus consultum* decreed that his portraits were to be destroyed, his *imago* was not to be displayed at funerals or in the family atrium, and his name was to be removed from inscriptions (Flower 1996: 23–31). Similarly, for the emperor, it appears that on the decision of the senate, although presumably under pressure from the new emperor, his name was removed from monuments, his statues destroyed, and his portraits erased or altered, thus effectively removing him from the history of the empire (Keppie 1991: 22). Only the personal name of the emperor was removed in these instances, whilst his filiation and magistracies were left intact: the individual could be obliterated from history, but the office was eternal. For example, a dedication slab from Chesters fort on Hadrian's Wall had the names of the two emperors Elagabalus and Severus Alexander erased, whilst their titles and ancestry were left (RIB 1465).

These images and titles would have been reinforced through other media. The most obvious of these is the coinage of the empire, bearing the head and titles of the emperor on one side and imperial iconography on the other. Seeing a statue or the titles of the emperor was not an isolated event to which the viewer brought no prior knowledge: the image of the emperor on these statues closely mirrored those on the coinage, and consequently each would be recalled in the act of viewing the other. For the people of Southern Britain, this knowledge may have pre-dated the Claudian conquest. John Creighton has persuasively argued for the adoption of Augustan iconography on the coinage of the Late Iron Age kings (Creighton 2000), and more recently he has argued for their adoption of Roman regalia and other symbols of power, such as sceptres and senatorial chairs (*sella curulis*, Creighton 2006 esp. 35–45). If his interpretation of the numismatic and archaeological evidence is correct, then it would mean that the people of these areas would have already been versed in the Roman language of the iconographic representation of the emperor, potentially blurring the pre- and post-conquest language of power.

The statues and inscriptions bearing the images and the names of the emperors, whether living or deceased, all had the effect of reproducing the physical being and the authority of the emperor within the everyday lives of the inhabitants of any community. Both through the act of erecting these memorials and through the repeated viewing of them, the people of these towns accepted his authority, recreating the ideology that the emperor was justified in holding ultimate political power. To be confronted by such an image and to acknowledge its significance was to replicate and to legitimate this power. However, we need to be careful not to overstate the homogeneity of this experience: Italica was an exception due to its imperial importance and here to move through the town was to be reminded of the emperor and the imperial family on a daily basis. Similarly Clunia, with its administrative role as a local *conventus* centre, was possibly more significant for iconographic display. In contrast, there are fewer example from towns without these connections, such as Bilbilis or Wroxeter, where such display was perhaps restricted to a statue or a dedication adorning the forum. The restricted adoption of epigraphic display in the urban centres of Britain would have had an impact on this distribution, limiting the frequency of such encounters (Revell 2007 for a more extended discussion). Consequently, although the visual impact of imperial power formed part of the common culture of the empire, it also served to differentiate the way it was experienced.

3.3 THE EMPEROR DEIFIED

As argued above, the statues present an ambiguous image of the emperor: simultaneously man and god. In this section, I want to look at the nature of the imperial cult and how it formed part of the localised encounters between the emperor as an idea and the people of the provinces. The evolution of the imperial cult has been well documented, although until recently much of this has been interpreted through an implicit, pejorative discourse of Christian belief (Price 1984, chapter 1). Recent approaches have instead considered the imperial cult through a sociological framework, influenced by the work of Clifford Geertz (1977), such as the studies by Hopkins (1978) and Price (1984) which have concentrated on the rituals and materiality of the cult. The seminal work on Iberia was published by Etienne (1958), and he argued that the origins of the imperial cult lay in *devotio iberica*, in opposition to the prevailing theory that it began in the east, based upon the Hellenistic ruler cults, and from there spread to the west. He mapped the distribution of the evidence, demonstrating the variation between and within the three provinces. The evidence for emperor worship has not been as systematically collected for Britain, and the discussion tends to be dominated by the monumental cult centre at Colchester and evidence from military contexts (for example, Henig 1995). Other approaches have looked at the imperial cult within the framework of Romanization and imperialism, as a focus for provincial communities and part of the spread of Roman culture from the time of Augustus onwards (for example Keay 1995; Curchin 1996).

One central problem remains the question of the processes through which the worship of the imperial family was adopted. Undoubtedly it was promoted from the centre, following the deification of Julius Caesar by Augustus, with the authorization of requests (not necessarily voluntary) from provincial communities for the inauguration of a cult. However, is it correct to see it as a forced imposition on unwilling subjects (for example Webster 1997a: 331–2), or as a more dynamic engagement (Whittaker 1997: 148-52)? An alternative is to envisage it as a blend of both: inaugurated and promoted by the imperial authorities, but maintained through the ongoing rituals of worship both in Rome and the provinces. In a similar vein, there has been much debate over whether the deification of the emperors and their families was a political veneer, or an internalised belief. Vespasian's deathbed witticism of "I must be turning into a god" (*vae puto deus fio*: Suet. *Vesp.* 23) could be taken to suggest a level of cynicism on the part of the Roman elite, but this must be tempered by the ubiquity of the cult and its rituals. We need to question how the people of the provinces experienced the imperial cult: the material and rituals which were bound up in an ongoing understanding of the emperor as a quasi-divine being. In this, there are three major forms of archaeological evidence: dedicated ritual space; the evidence for the various religious offices; and dedications to the deified emperors and associated deities.

Beginning with temples and shrines to the imperial cult, we are immediately confronted with a methodological problem. It is difficult to argue conclusively that a particular building was dedicated to the imperial cult without an explicit dedication on the building itself or a reference in a textual source, and in most instances these are not available. As an example, the large temple complex at Bilbilis has been attributed to the imperial cult, based upon the dedicatory inscription to Tiberius and the head of an imperial statue discovered within the area (see above for

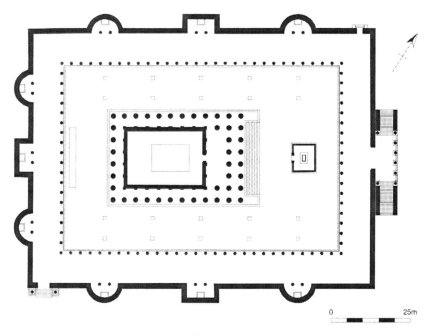

Figure 3.2. Italica: plan of Traianeum.

the problems of the statue's identification). From this, the excavators
have argued for a centre to the imperial cult, begun during the Augustan period and continuing under successive emperors (Martín Bueno
et al. 1985: 258; also Curchin 1996). However, this identification is contentious (Curchin 1996: 151 describes it as "problematic"), and thus we
hit upon a circular argument concerning temples to the imperial cult:
their dedication is based upon the ubiquity of such temples, but this
assumed ubiquity is in turn supported by the distribution of such structures (Alföldy 1996: 260). Similar caution should be applied to the other
case studies: another five structures have been associated with the cult by
various authors, with stronger evidence for some than for others.

Keeping these caveats in mind, one of the most plausible temples to
the imperial cult is from Italica, where the circumstantial evidence for
the so-called Traianeum being dedicated to the deified Trajan is certainly
persuasive (see Figure 3.2). The importance of the temple is demonstrated by its central location (León 1988: 45), and as the extension of
the town was probably a gift from the emperor Hadrian, it would have
been appropriate for the temple to be dedicated to his deified father.
Furthermore, one of the inscriptions within the temple precinct was

Figure 3.3. Munigua: view towards the Santuario des Terrezas.

set up by M. Cassius Caecilianus, *flamen perpetuus Divi Traiani* (CILA 2.343). As I shall discuss, the rituals of Roman religion in greater depth in the following chapter, I shall only make a couple of salient points here. The complex was dominated by the podium temple, which lies within a porticoed courtyard, aligned to the main axis running through the monumental entrance. Also on this axis was a large altar, its foundations over 6 m long and 3 m wide (León 1988: 44). We can envisage that people would have been drawn to the area for sacrifices, dedications and processions, with the central position of the temple making it a recognisable landmark in people's lives. The hill-top sanctuary at Munigua has also been ascribed to the imperial cult (see Figure 3.3) and this has been repeated as an almost certain fact (for example Keay 1998:76). In reality, the evidence is again problematic, based upon assumptions concerning the architectural layout and possible funding of the complex (Coarelli 1987). Nevertheless, the epigraphic evidence suggests that the imperial cult was a significant feature within the town, as the majority of religious dedications were to deities with the Augustus/a epithet, and there were

Figure 3.4. Clunia: probable shrine to the imperial family.

priests associated with the imperial cult (two *seviri*), all of which suggests the dedication of one or more of the three temples in the town to the imperial cult. The third plausible example is the shrine within the forum at Clunia (see Figure 3.4). It lay within the eastern row of shops and consisted of three rooms, the central one double width (Palol and Guitart 2000: 70–7). This central room contained traces of statue bases and some form of altar, as well as fragments of two large statues, one a bronze togate statue. Marble heads of a young Augustus and a young Nero, as well as other statue fragments, were found in nearby rooms, and one of the smaller adjoining rooms seems to have contained a bench for setting up statues. Again, the cumulative evidence points to an association with the imperial cult, but the differences in size and layout of the shrines points to a different form of ritual engagement to that at Italica.

The evidence from Britain for temples to the imperial cult is even more uncertain. The provincial cult was located in the large and elaborately decorated temple to Claudius at Colchester, and the dedications to aspects of the imperial cult at London point to activity there as well. However, elsewhere in the civilian sector, the evidence is sparse. The layout of the forum in the province differs from that elsewhere in the western provinces, with the lack of free-standing podium temples in most cases (Revell 2007). Instead, many of the forum basilicas contain an open room placed at the centre of the rear range of rooms, on the dominant axis through the complex from the entranceway. This is the case at Caerwent, where the central room had a wide-arched entrance and a raised floor (Brewer 1993), and this echoes those found at both Silchester and Caistor (Fulford and Timby 2000; Frere 1971 respectively). The most likely interpretation for this is as a shrine of some form, and it has been ascribed to the imperial cult based on analogies with the Shrine of the Standards in the corresponding position within the military principia, whereas in reality the architectural relationship between the civilian forum and the military headquarters are more problematic. However, the presence of an internal shrine is not unprecedented, and can be seen in the town forum at Tarraco for example (Dupré I Raventos 1995: 338–9, figure 3). If these shrines in Britain are indeed to the imperial cult, it would locate the worship of the deified emperor in the urban centre, within the most prestigious political building of the town. As at Clunia, the relationship between the architectural space and the public rituals would necessarily be different to that in towns with freestanding temples.

There is much clearer evidence for the priesthoods attached to the imperial cult, and the complex, multiple levels from municipal to provincial level. A key part of this was the provincial priesthood, which seems to have been a prestigious post within the magisterial career. The personnel for these were drawn from the province as a whole, and so the leading members of other towns of the province would have had the opportunity to serve as priest. From Italica, Caecilianus served as *flamen provinciae Baeticae* (CILA 2.343) and from Munigua, there is evidence for a priestess, this time to the Divae, or deified female relatives of the emperors (CILA 2.1055: *flaminica divarum Augustarum splendidissimae provinciae Baeticae*). This co-existed with the municipal priesthoods: at Italica, Caecilianus was not only priest of the provincial cult, but also served as *flamen divi Traiani* within the town (CILA 2.343); there is also mention of a *flamen Augustalis* (CILA 2.347), and from Clunia there are two references to the cult of Rome and Augustus (Clunia II 18, 28). There may also have been a *conventus* cult, but there is limited evidence for its widespread occurrence: for Tarraconensis it is patchy, and there is none for Baetica or Lusitania; therefore we must question how common it actually was (Etienne 1958:177–8, 180–2; Curchin 1996: 148). The evidence for a Conventus Cluniensis cult is dubious: Etienne cites CIL 2.6093 in support of this hypothesis; however, this inscription refers to a provincial priesthood. It is impossible to be certain whether the cult was situated at the *conventus* capital, and therefore what, if any, impact it would have had on the people of Clunia.

Other colleges of priests are evident from the epigraphic record. One of the more ubiquitous was the *sevir* and the associated *Augustales*. These were made up mainly of wealthy freedmen, and formed a way to incorporate them into the system of honours and munificence. The criteria for whether the local priests were accorded the title of *sevir*, *Augustalis*, or the two in combination is unknown, and in any case, there is unlikely to have been a strict differentiation. *Seviri* are attested at Italica (CILA 2.345; also possibly 515, 572) and Munigua (CILA 2.1054; also possibly 1094); there is evidence for a *sevir Augustalis* at Munigua (CILA 2.1061), and finally, for *Augustales* at Clunia (Clunia II 212), Italica (CILA 2.348, 388), and possibly Munigua (CILA 2.1094). Under Augustus, the traditional cult of the Lares was also renewed under the title of the Lares Augusti, and somehow incorporated into the imperial cult throughout the empire, with its own college of priests. This college is attested at Italica, with an inscription set up by a *magister Larum Augustorum* (CILA 2.385). In Britain, the evidence is more restricted: there is epigraphic evidence for an *Augustalis* at Bath (RIB 154), but otherwise the imperial cult is restricted to the military zone and the *coloniae* of Lincoln and York. However, there is the possibility that this under-representation may be a result of the lack of epigraphic evidence, as no priests are attested at Colchester, where we would expect a college of priests associated with the temple of Divus Claudius.

So far, I have dealt with religious architecture and priesthoods; the third theme I wish to explore is that of dedications. It would be expected that dedications to the deified emperor would have formed a major part of the cult; however, the evidence from both Spain and Britain is sparse. Indeed, Fishwick comments that overall, there are very few dedications directly to the emperor: they are more likely to be to another deity on his behalf (Fishwick 1987–2005:35; see also Price 1980 for a similar argument relating to sacrifice in Asia Minor). This phenomenon can also be seen in the evidence here. Dedications were set up to the Deified Vespasian and Titus by the townspeople of Munigua (CILA 2.1064, 1065), however more common are dedications to the emperor's Numen or divine spirit, such the example from Caerwent, dedicated to Mars Lenus and the Numen Augusti (RIB 309; other examples have been found in London, RIB 5, B7.2, and Bath RIB 146, 152). A variation on this is the DNMQE inscriptions: the dedication to the living emperor, followed by the name of the dedicant and *devotus numini maiestatique eius* (Etienne 1958: 310ff). Four third-century dedications from Italica use this formula (CILA 2.370–3), their date fitting with Fishwick's hypothesis that the Numen of the living emperor only flourished during the mid-third century (Fishwick 1969: 85–7). A more common way of incorporating the living emperor was to offer a dedication for the safety (*pro salute*) of the emperor, such as those found at Clunia, Italica and London (Clunia II 22, CILA 2.369, RIB 4 respectively). Another variant was dedications to the imperial house, such as the dedication set up to the Domus Divina at London (Brit. 7.2). Whether these can strictly be said to have been part of the imperial cult is unclear, but the mention of the emperor during the act of the dedication would have recalled his person and his authority when they were viewed.

An extension of the imperial cult can be seen in the cult of the Augustan gods and virtues. Various deities were given the epithet *Augustus/a*, which Fishwick has argued signified an association between them and the emperor, defining the sphere of the deities' powers as including protection over the emperor (Fishwick 1987–2005: 448). Over time, this epithet probably lost its precise meaning, and may have come to merely signify royal or imperial (ibid.). From the Iberian peninsula, there are a number of examples of dedications to deities with specific links to the imperial family, such as the Julio-Claudian claim of divine ancestry. Thus, from Italica, we have examples of dedications to Apollo Augustus and Mercury Augustus (CILA 2.342, 347 respectively); from Clunia, there is a dedication to Jupiter Augustus Ultor (Clunia II 8). Other deities were incorporated into this Augustan pantheon, from the traditional deities of Ceres Augusta and Hercules Augustus, both found in the main sanctuary at Munigua (CILA 2.1055, 1064 respectively), to deities imported from the provinces, such as the conflation with the African goddess Caelestis as Caelestis Pia Augusta found at Italica (CILA 2.348). Similar to the Augustan gods are the cults of the so-called Augustan virtues: the personification and deification of particular virtues which were incorporated into the sphere of the living emperor through the same epithet (Etienne 1958: 334). Examples have been found at Italica, with a dedication to Victoria Augusta (CILA 2.358), and at Munigua, to Fortuna Crescens Augusta (CILA 2.1064). As these were similar to the imperial personifications on coinage, this would have reinforced a pre-existing association with the emperor in the minds of the worshippers.

The evidence for the imperial cult from the temples, priesthoods and dedications tells us a certain amount about the incidence of the imperial cult, but it provides less evidence for how the cult formed part of everyday experience. For that, we need to look for evidence for the liturgy and ceremonies, through which the inhabitants of the towns would have understood and reproduced the ideology of the power of the emperor. However, we need to be wary in reconstructing these ceremonies due to the paucity of direct evidence for each community. The normative picture for the rituals of the imperial cult has been built up using the more abundant evidence from Italy and the eastern half of the empire, and then applied to the west; the danger is that without a level of sensitivity to the contextual detail, an isolated piece of evidence is used to validate the whole package (Fishwick 1987–2005: 588). Although not ideal, the picture presented is necessarily an amalgamation of the wider evidence, with the necessary caveat that the local detail may differ.

The imperial cult had its own calendar of festival days, geared towards specific imperial anniversaries. Various incomplete copies have been found throughout the empire (ibid. 483–99 for a fuller discussion of the evidence), including the *Feriale Duranum* from the cohors XX Palmyrenorum stationed at Dura Europus and dated to AD 224/5–235 (Fink et al. 1940). The calendar lists the religious festivals held throughout the year, and of the 41 extant, 27 refer to the imperial cult, both to the deified emperors and their families, and to the reigning emperor (ibid. 173). One typical example is that for September 23, the birthday of the deified Augustus, for which the sacrifice of an ox is prescribed (ibid. col.2, l.8). Similarly, on January 3, vows were to be fulfilled and offered to the living emperor, Marcus Aurelius Severus Alexander, with sacrifices to a number of other deities (ibid. col.1 ll.2–6). Inevitably, such calendars would have varied over time and space, but the evidence of a similar calendar from Cumae (CIL 10.8375) and a dedication referring to a calendar of festivals from Forum Clodii (ILS 154) both confirm that regular sacrifice formed part of the cult activity. Such calendars provide a flavour of how the religious year would have been organised around demarcated days celebrating significant imperial events, such as the birthday of living and deified emperors and their relatives, and celebrations of other noteworthy occasions (Fishwick 1987–2005: 500). Such festivals were marked out as special days, as demonstrated by the stipulation in the municipal law that political activities should not take place on the days of festival associated with the imperial cult (*lex Flav.* 31 and 92).

On these days, there were a number of rituals which might form part of the festivities. Firstly, the townspeople might process to through the town to the site of the temple or altar. Evidence from the eastern empire demonstrates that this was a regular part of the cult, and that the images of the emperor were carried on litters as part of the procession (Fishwick 1987–2005 550–3). The layout of the religious buildings in relation to the town grid suggests that such processions were part of the religious liturgy. At Italica, the Traianeum lies at the intersection of two of the major routes into the town, marked by a *quadrifons* or similar monumental archway just before the temple itself (Garcia y Bellído 1960: 79; León 1988: 19–21). These linked it to the amphitheatre, reinforcing the frequent connection between the imperial cult and public games or shows (Gros 1994: 27). To process from one to the other, the worshipper would follow one of the widest roads in the town. The altar was located at the axis between the entrance and the temple, and presumably any processions would have ended there. We know from epigraphic and iconographic evidence that sacrifice formed a prominent part of the rituals (Price 1980; Fishwick 1987–2005: 502–19): the *Feriale Duranum* stipulates which animals should be sacrificed during each festival, and other evidence suggests that incense or wine could be offered as well. The layout of the shrine at Munigua, reached via two formal routes, also suggests that processions formed part of the rituals there. However, it was not necessary to have a dedicated shrine: an altar alone could be sufficient. Therefore we should not discount the possibility of such rituals in the other towns for which we have no evidence of a temple or shrine; the processions and sacrifice could equally well have focussed on an altar in an open public space, which would leave little archaeological evidence.

The imperial priests wore a specific costume, consisting of a *toga praetexta*, with a cap ending in a spike of olive wood (the *apex*) and decorated with a thread of wool (ibid. 475–6). Depictions of such caps have been found at Tarraco, where friezes believed to be from the provincial cult centre show two different types, as well as a sacrificial knife and purification shaker (TED'A 1989: 162–3, fig. 9). The priest also wore a crown adorned with the emperor's image (Price 1984:170), and at Italica, the priestess Vibia Modesta dedicated her own golden flaminate crown in the Traianeum (CILA 2.358). As mentioned above, the festivals often incorporated public games or shows which the populations of the town would attend. Similarly, there is evidence from Spain of the *flamen* and the *flaminica* providing banquets, which may have formed part of the festivities (Fishwick 1987–2005: 584–7). Also connected with the rituals of the imperial cult, although not necessarily part of these festivals, are the numerous dedications mentioned above. Some of these represent the dedications of gifts, others, the complex rituals involving the taking of a vow and the dedication in thanks on its fulfilment (Derks 1995; see also Chapter 4).

It is clear from the discussion above that the evidence for the liturgy of the imperial cult from any single community is somewhat limited. However, it was through these practices, the processions, sacrifices and dedications, that the ideology of the emperor as a divine being was recreated and made part of the socio-political structures of the empire as a whole. The imperial cult placed the emperor amongst the gods, its rituals echoing those performed in religious festivals to the other deities, and the centrality and permanence of the temples and shrines provided a daily reminder of his divine nature. Less important to this discussion is the question of whether the worship of the living emperor formed part of the cult, for example in the debate over the dedication of the temple at Colchester (Fishwick 1972, 1995; Simpson 1994). These rituals, whether to a living or dead emperor, problematized the status of the emperor: he was human, but also divine, regardless of the precise moment when that divinity was reached. This anticipated divinity reinforced the ideology of the emperor as the head of the Roman political system. In the rituals for his worship, the people of the empire actively accepted and reproduced that ideology: it was not merely a one-sided imposition from Rome, but relied upon the actions of his subjects and their recreation of that power.

3.4 THE EMPEROR'S POLITICAL AUTHORITY

So far, we have seen how the provincial communities encountered the emperor as a somewhat abstract and remote being, but the emperor was also a political figure, with the power to have a real effect on their lives. His constitutional power was exercised predominantly through the political magistracies, with an emphasis upon judicial authority, benefaction and patronage, but his command extended to the provinces, binding them to the centre. This made it possible to form an ongoing relationship, but also that certain communities would have a closer or privileged association due to the inter-personal nature of such links. The workings of the political power of the emperor have been the subject of extensive research (for example Millar 1977; Hopkins 1978; Boatwright 2000), and it is clear that both his judicial authority and his role as benefactor were means of binding the provinces to the centre. However, these links and acts of donation can only be traced with total confidence through the epigraphic evidence and the historical sources, and so are difficult to detect from areas with limited inscriptions or which did not feature significantly in pages of the imperial histories. This could produce an unrepresentative picture of such links, and so any comparison of specific areas need to be treated with caution.

One aspect of the emperor's judicial role was the power to found a town or to change its constitutional status. Large numbers of *coloniae* and *municipia* were founded by Julius Caesar and Augustus, and this continued throughout the first century AD. However, by the second century ex novo foundations were much rarer, and change of constitutional status was more usual. In the preceding chapter, I argued that the town played a prominent role within Roman ideology, and was perceived as an almost supernatural entity, shrouded by quasi-religious ritual. Thus, for a town to be given a new constitution was a significant act, almost an act of rebirth. The town had to petition the emperor, and if it received a favourable answer it usually incorporated his name within its titles, a practice which Millar argues was adopted from the Hellenistic kings via Roman magistrates in the east during the late Republic (Millar 1977: 395–6). Thus, Bilbilis was presumably granted municipal status by Augustus and took his name within its new title of Municipium Augusta Bilbilis. Similarly, Colonia Aelia Augusta Italica commemorated being granted both municipal status by Augustus and colonial status by Hadrian. It is clear from urban charters that the emperor also possessed the authority to appoint the initial magistrates (*lex col.* 26), and when Italica became a *municipium*, the first priests were appointed by (or in the name of) the emperor. This act of patronage was an honour which L. Herius, L. Blattius Traianus Pollio and C. Traius Pollio celebrated in the text of inscriptions, increasing their own prestige through their association with the emperor (CILA 2.382, 383), whilst at the same time creating a written testament to his judicial authority.

A second element of his judicial power was his role as final arbiter in matters of law. When a judicial dispute arose between the provincial governor and the people of Munigua, the townspeople appealed to Titus for judgement (CILA 2.1052; see Millar 1977: 441–2). The letter from the emperor containing the judgement, addressed to the townspeople as a body, was then inscribed on bronze and publicly displayed in the forum; even though the emperor ruled against them overall, the fact that it was from the emperor made it a significant document. In this case, the people of Munigua clearly believed that they had the right to appeal to the emperor in person, sending delegates to Rome to argue their case before him, and presumably drawing upon the networks of patronage which spread from the province to capital in an attempt to sway his judgement in their favour. The wording of the letter maintains the idea of a personal relationship between the emperor and the townspeople, with the emperor addressing the *quattuorviri* and decurions directly.

The goodwill of the emperor might take a more physical form through the donation of building projects, either civic architecture or infrastructure. There is a tendency amongst provincial archaeologists to attribute substantial building projects to imperial benefaction on the coincidence of an imperial visit to the province and the broad construction date of the building. As mentioned in Chapter 2, a number of authors have argued as certain fact that Hadrian was responsible for the construction of the forum at Wroxeter, based upon the dedication of the building to him (RIB 228), overlooking the time lag between the inception of such a project and its completion. Trying to reconstruct these links more critically is problematic: within the case-studies, there are no examples of building work which can be securely attributed to an emperor. Nevertheless, it is highly probable that Hadrian acted as benefactor for the construction of the Nova Urbs (as discussed in Boatwright 2000: 162–7). The fact that it was the *patria* of the emperor suggests a privileged relationship, and the townspeople successfully petitioned him for colonial status (Aulus Gellius *Noctes Atticae* 16.13.4–5; Millar 1977: 408). The Nova Urbs substantially expanded the size of the town, incorporating substantial public buildings and opulent domestic residences, and it is widely accepted that this must have been the product of the intervention and personal patronage of the emperor. Furthermore, Hadrian also served as *duovir quinquennalis* of the town (HA *Hadr.* 19.1), the most prestigious magistracy, which can be read as both a means of honouring the emperor through the request, and as a conduit for his continued largesse.

This system of patronage, integral to the working of Roman politics, also allowed the emperor's benefaction to be extended to individual subjects, whether through formally constituted patron-client links, or through informal relationships of favours and obligation (Saller 1989 argues against a strict classification between these). Such links were exercised through personal relationships, with the idea of reciprocity from the client to the emperor and vice versa: in return for the favour of the emperor, the recipient was expected to provide political support and personal loyalty (Saller 1982: 41–78). Through this mechanism, the political power of the emperor was strengthened as increasing numbers of people became dependent upon his favour. Both Millar (1977) and Saller (1982) have discussed the various forms this took, demonstrating how they worked at a personal level, spreading the authority of the emperor through a network of intimate relationships. Rather than go through them in great detail, I only want to mention a selection. We have already seen the case of the three priests from Italica appointed by Augustus, who mentioned this honour on their dedications (CILA 2.382, 383; in this I have followed the interpretation of Canto 1981). The emperor could also raise members of the provincial elite to senatorial or equestrian rank through the process of *adlectio*, and Eck has argued for between 13 and 16 senators from Italica (Eck 1997a). Again, such personal relationships with the emperor could be recorded on stone. At Italica, a man raised to senatorial rank by Trajan included it on an inscription (CILA 2.403), emphasising the importance of the relationship to him and his family, and also that these acts were remembered after their initial event. There is the possibility that once elevated to senatorial rank, the nature of the relationship between such families and their local communities changed from one of direct involvement to more distant patronage (Caballos Rufino 1998: 142–5 for the evidence for and against equites maintaining direct contact). Richard Saller has argued that those going to Rome remained involved with their local *patriae* through links of patronage, *hospitium*, and inheritance, with some returning to their communities on retirement (Saller 1982: 185–7; also Eck 1997b). This brought the provincial communities into these networks at the highest level, with the attraction that they could acquire powerful patrons at Rome. On the other hand, these networks of imperial patronage could bring the emperor's favourites into the community through the appointment of officials over them. At Italica, there is evidence for a *curator rei publicae*, appointed by the emperor to attend to the affairs of the town (CILA 2.370–1, 379; Garnsey and Saller 1987: 34; Boatwright 2000: 73–8), again showing how the emperor had the authority to impact on the political life of the town.

The political influence of the emperor on provincial communities has tended to be understated as a consequence of the idea that the empire was administered through the local elites. However, it is important to remember that he still had the ability to have a very real impact on the towns of the empire both in an official capacity through his judicial authority, and in a more unofficial way through his position at the head of the networks of patronage and recommendation. These were networks into which the local elites were increasingly drawn, and as they were incorporated into the equestrian and senatorial ranks at Rome, they provided a link between the local and the empire-wide levels. Similarly, in any appeal to the emperor for legal redress, these were the people who would have acted on behalf of the towns, whether before the emperor himself or before his representative. Although there would have been a certain impact on the townspeople as a whole, for example when the emperor altered the legal status of a town, the political power of the emperor was something which ultimately would have been experienced differently between the elites and the non-elites of a town. Furthermore, the individual nature of these relationships suggests that it would also have been regionally variable, with emperors favouring specific provinces or towns as recipients of their favours, such as Hadrian's treatment of Italica. In particular the lack of members of the senatorial order from Britain strongly suggests a different level of engagement which could be explained either through the ongoing military presence within the province, or alternatively through the reaction of the people of the province to the cultural changes brought by Roman imperialism

3.5 AN IMPERIAL HISTORY?

The final aspect I want to look at is the question of whether the succession of emperors over time formed a shared historical narrative throughout the provinces. From Augustus onwards, the history of the empire increasingly revolved around the history of the emperor and his achievements; alternative histories were rewritten as a single mythological past and thus became communal memory. As Patrick Geary argues for the early Medieval period, the way a society remembers its history is a process of "transmission, suppression and recreation" (Geary 1994: 8). Specific events from the past (whether real or mythical) will be remembered and passed on because they are fundamental to the way that society, or a specific section of it, constructs its own identity. The minute details of that event will be selected, elaborated upon or even invented so that they might accord with the overarching ideology of the time. Furthermore, Geary argues that the creation of a communal history should be seen as political, with certain groups taking control of the past in order to further their own goals (ibid. 12; see also Hobsbawm 1993; Osborne 1996: 4–15; Gowing 2005: 7–15).

Memory should be seen as an active process of creating a history which is connected to the present, and which carries meaning in the present. The question here is whether, in the Roman empire, a political history was constructed which presented the empire as sharing a single history and mythology, narrated around the actions of the emperor. We should see this as political, and as part of an imperial discourse: many of the Roman towns were founded from pre-existing communities, but these histories came to be down-played or rewritten in favour of their Roman connections. In approaching this question, we are faced with a fundamental problem: the evidence from the communities themselves is largely archaeological. The historical sources we have were written by historians from outside these communities. Many were based at Rome, never travelling to Spain or Britain. Therefore, there is always the danger that these imperial histories might not reflect the shared histories of the provincial peoples (for example, Braund 1996 on Britain and its role in the Roman historical tradition).

Sue Alcock has argued for a materiality of memory, incorporating places and monuments which were given a situated and changing metaphorical meaning (Alcock 2002: 24–8), and has reconstructed the manipulation of the past in Roman Greece from the evidence of temples and the public spaces of the town. Some of the ways in which the emperor was encountered by the people of the provinces had the potential to be used to order or shape the narrative of the past. Perhaps the clearest example of this is in the statues and the inscriptions. Augustus used the iconography of the Forum Augustum as a way to recreate a history of Rome which responded to his own political needs (Flower 1996: 224–36), and Trajan may have had the same intention with the iconography of his forum (Gowing 2005: 147–8). In the towns outside Rome, the creation of groups of imperial statues, with associated inscriptions, may also have become not only an aide-memoire to an imperial history, but a way in which that new history was created and learnt. Based upon the epigraphic evidence, Garriguet has argued for a sequence of statues at Munigua which incorporated Vespasian, Titus and possibly Domitian (CILA 2.1064-6; Garriguet 2004; Gimeno Pascual 2003: 190–1 for contexts). The statues of Vespasian and Titus were donated at the same time, in the period between the deaths of Vespasian in June AD 79 and of Titus in September AD 81. The text of the dedication to Titus was altered to incorporate the title *divus*, and the statue of Domitian may have been added at the same time. This, allied with the genealogies included in the inscriptions, gives a chronological depth to the group which would have been identifiable to the viewer. They were discovered during excavations in the area below the forum, and so it likely that the forum itself was their original location, echoing the way in which such spaces became the site for the creation of an imperial gallery elsewhere in the empire (Rose 1997). We can see a similar thing at Italica, with its collection of imperial statues and dedications to the imperial family (Garriguet 2004: 78–9; section 3.2 above). The act of *damnatio memoriae*, with the removal of the images and the names of the emperors, represented a reordering of the past, with certain emperors obliterated from this historical narrative. The construction of a calendar for the commemoration of the *divi* and *divae* reinforced this creation of an imperial past through the ritualised commemoration of individuals and key events of their lives.

This may not only have been the creation of a historical narrative distant in space, but a narrative which some towns actively sought to share in, staking a claim in empire-wide events (see Carroll 2002 for the case of the Ubii). We have already seen how the emperor was involved in the refounding of towns in Spain such as Bilbilis or Clunia. This caused an intersection between the history of the town and the wider narrative of imperial succession, reinforced by their shared nomenclature. In some cases, the emperor might feature more prominently in this constructed history, such as in the case of Colonia Clunia Sulpicia, which was presumably named after the emperor Galba. This reflected its role in the events of the Civil Wars of AD 69, as recounted by Suetonius. When Galba was governor of Tarraconensis, the priest of Jupiter at Clunia reported to him certain signs and prophesies which predicted that some day the ruler of the world would come from Spain (Suetonius *Galba* 9.2), and this incident was said to be one of the factors influencing Galba's decision to enter the struggle for power. Whether this story is accurate or not is of secondary importance; it serves to demonstrate the way in which the history of a distant provincial town might be increasingly woven into the history of the empire, dominated by the figure and the actions of the emperors.

A similar interweaving can be seen in the case of the relationship between Hadrian and Italica. He was responsible for the town being given the new status of *colonia*, with the incorporation of his name Aelia into the titles of the town. His presumed benefaction in the construction of the Nova Urbs and the temple to Divus Trajan would have given him a place in the subsequent narrative of the town's history. Furthermore, Simon Keay has argued that at about this time that the inhabitants of Italica chose to emphasise the Roman elements of their history (Keay 1997a: especially 25–8). The inscription celebrating L. Aemilius Paullus' dedication of the spoils from the Battle of Zakynthos to the town was recut (CILA 2.377), and the second-century author, Appian, wrote that Scipio Africanus settled wounded soldiers there after the Battle of Ilipa, 206/5 BC (Appian

Iberica 38), an event which is not mentioned by Livy. Here we can see the inhabitants of Italica selecting certain incidents from their past as being more important than others, re-creating their own history within a changing political context. Again, debate concerning the veracity of such events obscures the active way in which they reinterpreted their own past to give their town a Roman history, worthy of its increased status and position as the birthplace of the emperor.

In a similar way, the mythology of Rome also became mythology of the empire. Augustus upheld his claim to power through an elaborate symbolic language which presented his reign as a new golden age, and exploited his alleged connections to a mythical Roman past (Zanker 1988). This imperial ideology was then adopted within the provinces, as can be seen in the architectural decoration of Tarraco and Merida, and this can also be seen at Italica and later at Bath. During the Augustan period at Italica, commemorative coins were minted modelled on imperial themes such as the she-wolf with Romulus and Remus (Keay 1997a: 37–8). This theme can also be seen re-used during the Hadrianic period on a plaque for a fountain depicting the she-wolf with the two children found in the monumental area of the Vetus Urbs (León 1995 no. 5). Martin Henig has argued that Augustan imagery can also be seen at Bath in the decoration of the temple, with the use of stars and the Oceanus-Medusa mask set on a *clipeus virtutis* and surrounded by a *corona civica* which is held aloft by Victories standing on globes. Tritons filled the corners of the pediment, recalling the Battle of Actium (Henig 1999: 419–23). The question of whether they had the same meaning in the provinces as at Rome is difficult to answer, particularly in the case of Bath, where it is possible that the imperial imagery was used by the local elite to reinforce their own positions of power. However, this iconography repeated the themes found on coinage, reinforcing the association with the emperor and his imperial authority. Whether or not the nuances of its significance were understood, such images represent a shared mythology and iconographic language, constructed around the emperor and reinforcing his authority.

Although the evidence is at times circumstantial, part of being Roman was sharing in a Roman history, and from the time of Augustus onwards, the history of the empire revolved around the emperor. Imperial actions such as urban foundations had an effect on specific communities, tying them into wider events and histories. The act of commemorating and remembering these histories, whether in the name of the town or through a distant folk tale, made them real. People actively created their own histories and literally made a place for themselves within the overall history of the empire, which depended on their participation, however insignificant, in events relating to the emperor. In addition, as Augustus created a mythical past to reinforce his own political power, so the adoption of those same myths as a communal heritage by people of the empire further recreated this power. Myths such as that of Romulus and Remus came to symbolise a shared sense of history, whilst at the same time maintaining the aura of imperial power.

3.6 DIFFERENT PLACES, DIFFERENT EMPERORS

There was no single mechanism by which the power and persona of the emperor were transmitted throughout the Roman empire. Instead, his authority was presenced through a variety of methods which produced a shifting and enigmatic picture. To take a holistic view of them in operation, this picture appears unproblematic, and the power of the emperor a tangible reality. The power of the emperor was written into the physical fabric of the provincial towns, with his images and titles adorning the public areas. The subjects of these statues echoed the ideological themes through which he legitimated his position of power: his roles as chief magistrate, as successful general, and as mythical hero/god. This last aspect was further developed through the imperial cult: his ambiguous position between mortal and immortal, evident in his portraits and titles, was negotiated and recreated through the rituals associated with the religious worship. This ambiguity formed one of the major ideological themes of his rule: his power was validated because he was more than mortal. Nevertheless, he was still a man, with political authority through his possession of patronage and benefaction. Whilst these roles seem contradictory, the overall effect of the imperial ideology was to make them consistent and coherent.

We can see this build up of imperial associations if we reconstruct the political ceremonies and their spatial context. According to the statutes of the Flavian municipal law, on their election, the *duumviri*, aediles and quaestors swore an oath in an assembly in the name of Jupiter, Augustus, the deified Claudius, Vepasian, Titus, Domitian and the Penates (*lex Flav.* 59). Over time the precise list of emperors would have changed somewhat, given the *damnatio memoriae* of Domitian and the deification of subsequent emperors. Nevertheless, the annual swearing-in ceremony for the new magistrates provided a repetitive reminder of the divine ancestry of the incumbent emperor. Although by this period it was a *colonia*, a similar oath was presumably sworn by the magistrates at Clunia in the forum in front of the rest of the community. We can begin to build up something of the impact of the emperor at such occasions. Imperial statues probably decorated the open area, including one of Julia, the daughter of Titus, found in the north-east angle of the forum. Furthermore, although none of the imperial dedications can be securely located to this area, two excavated fragments contained the letters AVG on them, one in letters 12 cm high (Clunia II 128, 157), possibly pointing to the emperor's name being set up prominently in the forum. There was probably a shrine to the imperial cult in one of the side ranges, decorated with more inscriptions and imperial statues, including heads of Augustus and Nero. Thus the newly elected magistrate stood at the political heart of the town, surrounded by the statues and written titles of the emperor and his family, in the area of a shrine to the imperial cult, and swore in the name of the deified former emperors to act according to the statues of the town. Each time the full name of the town was repeated, it also recalled the connection with Galba, and possibly the town's role in the events of his succession. Such ceremonies formed a repeated moment within which the power of the emperor was manifested and reproduced, and where the ideology of the emperor as the supreme political figure was made to seem part of the natural order of things. This gave it a legitimacy which made the authority of the emperor difficult to challenge, and at the same time, placed this authority within the individual towns of the empire.

However, this was not a uniform phenomenon, and as can be seen from the discussion as a whole, the picture was more complex. Repeatedly, much of the evidence has come from the same contexts: Italica, Clunia and Munigua, with less from Bilbilis and Britain. In part, this is a product of the epigraphic habit, as these are the towns from which we possess the greatest number of inscriptions. However, this does not negate the fact that there are major discrepancies between the ways in which the people of the empire experienced the power of the emperor. At Italica, we can see how the townspeople were fully integrated into the ideology of the emperor: its history was tightly bound up with that of Rome, with various emperors as powerful benefactors. The public areas were adorned with numerous statues of the emperor, and a dedicated cult centre stood at the heart of the town. For the people from Bilbilis, the situation was substantially different, with fewer dedications and statues, and perhaps a temple to the imperial cult. The situation at the civitas capitals of Britain was different again, with some evidence for the imperial cult, but overall fewer statues and inscriptions to recall his power. In particular, as these towns do not seem to have been fully integrated into the patronage links, they had less experience of the direct political power of the emperor. In this situation, we might expect the rituals of worship to be more important in informing their understanding of the emperor and his power, although again concrete evidence is sparse. The links of patronage also raises the question of different attitudes to the emperor within each community, with the local elites at least having the possibility (although for most probably not the reality) of a more direct relationship with him, mediated through the provincial council or through sending embassies to Rome. For the non-elites, his power would have been encountered in more abstract ways, through his statues, or the worship of his predecessors. As Barrett argues, we should not view this through a centre-periphery model (Barrett 1989): the emperor was a powerful presence in the activities of military life, and as the army was mainly stationed on the outskirts of the empire, spreading the ideology of the emperor to the very frontiers, we are presented with a more nuanced picture than this model allows for. Inevitably, the individual historical trajectory of each community and the way in which they were incorporated into the structures of the Roman Empire will have influenced their particular outcomes. However, it is enough to say that, whilst the emperor and the ideology legitimating his position were one of the social structures which determined peoples' understanding of being Roman, it was also one of the factors through which this experience differed across the empire.

FOUR

ADDRESSING THE DIVINE

4.1 ROMAN RELIGION AS PRACTISE

The need for a more powerful entity or supreme being to provide some form of order to the essentially chaotic nature of human existence is a phenomenon which can be seen throughout much of the past, and this is no less true of the Roman empire. For a Roman, the gods were everywhere, powerful forces with an interest in all aspects of life. At Rome itself, the senate could only hold their regular meetings within a *templum*: an area formally designated as religious space by the augurs. Before each meeting, the auspices had to be taken to ascertain whether or not the gods were favourable; any business transacted without divine sanction could be declared invalid (Beard et al. 1998: 23). Religion and religious activity were a key part of the cultural changes within the western provinces, with the spread of Latin dedications to both Roman and indigenous deities pointing to the complexity of these changes. In spite of this, religion has been something of a neglected topic in the study of Romanization and the western province (Woolf 2000 for a fuller survey), and past approaches to the topic have tended to concentrate on the deities and the temples. Much of this work has been carried out within the framework of Romanization, whether explicit or implicit, but in this aspect, perhaps more than any other element of Romanization, the relationship between imperial and indigenous is complex and dynamic.

This can be seen most clearly in the attempts to categorise the religions themselves. For the western provinces, the dominant discourse has been a dichotomy of Roman and native, or Roman and Celtic, with the eastern mystery cults sitting somewhat awkwardly as a third discrete strand. This is presented by many writers as a polar opposition with few, if any, overlapping characteristics, and often with one side somehow preferable or more authentic. Jane Webster has argued that this has in part been the result of an evolutionary paradigm of social progress, with Roman anthropomorphic religion a stage between Celtic paganism and Christian monotheism (Webster 1997a). In this vein, in her early work, Miranda Green sets up a dichotomy of Roman and Celtic deities, assessing the level (or lack) of movement from Celtic to Roman (Green 1976). For example, in discussing Silchester, she produces a clear and apparently unproblematic distinction between them:

> At Silchester true Roman religion is seen, for example, in the presence of a "lararium" and a Christian "church". Celtic influence reveals itself in Romano-Celtic shrines, Jupiter's presence as a wheel god, and Hercules Saegron. (ibid. 51)

Yet, this division is not unproblematic. The examples Green cites for Celtic religion are all syncretisms, raising the awkward question of their relationship to the original cult within an imperial discourse. To call a Christian church "true Roman religion" is to mask the shifting attitudes towards Christianity: essentially an eastern cult, it was a dissident religion for most of the imperial period, promoting very un-Roman behaviour and ritual. It is only from the early fourth century that we can describe Christianity as a Roman religion. Similarly for Roman Spain, Fear separates pre-Roman forms of belief, whether Punic, Celtic or Iberian, from the post-conquest cultural forms and discusses them as a distinct phenomenon which provides evidence for the continuation of pre-Roman culture, downplaying the complexity of syncretism and changing social contexts (Fear 1996: 227–69).

This polarization of Roman and pre-Roman is sometimes coupled with a consideration of the 'mystical' properties of the cult: how it fulfilled the spiritual need of the worshippers. Often the Celtic worship of nature, associated with fertility rites and totemism is contrasted with the post-conquest transformation, with new deities characterised as being symbolic of violence, trade and travel (for example, Woodward 1992: 51–65, especially 57–62). The religious satisfaction to be gained from the worship of Roman gods is dismissed, and it is presented as less authentic than Celtic beliefs, with Woodward arguing for "the replacement of the collective, naturalistic and elemental beliefs of the pagan Celts by the overt materialism and individuality promoted by the urbanized Roman elite and military machine" (ibid. 51). In a similar vein, it is easy to contrast eastern and Roman cults, arguing that the "ebullient alive, sympathetic and responsive" Oriental cults were more emotionally satisfying than the "staccato officialism of the Roman state cult" (Green 1976: 60). Such views can be criticised as something we can never hope to know about the people of the past (for example, MacMullen 1981: 65–7), but it also reveals the modern prejudices towards the various religious systems. Although we can characterise the nature of religious worship from the archaeological and textual sources, the strength of religious belief will always remain enigmatic. Ultimately it is very easy to be cynical about the motives behind the worship of Roman cults, but the danger is that such reactions are overly influenced by the continuing echoes of the past within both Judaeo-Christian religion and the hippie/New Age/Celtic movements popular from the 1960s onwards.

This trend of polarising Roman and Celtic worship is exacerbated by a split within the academic community, with separate personnel looking at religion Rome, and in the provinces, and with insufficient interaction between the two bodies of thought. This is mirrored by and probably the result of, a divergence in material studied. The religion of the city of Rome itself is largely reconstructed from literary, epigraphic and icono-graphic evidence; however, in dealing with the provinces, in particular the western provinces, we are left with a much poorer epigraphic and iconographic record, and must rely upon the enigmatic remains of the cult itself: the physical structures and ritual paraphernalia. There is often insufficient awareness of the nuances and pitfalls of the various forms of evidence across the disciplines. For example, Webster has argued for a millennial protest associated with the Druids in response to the Roman conquest of Gaul and Britain which changed the nature of Druidism, supporting her hypothesis with literary sources from Roman pre- and post-conquest writers (Webster 1999). However, as Beard, North and Price demonstrate, the textual evidence overall suggests a reformula-tion of the concepts of *religio* and *superstitio* within religious discourse at Rome (Beard et al. 1998: 221–2; see also Laurence 2001). In turn, their discussion of the religion of the western provinces is hampered by their over-reliance upon the epigraphic and iconographic evidence, not always plentiful in this area and subject to socio-political biases (Beard et al. 1998: 313–63, especially 319).

Many writers have approached Roman religion through the deities worshipped, looking at the distribution of evidence for their occur-rence, and the characteristics attributable to them. Most of this work has again been carried out through the Roman/native dichotomy dis-cussed above, particularly within what is traditionally termed the 'Celtic world'. The deity will be categorised as 'Roman', 'native' or 'eastern', the incidence of their worship noted, and their distribution mapped. It is easy to see how this approach then becomes part of the overall discourse of Romanization, leading to the equation of the Roman pantheon with Romanization, and the perceived continuation of Celtic deities with non-Romanization or resistance (for a fuller critique of this discourse, see Millett 1995, especially 93–5). This forms the core of Birley's approach to the deities of Roman Britain (Birley, E. 1986). The problems with his classification become evident when he deals with syncretism, which cannot be incorporated adequately within his categories. Similarly, his category of 'strictly Roman' excludes those imported from the east, such as Caelestis, Jupiter Dolichenus and Mithras; the limitations are most evident for Mithras, as it is questionable how far his worship actually reflects the eastern origins of the god, and how far it is the product of a Roman religious discourse of foreignness (Beard et al. 1998: 279–80). In the north-western provinces, where his worship was heavily associated with the military, this confusion over categorisation is particularly acute. By describing Mithras as an 'Eastern god', Birley sets an agenda which excludes the question of how Mithras was adopted within the western provinces: whether he was seen as an eastern deity, as part of a discourse of correct Roman worship, or as a predominantly military deity.

These problems with categorization are compounded by the fact that the majority of evidence for native deities is drawn from the Roman period, with the assumption that their worship was static and unchanging, and a direct reflection of the pre-existing situation. This view ignores the dynamic nature of religion, downplaying the complex nature of social change and the possible roles religion might play within that (Millett 1995). Jane Webster has argued that this act of *interpretatio* was essentially part of an imperial discourse, questioning whether the 'Celtic' element can unproblematically be identified within the later hybrid (Webster 1995a: 153). She further suggests that the equation of Roman and Celtic deities involved subjugating the Celtic deity within the Roman pantheon; it is then conceptualised within a Roman ideological framework and transformed from its original character (Webster 1995b: 178–9). Similarly, in her study of the epigraphic evidence from Hadrian's Wall, Amy Zoll (1995) has demonstrated that distinctions such as 'Roman' and 'native' are inadequate to account for the spectrum of worship. Approximately 20% of divinities fall outside this classification, and she concludes that this distinction might not have been important for the dedicators themselves (ibid. 136). How profitable this approach to deities, their classification and distribution is to the study of religion as a social institution and its role in social reproduction must remain open to question. There is a further problem with the nature of the evidence, as much of it is drawn from inscriptions and there is a danger that any distribution pattern is distorted by the epigraphic habit. MacMullen has argued that the highs and lows in the number of dedications to Isis in fact mirror fluctuations in the total number of inscriptions, concluding that the cult remained at a constant level (MacMullen 1981: 114–7, 144 n.31). Similarly, as the epigraphic uptake is also socially variable, there is the possibility that deities worshipped by the sections of society which are less likely to set up inscriptions will be less archaeologically visible.

The second approach to religion has been the study of the temples themselves. In the north-western provinces, where so-called Romano-Celtic temples are plentiful, much of this work has been similarly carried out within the native/Roman dichotomy which has again circumscribed the discussion of their role. The temples of Roman Britain have been researched most thoroughly by Lewis, who produced a catalogue of all known pagan temples and shrines in Roman Britain, with an elaborate typology of temple form (Lewis 1966). These were ordered by temple type; initially into 'Romano-Celtic', 'other temples', and 'Oriental cults'. The category of Romano-Celtic was subdivided into 'square type' and 'polygonal type'. Both groups were then analysed according to a secondary typology of hypothetical architectural styles: with a tower, with an all-over roof, or with an open *cella*. These had a further five subdivisions, dependant upon features such as open or closed porticoes and windows (ibid. 12–7, fig. 46). As a classification system this scheme is practically unworkable, as Lewis himself admits (ibid. 17). This typology is constructed within the discourse of Romanization, with each individual building, fitted into a scale of 'Celtic' to 'Roman' on the architectural detail of the main building alone (ibid. 10). The discussion of temple architecture in the Iberian peninsular is somewhat different, given the dominance of the Roman-style podium temple; in spite of this, they have similarly been approached through an overall paradigm of Romanization and used as signifiers for cultural change (for example, Mierse 1999). With both groups of material, there is the problem that in focussing on the temple building alone, its relationship to the surrounding complex and attendant features such as altars is ignored. It also fails to relate the temple to its broader context: how the people used the space, and other forms of material culture.

Such concentration on describing and categorizing deities and temples does not allow us to fully understand the nature of religious experience within the province. Much of this work lacks a clear theoretical framework, and the presence (or absence) of a 'Roman' god or temple is assumed to represent unproblematically Romanization and Roman power. In some cases, this leads to the search for a pre-conquest precursor to a shrine to bolster arguments for continuity in place, deity or even both (see for example Scheid 1995 on the Altbachtal at Trier). In contrast, I shall approach religion as a reproductive institution. Roman religion needs to be examined as a discourse functioning within both the context and the power structures of the empire as a whole, and the particular local conditions of any specific community. The issues I shall be dealing with in this chapter relate to Roman religious knowledge, how it is created, the form it took, and how it in turn reproduces Roman power and social structures. These lead to the core of a methodological problem when trying to understand belief systems in the past: as archaeologists we are constantly trying to access it through its material manifestations. We can never get into the minds of the people of the past, so we can never hope to 'prove' archaeologically what they actually believed, or how strong that belief was. However, this raises the question of how far the idea of 'belief' is appropriate in this context. Beard, North and Price have argued that it was not only who was worshipped but how they were worshipped, that is the form of cult being offered, that constitute correct religious practice (Beard et al. 1998: 214–7). John Scheid has similarly argued that belief and practice should be separated, and that the central requirements of Roman religion were related to *sacra* (such as sacrifice and vows) and divination (Scheid 2003: 18–28). These rituals constitute *religio*, which he defines as "a set of formal, objective rules, bequeathed by tradition. It was within the framework of those traditional rules and that system of 'etiquette' that an individual established a relationship with the gods" (ibid. 22–3).

This location of ritual as the core element of religion at Rome offers an alternative approach to the study of provincial religion and imperialism. From the archaeological evidence, we can re-construct the way religious practice formed a meaningful part of their daily existence and the way in which people of the past made sense of their world and how religious belief was written into their knowledge through ritual practice. Religion can be seen as both practical and discursive knowledge. The knowledge of how to act within a religious ceremony and the appropriate behaviour for divine worship resides within the practical knowledge of how to 'go on' in a social situation. As the Roman provinces were in many respects non-literate, it is possible that the majority of religious believers may have encountered religious truth through ritual: their religious knowledge lay in part within the repetitive ceremonies of worship (Asad 1983). Given the importance of *religio*, we need to be more critical of the relationship between the object of worship and the form of worship. A 'non-Roman' deity worshipped through 'Roman' religious practices challenges our assumptions of how imperial power was reproduced and raises question of whether adherence to ideas of *religio* was as important as worship of a deity of the Classical pantheon.

We should not see the literary sources as an ideal practice, or a paradigm for correct religious belief. As Dennis Feeney (1998) has argued, texts should be seen as one particular manifestation of religion: multiple and contradictory interpretations which contain the strategies and precon- ceptions of the author in response to a specific social discourse. There has been a tendency to view Roman religion as static and unchanging, whereas we should see it as a process of negotiation and adaptation: new cults, such as Bona Dea, the imperial cult or Mithraism, could add to and reshape the nature of religious knowledge. Provincial religion did not copy a rigid formula dictated in Rome, but entered into an empire-wide debate about correct worship. This discourse is a discourse of power, not only in the sense that certain people will use religious authority as a strategy for establishing their own social position, but in the sense that religion itself is the result of unequal power relations (Asad 1983: 237). Within an imperial framework, the form religious ritual took in the provinces was a response, whether acceptance or rejection, to Roman power (for contrasting conclusions about this, Webster 1997b; Whittaker 1997).

Religious knowledge was created through practice in the guise of reli- gious ritual: in the act of worship, people created both the preconditions for belief and the form belief took. Through these ritual acts, religious space became imbued with meaning, and this meaning was in turn read off in repetitive ritual use of these spaces (Graves 1989: 303). Representa- tions of deities provided a further means of constructing such knowledge: they formed a physical reality through which worshippers could con- ceptualise the divine as embodied beings, with their own attributes and histories (Elsner 1998: 12). Temples and shrines were places within which religious knowledge resided in the Roman Empire, and the repetitive acts of appropriate religious behaviour formed the encounters within which that knowledge was both written into and read off from these buildings. Therefore, a detailed, contextual study of these religious structures will provide an insight into the multiple and diverse ways in which local religious encounters were structured: which forms of knowledge and belief were being created. However, religious knowledge should not be separated from other forms of social knowledge (Asad 1983: 239): worshippers brought their understanding and experience of social norms from other aspects of their lives into religious worship.

Previous approaches to ritualised worship within the Roman provinces have been sketchy at best. There has been some work looking at the question of deposition as part of ritual behaviour. This includes the more spectacular deposits, such as those excavated at Conventina's Well where the context of a well shaft within an enclosure, filled with coins and other objects including altars to the goddess, make it relatively easy to identify the material as the product of ritual deposition (Allason-Jones and McKay 1985). Similar to this is work, such as that of Smith (2001), which looks at the distribution of material throughout the sacred enclosure. More problematic is the nature of deposition outside of an identifiable shrine, and in this, Hill's (1995) work on Iron Age deposition in Wessex has been influential. He argued that structured deposition is identifiable within the archaeological record, and as indicative of ritual activity. This has stimulated similar work with Roman material, for example, the identification of the ritual deposition at Pompeii and New-stead (respectively, Ciaraldi and Richardson 2000; Clarke 2000). There is still little work on the reconstructing ritual practice from the evidence of the temples and shrines themselves. In syntheses on Roman religion, it is dealt with briefly and in an uncritical manner, and with little attention to its physical context. Such accounts are methodologically problematic: both Green and Henig in their accounts of Romano-British religion provide surveys of the 'typical' picture for the whole province, divorcing the material from its archaeological context (Green 1976: 65–107; Henig 1995: 128–67). However, this approach has been criticised as invalid by Graves with reference to medieval Christianity, as producing a normative picture from decontextualized data, which is then reimposed uncritically onto the local context (Graves 1989:303). This results in the omission of local variation from the debate, and the nature of that religious discourse is obscured behind the mirage of 'correct practice'. However, variety characterised Roman religion, not only within the provinces, but in Rome itself. Therefore, in the rest of this chapter I shall look at the incidence of religion at a local level, using the detail of the physical remains to reconstruct the nature of localised ritual; from this I shall explore the question of how religion could reproduce the structures of the Roman empire. Furthermore, by examining the case studies individually, I shall argue that within this notion of Roman *religio*, there was still scope for local variability.

4.2 BATH: A CLASSICAL ODDITY?

The temple of Sulis Minerva at Bath is perhaps one of the most evocative images of Roman religion in Britain: the romantic image of the thermal springs evokes an emotive reaction, drawing on modern stereotypes of Celtic religion. Additionally, it is one of the few examples from Britain which conforms to the aesthetic ideal of Classical architecture formalised from the Renaissance onwards. The long history of excavation on the site, culminating in the important programme of work in the 1970s and 1980s, has provided the quality of data necessary for a detailed examination of the question of ritual practice. Here we can also see the problems with the rigid division between 'Celtic' and 'Roman' as categories applied to the post-conquest period. Sulis, (or possibly Sul), is presumably a Celtic goddess, possibly connected in some way with the Suleviae (RIB 151, see also 105 and 106 from Cirencester), although there is neither corroborating evidence nor any evidence that she was originally a local deity. She is associated with Minerva on some inscriptions, but is also worshiped in her own right, and her priest describes himself on his tombstone as *sacerdos deae Sulis* (RIB 155). Whether the temple had an Iron Age predecessor is also open to question: there is some evidence for late Iron Age activity with a possible enclosure pre-dating the later monumentalisation of the spring. The deposition of eighteen Celtic coins in the spring seems somewhat more promising (Sellwood 1988); however, this constitutes a small number of coins, and there are examples of such coinage being used for religious offerings during the Roman period (I. Wellington pers. com.). This meagre evidence tends to be given additional weight through the assumption that as the Iron Age population are characterized as predominantly nature worshipping, they would have worshipped at such an obvious watery location.

It is equally unclear who built the temple complex, and the debate follows the usual line of either 'Roman' or 'native' construction. In the excavation report, the authors suggest that the construction of the temple must represent a deliberate act of Romanization, possibly on the insti-gation of the provincial governor (Cunliffe and Davenport 1985: 179).

More recently, Henig has put forward the case for indigenous construction by Togidubnus following the defeat of the Boudiccan rebellion as proof of his loyalty to Rome (Henig 1999). Although discussion of the site has tended to concentrate on the temple and the spring, it is likely that much of the town was dedicated to the goddess, as indicated by its name of Aquae Sulis, and that the temple was part of a wider monumental area. It shared a physical and visual connection with the King's Baths, and there may have been a second precinct opposite it. Nineteenth-century clearances in the area uncovered a series of foundations opposite the entrance to the complex, and decorated blocks from a circular structure may also be from the area, incorporating a decorative frieze with a floral design alternating with figurative panels depicting deities such as Apollo with his lyre. Cunliffe has argued that this frieze belonged to a *tholos*, most likely located within a precinct represented by the foundations (Cunliffe 1989). Evidence for monumental architecture and dedications at the Cross Bath and the Hot Bath suggest that the King's Bath was part of a wider exploitation of the thermal springs, and there is a suggestion that there was a major reorganization of the centre of Bath during the middle of the second century AD (Davenport et al. 2007).

The precinct appears to have been marked off from the surrounding area by a stone wall, with a gateway on the principal axis protruding two metres into the street, possibly highlighted by a porch or free-standing arch (Cunliffe and Davenport 1985: 49, fig. 110). As worshippers entered the complex, they passed into religious space, with the boundary between the two clearly marked (see Figure 4.1). At this point, the view in front of them consisted of firstly the monumental altar, and behind, the large podium temple, possibly with the cult statue of the goddess visible through the door of the *cella*. It was only after entering the precinct that the worshipper would have been aware of the sacred pool, lying on a second axis of the overlooking windows of the baths, the spring itself, and the altar. Thus, the position of the spring within the complex is somewhat problematic. Interpretations which emphasise the spring and the reservoir as occupying the "central focus" of the shrine ignore the relationship between the various elements of the complex. The altar forms the architectural focus, with the two axes intersecting at this point (Cunliffe and Davenport 1985: 35). Also, the paved central courtyard, from the gateway to the temple steps, excludes the area around the spring, and appears to have been separated from it by a step or stylobate (ibid. 24). The reservoir was later enclosed, obliterating this second axis; after this time, there was visual access from the baths via the windows and physical access from the temple precinct through a small door. Thus, whilst forming the physical link between the baths and the temple, its role within the ritual use of the complex was dictated by difficulty rather than ease of access, and this restricted approach clearly increased over time.

The position and decoration of the altar both suggest that sacrifice formed an important part of the ritual activity of the shrine. We have already seen that initially the altar lay at the intersection of the two dominant axes. It stood on a base above the central paving, its size estimated at over two metres square, and nearly a metre and a half high (ibid. 35–7). The three surviving corners suggest an elaborate decorative scheme of Olympic deities. One depicts a naked male, probably Bacchus, holding a thyrsus and pouring wine to a panther at his feet, with a female figure holding a cornucopia and pouring a libation on the other side. The second depicts on one side Hercules holding a cup, and on the other a togate Jupiter with a trident, staff and eagle. The third is more worn, but appears to have been decorated with figures of male deities, one probably Apollo. Later alterations to the courtyard stress the importance of the altar: an additional platform was built extending the area it occupied, and later still a statue and another altar were built adjoining it. As part of the ritual worship, the worshippers had to first cross a clear boundary into sacred space to approach the altar. The large courtyard suggests that these rituals were envisioned as public occasions, a communal event for a body of worshippers. The theatricality of these occasions was emphasised by the platform surrounding the altar, its sheer size creating a space around it. Ryberg's analysis of reliefs depicting religious worship demonstrates the importance of animal sacrifice as a rite, with the repetitious motifs of the altar, victim, officiating priest and attendants (Ryberg 1955). The layout of the temple courtyard, with the dominance of the altar, is strongly indicative that sacrifice was a prominent feature of the cult at Bath. This collective sacrifice was performed in front of the temple, before the goddess herself in the form of her cult statue, and adhering to the idealised relationship described by Vitruvius:

> Altars should look to the east and should always be placed lower than the statues which are in the shrine, so that those who are praying and sacrificing, look up to the deity from unequal heights, which should be appropriate to the honour of the god.
>
> (Vitruvius *de Architectura* 4.9.1)

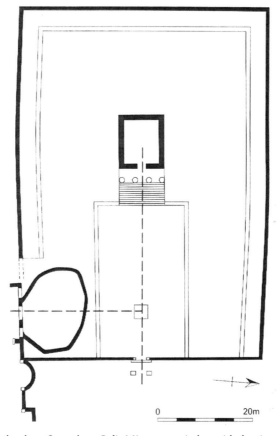

Figure 4.1. Bath: plan of temple to Sulis Minerva, period 1, with dominant axes shown.

As the priest and his attendants carried out the ritualized acts of preparing, slaughtering and butchering the victim, and then burning the appropriate offerings, the community collectively re-established their relationship with the goddess. However, it is clear that at Bath the rituals of such sacrifices were not static, but dynamic and subject to change over time. As the later altar and statue base were placed between the main altar and the temple, the priest could no longer face the goddess to perform the sacrifice. This would have altered the relationship between priest and deity, as represented by her cult statue, as well as the spatial arrangement of the rituals.

Evidence also points to pouring libations as a further part of the ritual use of the complex. Within the sacred spring, eight *paterae* were found, one of bronze, two of silver, and five of pewter. Of these, five bore the name of the goddess (Henig et al. 1988 nos. 24, 29–32), and a further two were inscribed (ibid. nos. 23, 25). These might have been votive offerings, but as they had been well-used and some repaired, it seems more likely that they had been used libations, with the worshippers offering water from the spring, or other liquids such as wine. The rituals of sacrifice and libations may have been led by a priest possessing special religious authority, as inscriptions have been found referring to a *sacerdos deae Sulis* and a *haruspex* (RIB 155, JRS 56.1 respectively). Such priests and other religious personnel may have worn special clothing, and it is possible that the lunate pendant and bronze openwork sheet found in the spring may have been part of such priestly regalia (Henig et al. 1988: nos. 1 and 2).

The spring and reservoir clearly formed a second area for worship within the shrine. At an early period, a containing wall was built around the spring to create the reservoir, with the top of the wall at the same level as the precinct floor (Cunliffe and Davenport 1985: 37–9), and there may have been a coping and a metal grill along the top of this wall (ibid. 42). Archaeological and geological investigations were carried out in the spring in 1979–80 and the range and quantity of material removed clearly indicate that deposition formed an important ritual (ibid. 22). We can see from this material that there were two forms of ritual deposition considered appropriate for the goddess: general material, mainly consisting of coins, and the curse tablets. To deal with the general material first, those which have survived are predominantly metal: jewellery, plates and bowls and some military items. There are also some wooden and leather items, as well as a number of gemstones (for full catalogue, see Henig et al. 1988). However, the most numerous finds are the coins: the partial excavation produced 18 Celtic, 12,595 Roman and 2 post-Roman coins. Presumably we are not dealing with the full range of offerings dedicated to the goddess: the worshippers may well have thrown items into the pool which have not survived. As Cunliffe notes, there is a lack of ex-voto offerings: representations of the area of the body healed by the goddess (Cunliffe 1988: 360). Although a tin mask and two representations of breasts were found in the spring (Henig et al 1988: nos. 3–5), this seems insufficient evidence to assume that the dedication of ex-votos played a substantial part in religious ritual. As there is no mention of healing in the curse tablets, we need to be wary of the assumption that Bath was a healing sanctuary: if it was, clearly the rituals did not include the thankful dedication of an ex-voto. Nevertheless, deposition was clearly a frequent part of the ritual, and the spring was considered the proper location for offerings to the goddess. The deposits were the product of an act which had some form of meaning for the worshipper, and to try and categorise it as true faith or superstition is to impose an anachronistic division. As the spring was unenclosed at this time, it would have been possible to make them from either the temple courtyard or windows in the baths overlooking it. Throwing a coin in seems to have been one of the most popular offerings, although it does not preclude the dedication of other objects. As this tradition continued after the spring was enclosed, when the majority of people presumably threw the offerings in from the baths, it seems that there was no formal ceremony involved, and that the dedications were a private act, as opposed to the public ritual surrounding the act of sacrifice.

The second form of ritual surrounded the dedication of curse tablets in the spring. These are often categorized as magic or superstition, but in his survey of the evidence from both Greek and Roman periods, Gager warns against separating curse tablets from 'correct' religious practice (Gager 1992: 12). As he points out, they were often dedicated to traditional deities, and at Bath we can see how they formed one part of a wider repertoire of rituals through which the worshipper might interact with the goddess. One hundred and thirty have been recovered from the site, and from these it is possible to reconstruct a number of stages in the ritual thanks to their comprehensive cataloguing and analysis by Roger Tomlin (Tomlin 1988). The majority were prompted by theft, and as Tomlin comments, the similarities in the word and thought indicate an established tradition where the thief or the stolen property was given over to the goddess, with a string of mutually exclusive clauses leaving open the identity of the thief (Tomlin 1988: 62–3). In the first stage of the ritual, the worshipper wrote out the tablet themselves, probably copying the correct form of address laid out by a temple scribe. Whilst Gager argues for professional scribes both composing and writing the magical formulae (Gager 1992: 4–5), the evidence from Bath suggests that this was not necessarily the case here: one text refers to the copying out of the written page (*Tab. Sulis* 8), and there are copying errors in the texts, but very few crossed out mistakes (Tomlin 1988: 98). No two tablets were written in the same hand, reinforcing the impression that the temple scribes did not actually write the tablets (ibid. 99–101; although one has been matched to the writing of a similar curse from Uley: Tomlin 2002). This was an essential part of the ritual, suggesting that the ritualised stages of writing the tablet were as important as the text itself in securing the compliance of Sulis Minerva. This could be one interpretation for the group of five tablets similar in form and in preparation, but written in unintelligible squiggles (*Tab. Sulis* 112–6): that the ritual required the petitioner to write out the curse themselves, and this was more important than it being readable. The repeated use of quasi-legal formulae suggests that there was a correct way to petition the goddess and ensure the effectiveness of the curse. As this language was distinct from their daily knowledge, it reinforced the special nature of the ritual, as well as forcing the worshipper to rely upon the religious expertise of the temple personnel in drafting the curses.

The second stage in the ritual was the concealment of the text. This might already have been in the mind of the dedicators as they wrote out the curse, as there are examples of texts reversed, or written in mirror image (reversal of script: *Tab. Sulis* 44, 62; mirror image: 61). In general, the folding of the tablet over and over, hiding the curse itself, seems to have been sufficient. Gager argues against this being a significant part of the ritual: he attributes the special forms of writing to a desire for the victims to suffer a similar fate, and the rolling as not primarily to prevent their reading (Gager 1992: 12). However, this ignores the repetitive and cumulative effect of the various stages of the ritual in producing the multiple levels of concealment. This culminated in the final stage with the deposition of the curse in the spring, hiding it completely from mortal eyes and thereby dedicating it to the goddess. This symbolically transferred the stolen goods or the thief to the goddess, making their recovery her concern (ibid. 174–6). The sense of place implied by the deposition in the temple precinct was reinforced through the number of times the shrine itself was mentioned in the texts, setting up a connection between the goddess and her sanctuary. The writer of one tablet hoped that the person who stole his gloves would lose their minds (sic) and eyes in the temple (*Tab. Sulis* 5); whoever stole Civilis' ploughshare was destined for a worse fate: he was to lay down his life in the temple (*Tab. Sulis* 31). Others less vengefully stated merely that the stolen goods should be returned to the temple (*Tab. Sulis* 10, 32, 45; temple of Mars, 95).

The layout of the shrine and the architectural treatment of the spring reinforced this secrecy. The majority of the tablets date to the period when the spring had been enclosed within a separate building, thus heightening the sense of secrecy and concealment surrounding the act of cursing. At the same time, the ritual of depositing the curse may also have changed. Once enclosed, there were two means of accessing the spring, one from the baths, the other from the temple courtyard via a small door. Its well-worn threshold indicates that it was used by some of the people visiting the shrine, and if they were depositing the curse tablets, it would have further increased the element of concealment which we have already seen surrounding their preparation. Furthermore, using the door from the temple precinct would have maintained the link between the curses and the temple itself, a link which would have been lost if they were deposited from the baths. In both the legalistic terminology and their ritual concealment, the curse tablets from Bath form a distinct group, with parallels found at the nearby shrine at Uley (Tomlin 2002). Here we see a good example of the dynamic nature of Roman religion in the provinces, with the worshippers taking an established aspect of ritual practice and adapting it to be meaningful and effective within the local context.

Another way for the worshippers to interact with the goddess was through dedications on stone. As discussed above, the traditional approach to interpreting these is to isolate the text, extract the name of the deity, and use it as evidence for their worship. However, this ignores the social practices and beliefs which led to their manufacture. They were the products of religious activity, an integral part of the religious experience and the articulation of the relationship between human and divine, and through their permanence, they continue to form part of future religious discourse. A high proportion of those from Bath have excavated contexts, although in the case of some, such as those from Lower Stall Street, we cannot always be sure of the building with which they were associated. There are 17 dedications in total from Bath, nine of which are to Sulis Minerva in various permutations (this excludes RIB141 which gives the name of the goddess in the genitive rather than the usual dative case). Not all of these are from the temple complex: dedications were also set up to her at the Cross Bath and the Hot Bath (RIB 146 and 150 respectively). She was worshipped throughout the town, and whilst the temple was her primary domain, she was not perceived as confined merely to that space. However, as we also have a dedication to Diana from the Hot Bath (RIB 139), it is clear that whilst her worship dominated the religious life of the town, it was not to the exclusion of other deities.

Two altars dedicated to Sulis Minerva demonstrate a number of the crucial issues. One was dedicated by Aufidius Eutuches and the other by Aufidius Lemnus, both freedmen of Marcus Aufidius Maximus, a centurion of the Sixth Legion (RIB 143 and 144 respectively). They were found in the 1790s below the Pump Room; their original location was presumably the temple courtyard. They have almost identical texts, even though the abbreviations and line divisions are different; for example the dedication from Eutuches has *libertus* contracted and misspelt (LEB), whereas the dedication from Lemnus as it written out in full. The dedication of Aufidius Eutuches reads:

[D]EAE SVLI
PRO SALVTE ET
INCOLVMITA
[TE] MAR AVFID
[M]AXIMI C LEG
VI VIC
[A]VFIDIVS EV
TVCHES LEB
VSLM

To the goddess Sulis, for the welfare and the safety of Marcus Aufidius Maximus, centurion of Legio VI Victix; Aufidius Eutuches, his freedman, willingly and deservedly fulfilled his vow.   (RIB 143)

These altars commemorated the act of worship, providing a permanent marker for what was essentially a transitory experience. This public declaration primarily denoted an individual act, the relationship between the goddess and the dedicator, and its articulation through a single ritual. However, the very public expression of that relationship fixed the goddess and her worship in that locality. The personal became communal, as future visitors to the temple viewed these offerings, using them to make sense of their own relationship with her: her power and their correct response to it. The use of the altar design for the inscription recalled the ritual of meat and liquid offerings and their importance at the heart of the Roman religion. Whether such inscribed altars were ever used is unclear; some appear similar to those depicted in representations of sacrifice, such as that on an inscription from Bridgeness, West Lothian (CSIR 1.4.68). This shows a high-ranking officer from the Legio II Augusta, dressed in a toga, pouring a libation over an altar which appears to be of a similar size. It should also be remembered that in sacrifice, only a small portion of meat was sacrificed to the gods, and so these small altars would be more than sufficient. On the other hand, it is clear that some altars dedicated to the gods were of such a small size that they must be purely symbolic, such as an altar to Jupiter Optimus Maximus from Clunia (Clunia II.10) which at 16 cm high was clearly of limited practical use. Whether used or not, the dedication of these altars recalled the importance of sacrifices and libations as part of religious discourse. Of the 17 dedications from Bath, 12 were on such altars, demonstrating how the visitors at the shrine now framed their worship of the gods.

Both *liberti* dedicated the altars as the fulfilment of a vow made to the goddess, the final, but archaeologically most visible stage in a complex ritual sequence. The wording follows the typical formula of the name of the deity in the dative, the name of the dedicator, and the characteristic abbreviation of V(otum) S(olvit) L(ibens) M(erito) (fulfilled the vow willingly and deservedly). The altar implies the earlier stages of the ritual, as explored by Ton Derks, beginning with the utterance of the vow itself (the *nuncupatio*), and ending with the repayment after its fulfilment by the goddess (Derks 1995, especially 114–22). Derks suggests that these personal vows were the result of a specific circumstance rather than a repetitive feature of the religious calendar. The primary thanksgiving offering was an animal sacrifice, as suggested by the donation of the altar itself and the iconography associated with it, but donations of statues were also found. This stage is well represented archaeologically; in contrast, evidence for the *nuncupatio* is much rarer. On this occasion we are given some indication of the nature of the vow: both freedmen record that it was for the safety of their former master, Aufudius Maximus. They viewed the continued safety of the centurion (possibly during a particular event which is not mentioned) as due to the favourable intercession of Sulis Minerva and the success of their vow. Such vows seem to have formed an important part of the religious experience at Bath, and 11 of the 17 dedications recorded favourable outcomes. However, there were other reasons for offering dedications to the divine. An unknown man (the text has only been partially preserved) set up a dedication for himself and his family as the result of a vision (RIB 153). This was dedicated in response to the goddess appearing to the man in person; clearly such direct interaction was not considered out of the ordinary, but rather an expected part of religious experience (Allason-Jones 1997). Further inscriptions refer to the dedicators donating gifts to the goddess, another popular way of gaining her good favour. On a statue base, the sculptor Sulinus commemorated an offering made to the Suleviae (RIB 151), and the priest Lucius Marcius Memor also recorded the dedication of an offering to Sulis on a base which originally stood in the temple precinct (JRS 56.1).

So far, I have only touched briefly upon the question of the relationship between the temple and the baths. It is clear that the two complexes were inter-connected: the spring which formed an integral part of the shrine, fed the baths, whilst initially visitors to the baths could look out over the spring and the altar. Yegül argues that this connection between religion and bathing can seen in thermo-mineral springs, although not in other forms of bathing establishment (Yegül 1992: 125). He further argues that this connection extended to divine healing through the thermal water and their curative powers. However, at Bath we lack clear evidence for the goddess as a healing goddess and the temple as the centre of a healing cult. Most noticeable is the lack of ex-voto offerings, usually found in abundance at healing shrines. Cunliffe, citing Potter's (1985) argument that this practice was in decline by the late Republic, suggests that the baths were seen as a more rational approach to medicine than the 'primitive' practice of divine healing (Cunliffe 1988: 360). However, Potter's argument applied to the republican healing sanctuaries in Italy, and the evidence from Gaul suggests that this was not the case in the north-western provinces. Two further hot springs at Bath were monumentalised, with some evidence for religious worship taking place there, reinforcing the connection between thermal springs and religious practice within the town (Cunliffe 1969; Davenport et al. 2007). Therefore, we can say that for the King's Spring, the close relationship between the temple and the baths, the goddess and the waters, is beyond doubt; that the relationship may have incorporated some form of curative aspect is plausible, but that the shrine functioned primarily and solely as a healing sanctuary, a form of Romano-Celtic Asclepeion, seems unlikely.

The archaeological evidence from Bath presents a rich picture of ritual activity. Whilst the shrine was dedicated to a syncretism of the pre-Roman goddess Sulis and the Roman Minerva, the nature of the pre-Roman worship is impossible to characterise due to lack of concrete evidence. For the Roman period, it is clear that there were a number of rituals through which the worshipper could call upon the goddess. The prominence of the altar indicates that sacrifice formed a major part of the religious experience, with the open courtyard pointing to large communal festivals. Alternatively, the worshipper could offer libations from *paterae* set aside for such purposes and ritually disposed of in the spring at the end of their life. Other rituals were more personal, forcing us to challenge the argument that Roman religion was a thin veneer cynically adopted. The epigraphic record indicates that some offered vows and dedications to the goddess, recording the act for perpetuity. These inscriptions, publicly displayed, then became a medium through which a ritual discourse was negotiated. For those who perceived themselves as being wronged, the power of the goddess could be requested to exact vengeance through a secretive curse. For many visitors to the spring, throwing a coin into the spring was perhaps enough. However, it is possible that different rituals were thought to be more effective by different groups. Of the 16 extant names of donors, six are connected with the military and a further two from other towns, indicating a cosmopolitan clientele. The remaining eight specify no origin, suggesting that the local elites may also have been setting up dedications at the shrine. In contrast, the curse tablets display no tria nomina and over half are 'Celtic' names, leading to the conclusion that the two forms of ritual were used by different members of the community of worshippers (Tomlin 1988: 96–7). However, to see this within a simple 'Roman' and 'native' discourse would obscure the way in which Roman religion was embedded in social hierarchies. Rather, we should see the religious activity around the site as multiple and dynamic, a combination of private impulse and communal set-pieces.

4.3 MUNIGUA: THE SANCTUARY ON THE HILL

Like Bath, the town of Munigua was dominated by a large temple complex and the town's importance seems to have been based upon its role as a sanctuary. Unlike Bath, it was a chartered town, becoming a *municipium* during the Flavian period, and so here we see the intertwining of religious and political space. The layout of the town was dictated by its hillside site, with the public buildings built on the slope of the hill, culminating with the main temple at the summit, the so-called Santuario de Terrazas (see Figure 3.3). Its dedication is uncertain: inscriptions have been found to both Fortuna Crescens Augusta and Hercules Augustus (CILA 2.1057 and 1060), but as both of the inscriptions are to deities with the epithet Augustus/-a, it is likely that it was associated with the imperial cult (Grünhagen 1959: 281–2; see also Coarelli 1987: 95–6 based upon the architectural similarity to other temples of the imperial cult). The shrine was built up on three terraces. The lowest was a long, open space, accessed from the town via ramps at either end (Grünhagen 1959; Hauschild 1991a). Two stairways led from this to the middle terrace, which incorporated a semi-circular exedra at the centre, and porticoed

Figure 4.2. Munigua: view of the approach to the main shrine, showing proposed processional route.

patios to the sides, each with a series of rooms presumably connected with the day-to-day requirements of the cult. Narrow, vaulted passage-ways connected these and the exedra. Above this rose the third terrace with the temple itself on a podium accessed from the rear, and a hemi-spherical portico to the front. The *cella* of the temple lay at the pivotal position architecturally: the series of symmetrical ramps and stairways are united at its entrance. However the three terraces did not share a strict common axis: the centre of the lower terrace lay off-centre to the exedra and the *cella* (Schattner 2003: 32).

The worshipper gradually climbed the hill to the shrine along a cer-emonial route, from the south gate of the town, up through the heart of the lower town, past the forum and the two-storey portico, past the later podium temple, and up a ramp to the lower terrace (see Figure 4.2). This was probably the main route, although it was mirrored by a second one from the other side, and the formalization of the northern route with a monumental structure to deal with both the bend and the slope points to both routes being used (Schattner 2003: 69–72). These cere-monial approaches point to the importance of public processions in the

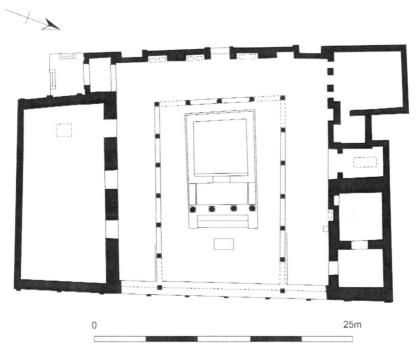

Figure 4.3. Munigua: plan of forum with temple and basilica.

ritual activity of the site, and that religious worship did not begin within the confines of the temple itself. Presumably these processions would have had a temporal element: they would not have been an everyday occurrence, but instead, would have been reserved for specific festivals, forming part of a local religious calendar. The details of such processions are difficult to reconstruct archaeologically, but they may have incorporated religious paraphernalia to be used at other stages in the festival, with the worshippers carrying images or even the cult statues of the deity, or leading sacrificial animals, if the procession preceded a sacrifice. Priests and others with specific roles in the rituals may have been assigned specific places within the procession. Ryberg's analysis of the Ara Pacis demonstrates that the procession depicted there had a formal order: Vestals, other priests, victims and attendants; then magistrates, priests and imperial family; finally senators and citizens (Ryberg 1955:42–4). This order reflects wider social hierarchies, and some elements may have been duplicated here. Such processions were often depicted with musicians playing flutes, trumpets and lyres: the Cancelleria reliefs from Rome show three trumpets, a flute player and a lyre player near the front (ibid.

75–7, figs. 37a–d), and would have made religious processions a noisy, bustling affair. It is unlikely that all the rituals would have been preceded by a procession; however, they would have established a sacred route, recalled in the minds of the worshippers when they approached the temple on other occasions.

These processional routes led to the lower terrace of the shrine through some form of gateway separating the ritual space of the sanctuary from the rest of the town (Schattner 2003: 30). Directly above this terrace, lying on the central axis of the sanctuary, was the semicircular exedra, possibly acting as some form of stage. It seems probable that the priests performed the main rituals within the exedra, with the audience of worshippers watching from the terrace below, the two groups of participants linked visually rather than spatially. No permanent altar base has been found during the excavations, although the excavators have speculated that it may have been positioned in this exedra, in which case ritual sacrifices would have been in front of the *cella* and any cult statue (Hauschild 1991a: 136). However, the lack of any archaeological evidence for a monumental altar within the complex stands in sharp contrast with those at Bath and Italica. Furthermore, as will be discussed more fully below, this phenomenon is also suggested in the other temples at Munigua. Finally, although this is not unique to Munigua, dedications to the various deities were not inscribed upon altars, with a single exception of the altar in the *aediculum*. Taken together, this does not rule out sacrifice, but it raises the question of how it was incorporated into the sacred space of the shrine, and the scale of such rituals. We might assume from temples and festivals elsewhere that sacrifice played a significant role, but this presents a very one-dimensional and static account of Roman religion, ignoring the choices and variation evident on a local level. It is not enough to assume that sacrifice was part of the religious experience: rather, we must ask how it was made part of the final setting of the religious space. Here, that incorporation is less visible as it lacks the architectural focus of a monumental altar which we saw at Bath. This does not mean that it did not form part of the ritual worship of the gods; rather that it was not accorded a permanent setting (CILA 2.1057, 1060).

A second temple was located within the forum which comprised a typical rectangular *cella* raised up on a lower podium, and almost completely filled the courtyard (Hauschild 1991b: 171; Figure 4.3). The quality of decoration shows that the temple was considered less important than the main sanctuary: instead of the elaborate marble decoration adorning the latter, the floor appears to have been *opus signinum*, and the walls covered in stucco and painted, with the column capitals and the cornice of moulded stucco (ibid. f/n 11, fig. 4). Following almost the same eastern-facing axis as the sanctuary temple, the forum temple looked out over the hillside, but although highly visible from a distance, it must have been very difficult to approach. Whilst the forum lay on the sacred route, to reach the front of the temple, the worshipper had to enter it through one of two doors, both of which faced the rear of the temple, and then go around the temple through the portico. As the temple filled much of the courtyard, there was little space for communal rituals, only those involving a limited number of people. As with the sanctuary, there is no archaeological evidence for a permanent altar, although again reconstructions include an altar lying on the same axis as the temple (ibid. fig. 5; in contrast with the plan of the excavated structures, ibid. fig. 2). Even if one existed, lack of space dictates that it cannot have formed a major architectural element. Once again, this does not rule out the possibility of sacrifice and libations forming part of religious practice, but we must question any assumptions about their importance, given the lack of a permanent marker, or their communal nature, given the lack of space.

A third temple lay between the sanctuary and the forum temple (see Figure 4.4). It was constructed in the early second century AD (Schattner 2003: 42), after the other two and shares some of the same distinctive local characteristics. It was set on a platform formed by a retaining wall and buttresses, and again was highly visible to the viewer, although this time, side-on with its axis at right angles to the other two temples (Hauschild 1991a: 138). It was set within a porticoed precinct, and built on a low podium; again, there is no trace of a permanent altar and the temple lacks the open space for communal rituals around one. It seems that the visibility of the large structure, set between the main sanctuary and the forum temple, was its dominant feature. It reaffirms the importance of the visibility of the temples in the layout of the town, with a succession of prominent religious structures built on a series of artificial terraces set into the hillside. The final religious structure from Munigua is the *aediculum* or so-called Shrine to Mercury (see Figure 4.5). The ascription of the shrine to the god is based on a plaque recording a dedication to him, although it is not certain whether it originally came from here (CILA 2.1061; Schattner 2003: 42–3). It lay on the sacred route, opposite the forum, and at a later date was incorporated into the two-storey portico. It was rectangular in shape with a small exedra to the rear, adorned with an architrave and Corinthian columns (Hauschild 1991a: 141–2). An altar with inscription was found in situ, and adjoining it a small table, possibly

Figure 4.4. Munigua: view of podium temple in foreground and forum temple behind.

for sacrifice. The inscription has been damaged, but records that it was set up in fulfilment of a vow by a freedman of Ferronius (CILA 2.1063). The position of the shrine, directly on the main route suggests that any ceremonies did not involve a large number of worshippers, but rather a smaller gathering, possibly a personal act of worship.

This reconstruction of ritual practice from the architecture can be augmented with the inscriptions. The inscriptions indicate a priesthood within the town, showing a formal organisation of religious practice and restricting of religious authority to a small number of prominent individuals (CILA 2.1054, possibly 1061). Those attested are connected with the imperial cult and are both freedmen, raising questions about the social context for this religious authority, providing an alternative route to social status for those excluded from the political magistracies, which cast some light on the motivation for consulting the divine. However, dedications to the gods from Munigua contrast sharply with those from Bath, where the majority of dedications record vows and their fulfilment by the deity. At Munigua, out the nine religious inscriptions, only one records a vow, and that is the sole altar from the *aediculum* already mentioned (CILA 2.1063). This does not necessarily mean that the

Figure 4.5. Munigua: remains of the aediculum shrine.

worshippers never made vows to the gods; however the ritual at Munigua did not include its fulfilment being recorded on stone. There were no permanent markers of such vows bearing witness to the success of such rituals in gaining the favour of the gods: the contract between divine and mortal remained private. Furthermore, there was no normative example of appropriate behaviour to guide future worshippers when they came to make similar vows. Instead, the act of donation was most frequently commemorated, with the remaining eight inscriptions recording some form of offering. One such came from the forum, and was a statue base dedicated to Bonus Adventus Augustus by the freedman Lucius Valerius Aelius Severus in gratitude for the god's part in securing his election as a *sevir* (CILA 2.1054). It was placed in a public place, in a niche in the north portico (Hauschild 1991b: 173); in this way the statue and the inscription continued to play a part in the formation of religious knowledge of those reading it. Also found in the north portico was a large granite pedestal from a bronze horse, dedicated to the Numen of Dis Pater (ibid.):

NVM[INI]
DITIS P[ATRIS]
L AELIVS Q[VIR]
FRONT[O]
EQVVM EXED[RAM]
EQVILEM DEDIT

To the Numen of Dis Pater; L. Aelius Fronto of the Quirina voting tribe, dedicated a horse and an exedra as a stable.   (CILA 2.1056)

This statue was placed in an open-fronted room leading from the portico (room 6): presumably this was the exedra which Fronto built as a stable (*equile*) for his offering of the horse. With both inscriptions, we can see the public display of these acts of devotion, and how this commemoration became part of the permanent city landscape.

A second feature of the dedications from Munigua is that two of them also commemorated deaths: Fabia Ursina stipulated in her will that a statue be set up to Fortuna Cresecens Augusta (CILA 2.1057), and a dedication was set up to Ceres Augusta in honour and memory of Quintia Flaccina by her friend and heir Quintus Aelius Vernaclus (CILA 2.1055). This inscription also records that a banquet was provided for both sexes, and this is also found in a dedication to the Genius Municipi (CILA 2.1058). These two inscriptions provide the best evidence for sacrifice in the town as the meat may have been from sacrificial animals. If this was the case, it suggests that the banquet was as important a part of the ritual as the sacrifice itself, and points to a different interpretation of the ritual to that we saw at Bath. These differences in the use of inscriptions are not only apparent in the text, but also in their design.

There is only a single inscription carved on a dedicatory altar: this was the one placed in the *aediculum*, which, as we have seen, is unusual as it is the only inscription recording a vow. Otherwise, the only other two inscribed altars are funerary altars, used as tombstones (CILA 2.1085, 1086). This phenomenon is not unique (it is also be seen at Italica), but it does reinforce the problematic role for sacrifice within religious discourse at Munigua and reflects the lack of monumental altars in the three temple complexes.

Compared to Bath, Munigua displays a very different picture: the worshippers here expressed their religious belief through somewhat different rituals. There were a number of religious spaces, with the hilltop sanctuary as the most important, and their visibility seems to have been the determining factor in their placement. The layout of the town suggests that processions played an important part in the religious experience of the worshippers, who would have climbed the hill to the sanctuary to worship the cult statue in the *cella*. However, the question of sacrifice as the culmination of these processions is problematic: both the layout of the various temples and the lack of altars question how much importance was placed upon the ritual. In contrast, there appears to have been a greater emphasis placed upon communal banquets, stressing a different stage of the act. The inscriptions demonstrate that offerings to the gods were an important ritual activity, but that in contrast, vows were deemed not worthy of recording on stone. We cannot conclude that rituals such as vows and sacrifice were completely absent, only that they were less visible, but this still demonstrates that the interpretation of ritual and its significance was essentially a local discourse.

4.4 RITUAL AT ITALICA

In looking at Bath and Munigua, we have explored the nature of the ritual experience in towns which were dominated by religious space; in contrast, Italica perhaps represents the more usual experience where temples formed an important part of the urban environment, without overwhelming other aspects of urban living. In previous chapters we have seen how at Italica religious and political space were intertwined, and here I want to develop the idea of how ritual was framed within these spaces, and how it too was an intermingling of the religious and the political. Religious space permeated the town, and was not confined to the large monumental temples, reinforcing the picture we have already seen at Munigua and Bath that religion cannot be neatly pigeon-holed into a discrete category, divorced from other aspects of society. There were a number of monumental religious structures within the town: the Traianeum, a large podium temple overlooking the theatre (Rodríguez Hidalgo and Keay 1995: 412), and a third controversial structure at Cerro de los Palacios. The remains of this monumental structure seem to have consisted of the cella of an archaic style temple, probably rebuilt during the imperial period. It has been interpreted as a Capitoline temple dating to the Roman foundation of the town, although both the interpretation and the dating have been disputed (Bendala Galán 1982; Keay 1997a: 29–30).

The Traianeum has already been discussed in detail in Chapter 3, but here I want to concentrate not upon the monumentality of structure itself or its imperial dedication, but the kinds of ritual which were carried out there. It was situated on a slight hill, at the highest point of the Nova Urbs (Léon 1988), occupying an important location in the network of streets: one route ran through a major gateway to the amphitheatre, another to a second main gate, whilst a third led to the Vetus Urbs and may have connected it with the political centre. These may have formed processional routes: although not as formalised as the routes at Munigua, they would have taken on this role for specific festivals. As the procession approached the temple, it reached a *tetrapylon* or arch only a few metres away from the precinct, which marked that they had reached their destination. As at Bath, the temple was enclosed within a precinct, here entered via a monumental staircase (see Figure 4.6). The complex repeated the axiality we have seen at previous sites: as the worshippers climbed the stairs of the main entrance and passed into the enclosed courtyard, they would have seen the monumental altar and beyond it the podium temple, with the cult statue within. The prominence of the altar and its massive size (the foundations were over six metres by three metres) symbolised the importance of sacrifice. The large open space of the courtyard indicates that such rituals were expected to be public, with large groups participating in the act of worshipping and communicating with the divine through the sacrificial act.

Within the courtyard of the temple were lines of bases, and four dedications from the site, which may have been from these bases, give an idea of some of the rituals being carried out here. One was in fulfilment of a vow to Jupiter, and the Genius Coloniae is also mentioned in the dedication (CILA 2.344). The other three point more explicitly to the act of dedication, predominantly of statues. One recorded the dedication

Figure 4.6. Italica: dedication to Nemesis in floor of amphitheatre entranceway.

of a statue to Apollo in thanks for election as duovir (CILA 2.342) and a second commemorated the dedication of four statues to the Genius Coloniae, again in thanks for election as magistrate (CILA 2.343). A third inscription from Vibia Modesta dedicated a silver statue adorned with jewellery and a jewel-encrusted golden crown to the goddess Victoria Augusta, probably in thanks for her election as *flaminica* (CILA 2.358). In addition, she deposited in the temple itself her flaminate crown of gold, and busts of Isis, Ceres and Juno Regina. These offerings were made in thanks for some form of success, or in fulfilment of a vow, suggesting that the relationship between human and divine was perceived to be an interactive one of obligation and reciprocity. These objects in turn shaped future worshippers' understanding of this relationship and the correct form of behaviour through which to approach the gods: a symbol through which religious discourse was continually interpreted and reinterpreted. They also indicate the relationship between religion and politics, with all four advertising their political offices in the text, and some being dedicated explicitly in thanks for political success. Further, the link with the Genius Coloniae in two of the inscriptions indicated the relationship between urbanism and public cult. The dedication and display of these statues and inscriptions within the temple precinct points to one feature of Roman temples which is often overlooked in modern reconstructions. Instead of the pristinely tidy spaces often depicted, these spaces were cluttered with dedications and may well have been somewhat smoky, smelly areas from the burning of offerings (both animal and non-animal) to the gods. These visual and olfactory reminders formed part of the everyday encounters of the townspeople with the gods: if they were not involved in the rituals themselves, they would have been aware that they were taking place, reinforcing the importance of religious activity within the town.

As we have already seen, a processional route physically linked the Traianeum with the amphitheatre. This suggests that *ludi* formed an important part of the religious festivities, with the worshippers enjoying gladiatorial games as part of the religious celebrations. The theatre also seems to have been spatially linked with a major temple: traces of a monumental building have been discovered on the hillside above which shared the axes of the theatre, and the two building were connected through a formal access (Rodríguez Gutiérrez 2004: 273–6). The remains of the temple date to the Trajanic period and comprise a terrace with a series of walls for some type of enclosed area, probably a temple. Colossal statues of Venus, Diana, Hermes Dionysophorus and the imperial family have been found in the area which may have been displayed in this complex; these images aided in the formation of the religious discourse of the viewers, providing an image through which to conceptualize the divine. A pedestal from the forum area records the donation of *ludi scaenici* by the freedman, Lucius Caelius Saturninus as part of the celebrations for his adoption as *sevir* (CILA 2.345). Such *ludi* were a frequent part of Roman religious festivals, and the *lex Coloniae Genetivae* sets down that the urban magistrates of the colony were responsible for shows or dramatic spectacles lasting three and four days in honour of the Capitoline triad (*lex col.* chapters 70 and 71). These extended festivals shaped a local religious calendar, forming an important part of the communal religious experience. They also formed a further part of the link between political hierarchies and religious activity, confirmed by the inscription itself which acknowledges that these games were connected with Saturninus becoming *sevir*.

This connection between the secular and the religious can also be seen at the amphitheatre with a series of dedications to the goddess Nemesis found in the eastern entrance. These so-called *plantae pedum* inscriptions consist of eleven inscribed marble plaques, one bronze plaque, and three anepigraphic marble plaques (for full catalogue, Canto 1984: 184–5). The typical form was a marble plaque, inscribed with between one and three pairs of feet, and an inscription consisting of the name of the dedicator and sometimes, although not always, the name of the deity (Figure 4.6). Just over half of the dedications gave the name of the recipient: Nemesis was the most popular, and others named included Caelestis and Domina Regia. This has led Canto to argue that this represents a syncretism between Nemesis and Caelestis, representing the Punic and Hellenic influences within Baetica (Canto 1984 186–7). These dedications were from members of the elite and local magistrates, appealing for the goddess' goodwill during their period of office (ibid. 189–92). This is reinforced by Hornum's assertion that throughout the empire, magistrates were the most frequent dedicators to the goddess (Hornum 1993:70–3). Hornum also argues for a close link between Nemesis and gladiatorial games, with dedications concentrated in amphitheatres in the western empire (ibid. 43–56), suggesting that this tied in with the relationship between games as an exhibition of power and her role as maintainer of the correct social order (ibid. 88).

These inscriptions point to the worship of Nemesis being conducted through the usual rituals of vows and dedication. Four point to the fulfil-ment of a vow: for example, Caius Servius Africanus and his children set up a dedication to Caelestis Pia Augusta in thanks for the goddess' favour (CILA 2.348). Two inscriptions also refer to an offering to the goddess: one man records that he donated a gift (*donum*) and the inscription (*ves-tigia*) as the result of a vow (CILA 2.352). However, they differ from the more normal statue base or altar in that they were set into the floor and the images of the feet seem to be an important part of the ritual, as it is the feature common to all the inscriptions, including the three anepi-graphic examples. Katherine Dunbabin has demonstrated that this was not an isolated ritual, citing examples from around the Mediterranean associated with other deities, such as the two *plantae pedum* inscriptions found in situ in front of the entrance to the temple of Isis at Belo (Dun-babin 1990, especially figs. 4 and 5). However, it is only at Italica that they were associated with the worship of Nemesis (Hornum 1993: 77); instead, the majority were associated with Egyptian deities, especially Isis and Serapis, although they are also found with traditional Graeco-Roman deities such as Saturn at Thugga and Demeter at Acrocorinth. It is unclear what they signify, whether they are meant to denote the goddess or the worshipper, but Dunbabin has suggested that in certain circumstances they may have had apotropaic powers, almost like a good luck charm (Dunbabin 1990: 195–6), which would reinforce the idea that the dedications were connected to success in office.

The remaining inscriptions from Italica suggest other aspects of reli-gious activity: the interaction between human and divine, ritual practices and religious personnel. One person, who remained unnamed, dedicated an altar on the instructions the god (also unnamed) in fulfilment of a vow (CILA 2.361). A curse tablet has also been found, very similar to those from Bath (CILA 2.362). The author used the same formulae, asking the goddess to recover his stolen boots and sandals. The appeal is directed to Domina Fons Fovens, presumably the guardian spirit of a spring or fountain, although it was found within the Casa de la Cañada Honda and not deposited in the spring itself (Gil and Luzón 1975), and it does not seem to have been ritually 'hidden' in the same way as those from Bath. Dedications also confirm the rituals of sacrifice and libations within the town. There are a number of altars, although they are not common, and all seem to have been purely votive (for example, CILA 2.360 to Asclepius is 13 × 23 × 15 cm). As was a common practice, some bases were decorated with sacrificial iconography, such as *urcei*, *paterae* and *praefericula* (CILA 2.345, 347). It is clear that religious authority was given to a number of religious officers, both male and female, with the usual range of titles. We have evidence for the presence of augurs (CILA 2.342, possibly 346), *sacerdotes coloniae* of both sexes (CILA 2.351, 358, 387), and *pontifices* (CILA 2.382, 383). The most frequently attested priesthoods are those connected with the imperial cult, with a total of six different titles recorded. It seems to have been possible to hold more than one priesthood at once, and Vibia Modesta served as both *sacerdos coloniae* and *flaminica* of the imperial cult (CILA 2.358).

For the people of Italica, religious space was everywhere in the city, with a plethora of temples and shrines. The intermingling of spaces and activities which we might term 'sacred' and 'secular' denies any argument for universal categories: their meaning must be seen as contextual. Many of the rituals we have already discussed can be seen here: sacrifice, donations, vows, processions, and there are others which were absent at Bath and Munigia, but common elsewhere in the empire, such as the *ludi*. However, again we can see that there was a local character to the forms of worship, with the *plantae pedum* to Nemesis apparently a unique feature. We also see here the overlaps between politics and religion, both in personnel, but also in the way rituals were incorporated into the political sphere.

4.5 MULTA EX PARVIS

The examples discussed so far are particularly well documented, both in terms of the excavated evidence and the epigraphic record. However, it might be argued that the majority of religious sites do not provide the same level of information, and that for these we are reliant upon generalisation and analogy. Nevertheless, for any particular town, we can still move beyond the uncritical application of a general paradigm, and

Figure 4.7. Bilbilis: temple, with theatre below.

produce a more nuanced interpretation based upon a detailed exploration
of the available evidence. Even in cases where the epigraphic evidence
is limited or non-existent, it is possible to reconstruct something of the
ritual observances from the structural evidence alone.

Bilbilis is at first sight a poor relation of Munigua and Italica, both
in terms of past structures and present evidence. There are a number of
religious buildings: the main podium temple, the small shrine to the rear
of the theatre, and another podium temple further down the hill near the
pedestrian gateway. In the case of the main temple, many of the features
we have already seen at other sites are also present here (see Figure 4.7).
Access to the precinct was via a steep ramp in the north-eastern area. At
the foot of this the remains of a podium have been found, either for a
statue or small *aediculum* (Martín-Bueno 1987: 107), which may mark the
start of the ceremonial approach to the temple itself. This led into the
lower courtyard: a large space, suitable for a sizeable number of people
and suggesting communal festivals. From here, a monumental stairway led
up to the smaller temple precinct, with this axis continuing up a second
stairway to the *cella*. Again, we see the dominant visual axis repeated: any

ritual activity taking place in the temple precinct would be visible both to the deity and to the participants in the lower courtyard. It also creates the possibility of a spatial hierarchy in these rituals, with only those with religious authority or specific roles allowed into this upper area. It is unclear whether there was an altar in front of the temple: as at Munigua, no archaeological trace has been found, but here the structures around the temple have been so badly destroyed that the possibility cannot be discounted (Martín-Bueno et al. 1985: 259). Fragments of wall-painting have been found which depict a ladle and a bucket, suggesting that the inhabitants were at least aware of the ritual paraphernalia for libations and sacrifice (Guiral Pelegrín and Martín-Bueno 1996: 119–20, frags. 257–8, lam. 258).

A further staircase led from the lower courtyard westwards to the theatre; its decoration with fountains and other architectural elements, now badly preserved, suggests an important conceptual link between the temple and the theatre (Martín-Bueno 1982b: 86). The implication that the theatre played a part in ritual activity is reinforced by the presence of a small temple, centrally placed above the *summa cavea*. Although few details have been published, it followed the same orientation as the main temple, facing southwards over the plain. Thus it seems likely that ritual worship at both would have been associated with theatrical performances of various kinds. We can imagine that such religious festivals would have extended throughout the day, incorporating the community as a whole. These may have involved offerings or sacrifices to the various deities at the main temple, followed by a procession, possibly carrying statues of the gods, to the theatre and then a theatrical display of some kind. There may have been more offerings and dedications at the small theatre temple, but as there was no open area around it, these would have been confined to a smaller subgroup.

Perhaps the main point to be made from Bilbilis is a methodological one: the buildings themselves can only tell part of the story, and ritual activity requires a more nuanced exploration than the checklist approach of '3 temples + 1 theatre = Roman religion.' The open setting of the hilltop temple suggests communal worship, probably preceded by processions, possibly incorporating sacrifice. There appears to be an important spatial connection between the temple and the theatre, with theatrical performance forming part of the religious festivals. The small temple at the rear of the cavea points to varying levels of participation in the ritual, establishing hierarchies of religious experience and authority. The lack of inscriptions from the town not only leaves us in the dark concerning activities such as dedications and vows, but indicates that for the people of Bilbilis, these permanent markers did not form a way of negotiating religious discourse and appropriate behaviour.

A similar rejection of inscriptions as a means of constructing a discourse of correct religious practice can also be seen in Britain, where it has long been noted that there is a general lack of epigraphy from urban contexts. However, this is compensated for by the distribution of Romano-Celtic temples, which are concentrated in the southern, predominantly civilian area. John Creighton has demonstrated that in some towns, such as Silchester and Verulamium, temples formed an important determinant in structuring the layout of these towns (Creighton 2006). Nevertheless, temples were not always prominent within the urban landscape: at Caerwent, the only known religious structures dating to this period are those within the basilica (the Romano-Celtic temple in the centre of the town dates to the fourth century AD). Room 4 has long been identified as a possible shrine; furthermore, its similarity to room 5 suggests that the latter may have been a second shrine (see Figure 4.8). Both had wide, open entrances, with raised floors, and at a later date the south wall of each was widened on either side with brick plinths (Ashby et al. 1909: 571; Frere 1988: 422; Burnham et al. 1994: 252). In addition, room 4 may have been separated from the nave by a wooden screen, and room 5 had a mosaic floor inserted at a later date. Set at the rear of the basilica, albeit within a central position, the rituals carried out to the gods within these shrines must have taken a very different form to those we have been discussing so far. Presumably any large-scale communal festivals would have taken place in the forum courtyard, removing the physical connection with the deity. Whereas in other examples, the cult statue was able to symbolically watch over the proceedings and receive any offerings, here at Caerwent, they were banished out of sight, becoming a remote figure. Alternatively, any ritual taking place within or in front of the shrine would either have been invisible to the majority of the worshippers, or involved only a small number of participants. Whichever is the case, we can see from the spatial layout of this religious structure compared to Bath for example, that the religious experiences and the forms of religious knowledge created would have been very different. Caerwent also demonstrates another frequent feature of religion in Britain: the lack of inscriptions referring to a priesthood. The only examples attested within civilian contexts are the two from Bath (RIB 155, JRS 56.1). The rest are either from the military *coloniae* of York and Lincoln, and from forts in the north (for example, *sacerdotes* are attested at Birdoswald, RIB 1915, and Wallsend, RIB 1314); even if these are not military personnel, they are the product of a different cultural milieu.

Both Bilbilis and Caerwent highlight the need for methodological rigour when discussing ritual practices at Roman shrines. The lack of inscriptions make both, at first sight, difficult to deal with: we have no explicit guide and so the temptation is to fall back on the picture of a 'typical' religious practice. However, as we have already seen in this chapter, there is no such thing as a 'typical' religious site. Each has a distinctive local character: a form of *religio* which we might think of as broadly 'Roman', but within which remained the possibility of diversity and individuality. It undermines the usual methodology of building up a picture of 'typical' ritual practice, demonstrating that through critical examination of the religious buildings and the possibilities of movement and sight we can begin to describe how the worshippers might encounter the divine.

4.6 RECONSTRUCTING ROMAN RITUAL

In this chapter I have raised the question of how we should investigate the phenomenon of Roman religion through looking at some of the complexities of religious practice, and variation both within and between towns. However, rather than attempting to categorise deities and temples, I have concentrated on the idea of the interaction between the human and the divine, and the way in which ritual informed people's knowledge of the divine. Ritual should be seen as a form of discourse, the local setting through which Romans gained the practical knowledge of how to 'go on' as a Roman, and through which they understood their relations with each other, with the wider Roman world, and with the divine. This understanding did not only reside in the deities worshiped or the form of structure used, but also in the physical performance of religious ritual. Here we can see the people of these communities entering into the discourse of *religio*, and adopting new ideas of what was considered the appropriate way to interact with the divine. This knowledge was written into the very fabric of the town and 'read off' through the repetitive acts of worship. The material evidence did not merely symbolise a particular form of religion: it was both the product and the medium of that discourse.

In looking at religion in this way, we are confronted with the problem of the individual and the general, that is the perceived dichotomy between local variability and a paradigm of 'Roman'. A detailed, contextual

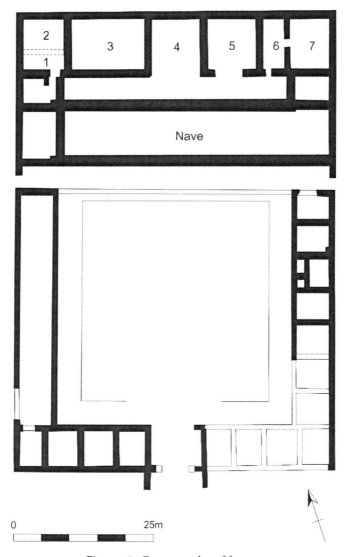

Figure 4.8. Caerwent: plan of forum.

reconstruction of the ritual practice at a number of sites will produce both similarities and differences: each is broadly similar to the next, but with a clear pattern of individual features. In the case studies examined in this chapter, certain rituals have been evident throughout: vows, dedications, sacrifices, processions, dedicated ritual space and inscriptions. Nevertheless, this does not amount to a blue-print for 'correct' ritual practice; rather it forms a range of possibilities. Thus, as we have seen, ritual worship at Bath is very different to that at Munigua, which is different again to Italica. This raises a fundamental methodological problem for the study of Roman ritual. The usual approach is to build up a provincewide picture, regardless of whether the individual sites might be treated as a homogenous group or not. This general picture is then overlaid back onto the individual sites, with little attention to the local features. I would suggest that this can no longer be seen as a viable methodology: firstly because there is no universal form of worship, and secondly because it ignores the particular local characteristics.

In order to explore the character of Roman religion, we need to see material culture not as a mere representation of a particular form of worship, but as active in the construction of that discourse. The inhabitants of any community encountered the divine through the medium of these artefacts; religious truth was embedded within the rituals which in turn reproduced the structures of the Roman empire. To concentrate on the individual deities ignores the fluid and inclusive nature of Roman polytheism: the adoption and appropriation of foreign gods was part of an imperial discourse, problematising the categories of Roman/indigenous, state/private, Romanized/resistant. Furthermore, a more critical awareness is needed of the relationship between who is being worshipped and how: what does it mean when a pre-Roman religious complex to an indigenous deity is then rebuilt with a different spatial arrangement and different ritual practices? The continuity in the object of worship belies a fundamental change in the way in which worship was being formulated.

Religious space was the theatre for ritual worship, and in reconstructing the details of these rituals, we can explore the characteristics of local worship. The physical differences between the examples produced very different religious encounters: the communal and highly visible acts of worship at Bath for example contrast sharply with the experience of those at Caerwent. Similarly, the emphasis on sacrifice at Italica contrasts with its invisibility in the archaeological record at Munigua. The epigraphic record should be treated not only as an historical text, but also as a form of material culture. The act of recording a ritual in stone becomes part of the religious discourse: certain actions are deemed worthy of commemoration, and these permanent and visible markers then play a part in the creation of a normative form of interaction between human and divine. However, we need to be careful of how we use negative evidence. The lack of evidence for sacrifice at Munigua cannot be used to argue that it never occurred, only that it was experienced and interpreted in a different way: the construction of permanent altars was not deemed appropriate and only the final act of the banquet was commemorated in the inscriptions. Again, this leads us to the idea of similarity and difference: that although there was a form of religious ritual which could be broadly classified as 'Roman' evident at all sites, it was not an identikit phenomenon, but one subject to local variability.

FIVE

A QUESTION OF STATUS

5.1 INTRODUCTION

In the course of the previous three chapters, I have explored some of the structures through which Roman power was reproduced by urban communities at a local level, and the ways in which a discourse of a shared identity was located within the fabric of the town. The idea throughout has been that whilst there was an overall level of similarity between the various towns, the way in which these social structures were reproduced was in each case slightly different. In this way, the understanding of what it was to be Roman varied subtly between communities. However, both unequal power relationships and shared group identities can exist at various levels. In seeking to understand the nature of Roman society, we need to be able to move between scales, from the global to the local (Gardner 2002). Unequal relations of power existed at the wider level between centre and province, but also at the local level within individual communities. Although identity, hierarchies and power existed on these different scales, the ways in which they formed part of a lived experience rested upon the same social practices and the same material culture. Given this multivocality of material culture, the public architecture of a provincial town could be used in the reproduction of imperial power at the same time as the articulation of local hierarchies and identities. Furthermore, one consequence of this duality was that made possible different experiences of being Roman within the broader discourse of Roman-ness.

The cultural changes in the provinces following their conquest and incorporation into the administrative structures of the empire went beyond the changes in ethnic identity. It also encompassed new ways of expressing other aspects of identity within the local society. Social rank or status was understood in new ways: expressed through wealth and political privilege rather than, for example, warrior leadership. These changes spread beyond the elite themselves, and extended to aspects of identity around axes of elite/non-elite, free/un-free, male/female, adult/child. The structures of urbanism and religion, for example, which we have already seen forming part of a shared ethnic identity, also became ways in which ideas of social rank were expressed. Age and gender, for example, revolved around ideas of citizenship of the town: eligibility to participate in the running of the town, such as the annual election of the magistrates, became one way of distinguishing between men and women, and similarly of marking the transition from adolescence to adulthood. In turn, these aspects of personal identity were negotiated through the political spaces of the town, and the public ceremonies of voting, for example, which were enshrined in the town charters.

The identity of any individual person forms a complex and continual negotiation of a number of elements: ethnicity, rank, gender, age and occupation. The use of public buildings not only reproduces an ethnic identity, but the differential use of these spaces also becomes a resource for the negotiation of these more local forms of identity. Different social groups had different levels of access to the various areas, and different roles to play during the social rituals enacted within them. The privileging of certain groups, through access to restricted areas, carrying props or wearing specific costumes, leads to the creation and negotiation of power hierarchies. The combination of the different activities carried out within the various buildings accumulates to form a single field of discourse, with the roles carried out within one building or ritual carried forward to other buildings or rituals, to be reaffirmed or undermined. These activities carried out within public buildings formed part of a discourse of correct behaviour. Central to this is the idea of the body: its position, movement and decoration are bound up in how someone internalizes the wider rules and ideologies of the society within which they dwell (Giddens 1984: 36). This forms a discourse of the body: it is culturally constructed, literally embodying the norms and the prejudices of that society.

The idea of identity as a discourse rather than a fixed given is one which has become influential within archaeology as a means of understanding social relations in the past. Thus, for example, gender has entered the agenda as more than a search for women in the archaeological record, but as a discourse to be explored within its own right as one of the structural components of past societies (Scott, E. 1996: 126). Material culture is implicated within these behaviours, as it becomes the resources through which the social agent understands and reproduces their own gender as opposed to other possibilities. A similar approach can also be adopted to age and rank: rather than looking for discrete categories (such as children or adults), these can also be seen as residing in particular social discourses, which can be explored through the material record. However, we should not assume that these identities are neutral; instead, they are judged through the ideology of the society, producing hierarchies of power. Roman society privileged certain experiences, in particular those of the most powerful, the adult, wealthy male, making this the normative experience (Foxhall 1998), creating hierarchies of male/female, adult/child, free-born/slave and wealthy/poor.

Roman archaeologists have tended to be seduced by the rhetoric of the material record and have followed these same biases. They have taken this privileged experience as the paradigm for Roman behaviour rather than one of a series of possible experiences. Other identities, especially women and children, have been written out of the archaeological story and repeated calls for gender to be addressed within an explicitly theoretical framework have largely fallen on deaf ears (for example, Scott, E. 1993: 2–3; Laurence 1999a: 388–9; Hill 2001; Baker 2003). In her analysis of general accounts on Roman archaeology, Eleanor Scott has identified three ways in which women in particular come to be ignored: firstly, through exclusion, secondly, through pseudo-inclusion or marginalization, and thirdly, through alienation, or being seen as anomalies within an androcentric perspective (Scott, E. 1995: 176–9). We can apply these three means of excluding gender to both age and the free/unfree dichotomy: these have similarly been marginalised as research agenda within Roman archaeology. This contrasts markedly with the situation within the fields of Ancient History and Art, where the study of women, children, the family and slaves have been central to research for the past two decades. This is not to deny that these topics have been considered by a few Roman archaeologists, but they have yet to be accepted as central research questions for the discipline as a whole and incorporated into discussions of imperialism and cultural change.

The aim of this chapter is to examine how different social groups negotiated their sense of their own identity through their use of public space. I shall look at how a privileged experience was created, and how others were written out. In doing so, I shall explore how the social experience of the wealthy, adult male was negotiated in opposition to other, less privileged ones and so how this discourse also provided the conditions necessary for the maintenance of other identities. However, there is an inherent bias within the evidence when trying to locate the less powerful in the use of public buildings. In the Roman period, the social use of space was drawn into privileging the identities of the elite, separating them from the rest of the community. This has led to the interpretation of Roman material culture as the culture of the elite. Whilst this is not completely inaccurate, it has tended to constrain the debate, producing a polarity between the elite and non-elite, which echoes that of the Roman and native in earlier discourses. There is a temptation to see them as bounded groups with isolated material lives.

The spread of Romanization outside of the elite males is one which has yet to be fully addressed within accounts of cultural change. Millett's proposed model (1990a, b) is based upon the idea of the elites driving the process as a means of maintaining their power within the changing imperial context. The non-elites then acquire these same material goods through the process of emulation. This has perhaps understandably formed a fundamental problem with the overall model, and the idea of discrepant identities is one attempt to address the range of material lives (Mattingley 2004, 2006). Paul Zanker's work on the so-called garden houses of Pompeii provides something of a more nuanced interpretation (Zanker 1998): he argues that the owners of a series of medium sized houses used the spaces and decoration of their gardens and peristyles to express their own sense of status within the community. Whilst his association of these houses with the rise of a middle class of freedmen is tenuous and based upon a controversial reading of the epigraphic evidence, it still demonstrates how a non-elite group within the city were adopting the material culture in a very knowing manner, which goes beyond any idea of blind emulation. Nevertheless, other community members are less visible archaeologically, and we are left with the problem of reconstructing their experiences. This problem is not unique to Roman archaeology, and as Barbara Bender has argued for Stonehenge:

> To some degree, the world of the less powerful has to be reconstructed from the absences in the record, for example the lack of permanent burials. The world of the less powerful is also imagined in the 'discourse' of the powerful: spaces were constructed to keep 'them' at a distance, to prevent them from 'seeing' even though their labour created those spaces. (Bender 1992: 752)

The temptation, when writing about the use of a building, is to present this privileged experience as the norm, masking other experiences and thus mirroring the gaps in the past with gaps in the present. Many of the more visible forms of material culture, such as inscriptions, architecture and sculpture, served both as symbols of a Roman ethnic identity, but also of a specifically elite identity. However, this did not mean that they were exclusively reserved for the elite. Much of the epigraphy and sculpture from the towns was on display within the public spaces of the town: designed to be seen and interpreted by the non-elite. In writing the story of the elite, we need to explore how they were dependent upon the creation of the less powerful, and even if we cannot securely locate the women, children and poor of the Roman empire, we should at least appreciate how they became written out of the archaeological record. We need to be explicit about the gaps in the material culture: the ways in which these other groups became invisible in Roman society. Furthermore, we can also concede that the powerful did not exist in a vacuum: in a hierarchical society, elite status required differentiated from the non-elite, but their position rested upon the acquiescence and even the support of other members of the community.

In this chapter, I shall look at how urbanism became one way in which local-based identities, and in particular class-based identities, were formed, and how they were expressed through the physical fabric of the town. This expression of elite identity also rested on the creation of less privileged experiences of space, whether based upon rank, gender or age. The various types of public buildings, their layout and the ceremonies conducted within them were all drawn into the negotiation of these varying positions within the local community. Through using the accumulation of the evidence, I will explore the architectural language of these buildings in more detail, building up a composite range of possibilities. The various type of public building in reality act in a cumulative way, as the use of one becomes implicated in the use of others, each strengthening or undermining the power hierarchies established elsewhere. The range of identities is ultimately infinite, as the various aspects of identity are often presented as dualities, but in reality form extremes within a continuum. As any individual will ultimately experience a building based upon own position within a range of these different aspects, it is necessary to temper the broad brush interpretation of general experiences with the recognition that any individual's role within the social situations will inevitably be a compromise between the various elements of their own social identity.

5.2 BUILDING FOR POLITICS

As I argued in Chapter 2, political activity formed an important part of the ideology of Roman urbanism, and it is therefore unsurprising that it played a role in the negotiation of social identity at a local level. Eligibility for political office was restricted through criteria of age, gender, status and wealth to adult men, free-born and able to satisfy certain property qualifications. Within the Republican system, progression through the ranks of magistrates was linked to specific age qualifications (Beard & Crawford 1985: 52–5), and during the imperial period, it continued to be used as the model for deciding who was suitable to hold power within the local communities. In the municipal charter, eligibility for office is restricted to those who were male, free-born and over 25 years of age (*lex Flav.* 54); in the case of a drawn election, the deciding issue was then whether the candidate was married, and how many sons he had (*lex Flav.* 56). Thus, eligibility for election was drawn into the definition of elite status, and for those barred from political office, it formed a way in which their inequality was expressed and internalised. These inequalities were played out in the rituals of urban politics, in the formalised events connected with the running of the town. They were expressed in particular in the political space of the forum and the basilica, and in particular the *curia* or council chamber and the tribunal. These were both areas to which the magistrate had privileged access and an examination of the ways in which they were highlighted architecturally within the basilica as a whole will enable us to understand how the experience of the magistrate was privileged amongst users of the building.

Beginning with the area of the *curia* or council chamber, from analogy with other fora and explicit mention of the town council or meeting of decurions in many inscriptions, we can surmise with a reasonable degree of confidence that there would have been a *curia* in each forum. However, its certain identification is more difficult, particularly in cases where the forum has not been fully excavated. For example, it is often repeated that the room forming the east side of the basilica at Clunia was the *curia* (Palol 1991d: 387–8), but as the area is unexcavated, its identification remains uncertain, and it has been argued that an alternative location might be the structure to the north of the basilica which is usually identified as a temple (Balty 1991: 340). Similarly, the supposed *curia* from Munigua has produced no definite evidence for its use and with three open entrances into it from the portico, its identification is questionable.

Nevertheless, we can be more confident about the *curia* at Caerwent based upon its position, decoration and internal layout, and recent excavations have increased our understanding of how the spatial rhetoric of these areas might be constructed. It lay in the range of rooms to the rear of the basilica and could only be accessed from an antechamber, which was initially a single room, but later divided into two. This distanced the councillors from the rest of the building and, by extension, the rest of the community through an increasingly convoluted approach. Its importance was reflected in its decoration, with remains of two phases of wall-painting and a later mosaic floor (Ashby 1906: 128, plate 19). As the political elite physically set themselves apart from the rest of the community through their use of this room, so they metaphorically marked out their elevated social position. Within the room, slots were found in the floor for benches, and the remains of a dais at one end, which reinforces the identification of the room as a council chamber, but also indicates a hierarchy within the magistrates themselves (Frere 1989: 264). Entering this room for council meetings marked the social and political status of the councillors, and reconfirmed the criteria for their eligibility, forming part of the discourse though which hierarchies of gender, age, wealth and class were negotiated between those who could and could not enter.

The tribunal formed a second area of the building to which the magistrates had privileged access, and this was also highlighted through the architecture of the building. The basilica at London seems to have had a single tribunal at the eastern end which comprised a raised platform set within a circular apse with an antechamber separating it from the main part of the nave (Brigham 1992). This was accentuated through columns and pilasters which framed the apse. The reconstruction of the decoration, based upon the contexts of fragments of wall painting, indicates that the more elaborate decoration was concentrated on the antechamber, with a scheme of red panels with borders of green and yellow pennants and a second border of narrow white bands. The red panels, some bordered with blue, were decorated with designs of spiralling green stalks and coloured flowers, and a robed figure of some kind. However, there is no firm evidence for the decoration of the apse, although traces of plaques in the plastered wall suggest that it might have been lined with marble veneers.

This architectural language can also be seen at Caerwent (see Figure 5.1), where the tribunal at the east end of the nave was set within a

Figure 5.1. Caerwent: view down the basilica nave towards the tribunal.

rectangular apse, its raised floor and possible screen separating it from the main body of the nave. It was further delineated visually with engaged columns, rendered and painted white. There were two means of access: through the nave itself, and from a door to the north aisle. Again the hierarchies of space were reinforced by differences in decoration compared to the rest of the nave: there are traces of at least one layer of wall painting, the tessellated floor contrasted with the *opus signinum* elsewhere, and a hypocaust was later added. Likewise at Wroxeter, the tribunal formed an extended platform at the south end of the basilica nave, reached by one or two steps, with some form of screen across the front (Atkinson 1942: 98). It was set within a rectangular apse, with access from the nave itself, or via a door into the east aisle. Slightly different in form was the tribunal at Clunia: it was undoubtedly more opulent than either of these examples and the layout varied slightly, but spatial analysis reveals that it was the product of a similar spatial rhetoric (see Figure 5.2). It was set within the nave, with walls to the sides and the back controlling the points from which it could be seen, its raised floor increasing its visibility (Palol and Guitart 2000). The architectural decoration likewise reinforces the idea that this was a focal area: the walls were lined with marble, and the floor decorated with *opus sectile* of multi-coloured marbles in geometric and floral designs. The main differences between this and the examples from Caerwent and Wroxeter are that it was a freestanding structure to one end of the nave with no side doors or screen.

The tribunals were privileged areas, highlighted architecturally and decoratively. Those with access would thus have been physically set apart from those in the nave and the side aisles, and the raised platforms would have made these people and their activities more visible to the audience. This was a prestigious area, enhanced by its higher quality decoration and richer materials. Although there are clear differences in quality between the four examples, in each the spatial language is similar. It could be argued that the basilica was built to conform to a model from Rome and did not reflect the awareness of the local population; however the evidence of alteration and rebuilding suggests that this was not the case. At Caerwent, there was an emphasis on this area during redecoration, and it was later furnished with a hypocaust, suggesting that this was perceived as a focal area by those who continued to use the basilica. The major difference between these examples is the means of access. Those at Caerwent and Wroxeter possess an additional door from the side nave; in contrast the tribunals at Clunia and London could only be reached through the body of the central nave. Thus, the dynamics between those on the tribunal and those in the nave must be different, a point which will be discussed more fully below.

The tribunal would have been used by the local magistrates and imperial officials in the course of their political duties, with these two levels intersecting spatially, leading to each being recalled and re-interpreted during the other, shaping the way in which political identity was understood and the criteria through which the quality of the performance judged. The architectural layout of the basilica, which served to highlight any activity and increase its visibility, accentuated the theatricality of the occasion, but also produced the tension and contingency within the demonstration of political power. It raised the possibility of failing before the community, for example by delivering an unpopular judgment

Figure 5.2. Clunia: tribunal set within basilica nave.

before a disapproving audience, and consequently of being judged unfit for office. At Clunia and London this interaction was increased by the means of accessing the tribunal, as a magistrate would have had to enter through the collected body of the local citizens. This provided a further opportunity for those without formal political power to express their approval or disapproval. At Caerwent and Wroxeter, the possibility of entering the tribunal from the side-door removes this moment of contention, separating the two groups more rigidly and symbolically distancing the magistrates from those in the nave. This remoteness is further emphasised by the balustrades or screens which provided a physical barrier between them. These differences seem to suggest that the magistrates at Clunia and London were subject to constant scrutiny: failure to conform to the standards expected by the audience would be a constant threat. In contrast, the magistrates at Caerwent and Wroxeter were distanced from the rest of the community and as they were less visible, were not placed under the same direct scrutiny. They could enter the tribunal through the side doors, and the presence of screens gave them less physical interaction with those in the nave; consequently their power could not be challenged in the same way. It suggests that these differing layouts, although apparently a minor architectural difference, in fact framed somewhat different social encounters.

The performances enacted within the basilica formed an important occasion when a magistrate validated his elite position within the local community, and when his performance was judged through communally held ideas of appropriate behaviour. This brought with it the constant danger of that if he acted in an inappropriate way, he would then undermine his social position. The tribunal literally formed a stage upon which suitability to govern was demonstrated in the presence of an audience. It became a way in which a certain type of identity was expressed, that of the elite male with his privileged access to certain privileged forms of knowledge. Similarly, in the *curia*, whilst the audience was that of his social and political equals, it too formed an area within which his authority was judged. During the Republic, part of being a good magistrate was being a good orator (Cicero *de Oratore* 1.8.30), and although the importance of oratory has been seen as declining in the imperial period (Clarke 1953: 100–8), it continued to form part of elite education through its role in the law courts and declamation. During a speech, the magistrate justified his position of power and his authority as the leader of the community, thus reinforcing the unequal power relations within the group. Standing on the tribunal in front of an audience, his self-reflexive control of his body became an indicator of his fitness for social power. Throughout the oratorical handbooks, there is a clear emphasis on the importance of the body, of dress, gesture and movement, demonstrating the anxiety and the need for control. There are elaborate rules for how the toga should be worn, for example: how it should hang and the folds should be arranged (Quintilian *Institutiones Oratoriae* 11.3.137–49). Similarly, gestures were subjected to the same stringent control (11.3.84–116). These instructions may seem minor, and clearly they would not have been adhered to in such detail. However, they do demonstrate that political status rested upon correct presentation of the body. Furthermore, there was a moral element: oratory was seen as a skill which could only be successfully mastered by the upright man, the *bonus vir*, creating the ideal that government lay in the hands of those morally suited for office (Quintilian *Institutiones Oratoriae* 1.pr.9–10). Thus for a magistrate, there was the danger that any substandard performance was an indication of moral turpide. If he appeared too like an actor, he might be seen as *infames*, or devoid of honour (Edwards 1997; Cicero *Auctor ad Herennium* 3.15.26; Quintilian *Institutiones Oratoriae* 1.11.3), or similarly, if he did not appear manly enough, he risked appearing *effeminatus*, thereby making the audience doubt his masculinity (Richlin 1997). Through the act of delivering a judgment, a petition or any other kind of speech, a magistrate asserted his moral superiority within the community, restating his authority as a leader.

It is very easy to trace this discourse at Rome; however, can we be sure that the same preoccupations and power structures were operating in a provincial context? In all four examples discussed, the tribunal was clearly a focal and privileged area, designed to heighten the theatricality of any event: the architectural layout increased its visibility and at the same time controlled how it was viewed. All this suggests that the public performance of political authority was an important part of the use of the building. However, in such encounters, it was not simply a case of the magistrates demonstrating their right to rule, but also of the audience judging their suitability. The criteria by which the performance was judged may not have been the same as those laid out in the oratorical textbooks, but as oratory formed part of a boy's education, it would have been part of the way a magistrate monitored his own performance (for example Woolf 1998: 1 for oratorical schools in Gaul). The importance of political activity in the self-definition of an elite man can be seen in the prominence of togate statues within the iconographic repertoire, such as the togate statue found in Munigua (now in the Museum of Archaeology, Seville). A similar example was found in the vicinity of the theatre at Clunia, and a further two at the nearby Coruña del Conde (Palol 1991b: 29; 1991e: 327).

As Richlin has argued, the Roman forum was engendered space: "[it] was ringed by buildings in which the (male) business of running the Roman state was carried on" (Richlin 1997: 92). The archaeological examples from Spain and Britain demonstrate how space was differentiated in the basilicas. The *curia* and the tribunal were highlighted as focal areas through the layout of the building and their comparatively opulent decoration. However, the way in which they were used differed. The *curia* was remote and hidden, the tribunal highly visible; status was established through being hidden from and revealed to the community on different occasions. They formed an area where certain members of the community, the adult, male urban magistrates, could create and maintain their political power and social position: power was written into the very fabric of the basilica. The tribunal structured these encounters as a performance, making the body of the magistrate a symbol of his ability to govern. At the same time, the rest of the community was written out of these privileged areas, using the reasons for their absence (gender or age for example) as a way to make sense of their own place within the urban community.

5.3 BUILDINGS FOR RELIGIOUS RITUAL

The repetitive activities of political life privileged one particular section of the community, the wealthy, adult male, and this extended into the sphere of religious ritual. As we have seen in previous chapters, the urban priesthoods were integrated into the political system of magistracies: the various offices of *flamen* and *sacerdos* were integrated into the *cursus honorum*, and the epigraphic evidence demonstrates a substantial overlap in the men holding political and religious posts. Consequently the temples and shrines of the towns can, to some extent, be seen as an extension of political space, and the rituals of sacrifice and dedication which formed the core of religious practice also formed a strategy through which such men were able to maintain their social position within the local hierarchies. However, religion also brought others into public life, and in particular wealthy individuals excluded from political office such as wealthy women and freedmen. This allows us to develop the picture, and to explore how different roles within the rituals problematized social authority.

There are certain problems of definition when dealing with religious authority, as authority to officiate was not restricted to named priesthoods (Scheid 2003: 129–30). There was no distinction between the political and religious officers, and so there was not a dedicated religious personnel; furthermore, other personnel were involved in sacrifice, extending religious knowledge beyond the priesthood and requiring their relative statuses to be strictly policed through other strategies such as distinctive clothing (North 1990:52–3). The priestly colleges formed an important part of the *cursus honorum*: at Rome a young man might expect to hold the title of augur as his first magistracy (Szemler 1986: 2328–30), and epigraphic evidence from the provinces makes it clear the leading men of any community would hold both political and religious offices. Priests acted as interpreters and intermediaries between human and divine, advising the community on the will of the gods and the meaning of messages believed to be of divine origin. This gave them privileged access to special forms of knowledge not possessed by the rest of the community. Access to the priesthoods was marked by specific criteria: most priesthoods were confined to adult males, presumably with the same qualifications of wealth and birth as for the political magistracies. To act as a priest was to differentiate between men and women, mark the transition from child to adult, and to demonstrate a position within a ranked society.

Urban charters confirm that within the provinces, priesthoods were subject to similar demarcation and honours. The colonial charter from

Urso does not give the precise criteria for eligibility for priestly offices, but stipulates that the first were chosen by the founder of the colony, and their successors co-opted by the rest of the college of priests, giving them the opportunity to restrict the priesthood to a specific social group (*lex col.* 26–7). They were granted a number of privileges: they and their children were exempt from military service, they could wear the *toga praetexta*, and they were entitled to seats amongst the decurions at theatres and amphitheatres (*lex col.* 26). From the evidence in Spain, Nicola Mackie has demonstrated that the main priesthoods appear to have been held by men eligible for public office, and often feature with political magistracies (Mackie 1983:42; also Curchin 1990: 43–4). At Italica, a range of priesthoods are attested, some of which were held in conjunction with the political magistracies. For example, Caecilianus served as *flamen perpetuus*, *flamen provinciae*, and *duovir* (CILA 2.343).

At Rome, the priests were marked out by their distinctive clothing, with different costumes for the various colleges. Augurs wore the *toga praetexta* with their heads covered during sacrifice, and carried a *lituus* or curved staff (Linderski 1986: f/n 411). The *flamen* sometimes wore a *laena*, or mantle, draped around both shoulders, and a felt cap topped with a spike of olive wood (*apex*) and a thread of wool (*apiculum*) (Fishwick 1987–2005: 475–81). Access to specialised religious knowledge, for example the books of augural law, was a further way to separate their role from the rest of the worshippers (Linderski 1986: 2241–56). It is difficult to be sure how far these items were adopted outside Rome and Italy, but iconographic evidence from the Iberian peninsula suggests some familiarity with them; for example, friezes from the provincial forum at Tarraco depict two types of *apices*, a sacrificial knife and a purification shaker (TED'A 1989: 162–3, fig. 9; see Curchin 1996: 152 for other examples). At Bilbilis, a fragment of wall painting was decorated with a small ladle, a bucket for drawing water, another purification shaker and a *lituus* (Guiral Pelegín and Martín-Bueno 1996: 119–20, nos. 257–8, lam. 258). Even if not identical to the costumes at Rome, wearing distinctive clothing and carrying special objects set the priests apart, and acting in an authoritative manner and interpreting the will of the gods demonstrated a knowledge not available to the rest of the community.

As we saw in Chapter 4, sacrifice was frequently a public event, making it a moment when local hierarchies were acted out in a communal setting. The right to preside over a sacrifice was limited to those with *auctoritas*, such as the *paterfamilias*, magistrates and priests (Scheid 2003: 79–92). The presiding official might lead a procession to the altar; he would then pour wine over the animal's brow, sprinkle its back with salted flour and pass the sacrificial knife over its spine to symbolise the transfer of the offering from human to divine possession (ibid. 89–92). After his attendants had killed it, he inspected the entrails to decide whether it was acceptable to the gods; if it was, the entrails were burnt as offerings before a sacrificial banquet of the rest of the meat. So, for example, at the temple at Bath, whoever officiated at the sacrifices would have had special access to the altar which formed the pivotal point of the whole complex. He would have stood apart from the rest of the community during the whole process, as the person with the authority to transfer the offering to the divine realm and to interpret whether it had been accepted. Furthermore, at the moment when the entrails were burnt, he would have had a prominent position near the altar, and this conceptual link between priest and altar can be seen in iconographic representations of religious rituals, both sacrifice and libations, where the person presiding over the proceedings is depicted next to it. The Altar of Vespasian at Pompeii depicts such a group of victim and priests around a central altar, the priest dominating in spite of the greater size of the victim (Ryberg 1955: 195; see Figure 5.3). Through his central role in the ritual, a man would reinforce his authority and status, and also other elements of his identity: his age and his gender. However, the magistrate did not carry out the act of slaughter itself: the victim was killed by the *victimarii*, giving them the potential to undermine the status of the magistrate through their active role at the moment of the slaughter. The contrasting clothing of the priests and *victimarii* served to indicate their relative status: the priest wore a toga, with his head covered to signify the *pietas* of the occasion, whilst the *victimarius* is usually depicted in a short skirt and bare-chested to depict his servile status. In spite of this, the success of any sacrifice relied upon the compliance and co-operation of all parties involved in the ritual.

A second means of interacting with the gods was through the act of dedication. These could range in value from a few coins to substantial building works. Inscriptions could serve as a permanent marker of the more generous, marking the largesse and the *piestas* of the dedicator. Such texts vary in the amount of information they provide: in some cases they explicitly state the form the donation took, and even what it cost, and on other occasions we can deduce the nature of the offering from the physical form of the inscription, such as at Caerwent where the truncated feet on the base suggest that the offering was a statue was of Mars and a goose (RIB 309). As access to wealth underpinned the hierarchies within

Figure 5.3. Pompeii: altar of Vespasian depicting priest presiding over a sacrifice.

the Roman system, the frequency with which the inscriptions mention how much the offering cost or the weight of metal used demonstrates the importance of the cost of the donation. It not only represented the *pietas* of the donor, but also their disposable wealth. When Lucius Aelius Fronto dedicated the statue of a horse to Dis Pater (CILA 2.1056), he built an apse in the forum for it, a public place visible to the whole community, commemorating the offering with an inscription, the public setting for the dedications turning a private act of religious worship into a public declaration of rank.

Religious buildings differed from the political spaces of the town, as they formed a way for women and freedmen with access to a certain level of wealth, and who might therefore have been of some standing within the community, to appropriate something of the status of the magistrate. The priesthoods in particular brought women and freedmen into the system of public office, albeit at a somewhat restricted level. At Italica, Vibia Modesta served as priestess of both provincial and local cults: as *flaminica provinciae Baeticae* and *sacerdos coloniae* (CILA 2.358). Interestingly, the latter title is also attested as being held by two men (CILA 2.351, 387), showing how flexible these priesthoods actually were. The evidence collected by Delgado y Delgado for Baetica and Mauretania indicates that it was mainly wealthy women from the upper ranks of society who held such offices, showing the interplay between gender and rank and suggesting that their wealth and family ties allowed them to overcome the restrictions imposed on women in eligibility for political office (Delgado y Delgado 1998: 74–5, 80). Similarly, *seviri* are attested at Italica and Munigua, and, again, the general picture from Spain suggests that they were usually wealthy freedmen. Nicola Mackie has suggested that perhaps they needed to make a more strenuous effort to overcome the ambiguity of their status and that their lack of political power resulted in heavier financial demands being placed upon them (Mackie 1983: 42). Their official duties are sometimes shown on their tombs, such as scenes of sacrifice around a tripod or altar (Ryberg 1955: 100–1). In contrast, women were traditionally barred from presiding over sacrifices, and it is unclear precisely what their religious duties involved. For both women and freedmen priests, their special roles were marked out by specific costumes which repeated elements of those of the political magistrates: *seviri* were often granted the *ornamenta* of the decurions and magistrates, possibly including the *toga praetexta* (Mackie 1983: 64; Curchin 1990: 81), and at Italica Vibia Modesta wore a flaminate crown as part of her priestess' garb (CILA 2.358).

Those with wealth but no political office could also use religious donations to establish their position within the community. Fabia Ursina at Munigua, for example, stipulated in her will that a statue be dedicated to Fortuna Crescens Augusta and the resulting inscription gives its weight in silver, thus reinforcing the idea of offering and wealth (CILA 2.1057). Quintia Flaccina also dedicated a statue to the Genius Municipii, with a shrine and exedra, presumably to house it, and celebrated the event with a banquet (CILA 2.1058; it may have formed a pair with 1059; she may also have been responsible for 1080). At her death, her heir Quintus Aelius Vernaculus dedicated an inscription to Ceres Augusta in memory of her (CILA 2.1055; see Gimeno Pascual 2003: 183–4). All four inscriptions associated with Flaccina recorded that banquets were provided for both sexes, suggesting that the sacrificial banquet might be restricted to certain members of the community, and that ideas of inclusion and exclusion at such events might form one way to demarcate specific groups within the community, whether by gender, rank or membership of a *collegium*.

Religious display formed a setting for the establishment of a religious hierarchy which was embedded into the wider social hierarchies. The majority of the various priesthoods were seen as part of the magisterial system, bound by the same criteria of gender, age and wealth as qualification for the political magistrates. However, within the religious sphere the hierarchies begin to blur, as sufficient wealth or family status granted those excluded from the political magistracies a more elevated position. The various priestesses and *seviri* were able to negotiate a place for themselves within the local hierarchies through the rituals of worship. They did not necessarily challenge the dominant power structures; rather, as power was based upon an ideology of wealth, such religious offices allowed a place in the system for those who were wealthy, but outside the main political structures.

5.4 BUILDINGS FOR ENTERTAINMENT

A third type of building associated with the political and religious activities already discussed consisted of the theatres and amphitheatres found in many Roman towns, and so these spaces can be thought of as an extension of the more formal public spaces of the towns. Whilst the activities carried out in the two forms of building are very specific, the rules governing their use were broadly similar, and so they can be dealt with together. Although it is usual to concentrate on purpose-built venues for these events, such architectural structures were not necessary; for example, gladiatorial games could take place in spaces other than a permanent amphitheatre, whether temporary wooden structures build for a specific event, or permanent structures which had other primary uses, such as the forum (Gros 1994: 13; Hopkins 1983: 5). Therefore it is possible that even in towns where there is no archaeological evidence for monumental theatres or amphitheatres, the gladiatorial games and theatrical spectacles still took place and so formed part of the way in which social identity was understood.

The games and events which were held in the theatres and amphitheatres formed formal events which were bound up in the magisterial system and local hierarchies. In the colonial charter from Urso, the leading magistrates were responsible for organising such spectacles for the community from a combination of public and private money (*lex col.* 70–71). The *duoviri* were to produce four days of shows or dramatic spectacles, and the aediles three days, as well as a day of games in the circus or of gladiators in the forum. Inscriptions from Italica record the presentation of *ludi* by the wealthier members of the community (for example, CILA 2.392). This was a part of the elite's obligation of munificence towards the wider community, forming a further expression of their wealth. This may then have been expressed through the physical layout of the buildings, with the sponsor of such spectacles granted a special seat within the theatre, highlighting their role to the rest of the audience. Within the amphitheatre at Italica, two tribunals or boxes were marked out as high status areas through their architectural position and the facilities available for those using them. They were accessed from the lower galleries through private antechambers which had two vaulted niches and traces of stucco and red paint on the interior walls (Corzo Sánchez 1994: 197; Roldán Gómez 1993: 239). Here the presiding donor and other distinguished members of the audience had access to private rooms and prestigious seating areas. In addition, the colonial charter states that the person giving the games would lead in the audience, allocating their seats in accordance with the rules of the decurions (*lex col.* 126). Presumably referring to the *pompa*, or procession, it further emphasizes the role of particular members of the group.

Whilst embedded in political authority, as with religion, producing such games formed an important opportunity for those barred from political office to show off wealth, and consequently their potential influence. At Italica, the freedman Lucius Caelius Saturninus produced *ludi scaenici* to celebrate his election as a *sevir* (CILA 2.354). Ryberg has noted that *seviri* often depicted their official duties on their tombs and that one of the most frequent themes represented was the games they produced in honour of the deified emperor (Ryberg 1955: 98–100). Such images might show the *sevir* presiding over the display, perhaps surrounded by gladiators in combat, or another popular theme was the *pompa* or procession preceding the *ludi*. As the wealth of the *sevir* granted him a position of power within the community, it is perhaps unsurprising that the production of games, a visible demonstration of that wealth, should form an important means of counteracting his lack of direct political power.

However, the games were not only an occasion for the expression of elite identity. Rawson has argued that Augustus, as part of his social reforms, enacted a law stipulating the seating for certain social groups at

Rome (Rawson 1987). She has recreated the way in which the particular social groups were divided and where they were seated within the
auditorium. There was a hierarchical order, with the front rows of seats
considered the most prestigious, and the standing room at the back the
least desirable. The front fourteen rows were reserved for the equites,
and the most privileged positions were allocated to the senators; in the
theatre, this was the *orchestra*, in the amphitheatre the very front rows.
Certain colleges of priests had their own seats, and front seats could also
be granted to individuals of merit. The *plebs* occupied the main part of
the *media cavea*. Other groups might have their own places, and Rawson
suggests that certain areas may have been reserved for soldiers, the paid
attendants of the magistrates, married men and the various *collegia*. She
argues that slaves and the toga-less poor were confined to the *summa cavea*,
and similarly, women's seats were near the back, although if a woman was
to be specifically honoured, she was allocated a seat at the front with the
Vestal Virgins. This law was the product of a particular ideology, which
favoured wealthy over poor, men over women, and adults over children,
and when the audience was seated, this social ranking was made explicit
and internalized by the participants.

Rawson's reconstruction rests on evidence from Rome, and consequently we are left with the problem of how far it was applicable outside
of Italy. The *lex colonia Genetivae* grants decurions and those with *imperium*
privileged places, with a 5000-sesterces fine for those sitting in seats to
which they were not entitled (*lex col.* 25); furthermore, the *orchestra* of
the theatre was to be reserved for magistrates of the Roman people, senators and the sons of senators and possibly for the decurions (*lex col.* 27).
In contrast, the municipal law states that seating at games was to be
in accordance with previous custom, provided it was confirmed by the
decree of the decurions (*lex Flav.* 81). Thus, we cannot be completely
certain that the elaborate terms of the *lex Julia theatralis* were applied with
all their details to the whole of Spain and Britain. Nevertheless, the physical evidence of the buildings themselves points to divisions within the
audience from the time they entered the building. In the amphitheatre
at Italica, the layout of the entranceway separated the different groups
(Roldán Gómez 1994: 218–223). The most powerful men had the easiest
access to their front row seats, via two doors either side of the main
entrance; they could then use the rooms grouped around the entrance,
before reaching their seats through a wide perimeter corridor with pro-
portionately more stairways per seat. In contrast, those in the upper tiers
by-passed the rooms in the entrance area, and were funnelled through

narrower passageways and fewer stairways. Once the spectators reached
their seats, they were still separated into groups through divisions within
the auditorium through the *caveae* and *cunei* (see Figure 5.4). At the theatre at Bilbilis, for example, the *media* and *ima cavea* were divided by a
circular wall (Martín-Bueno 1982b: 80); likewise, at Italica the *summa*
and *media cavea* were separated by a narrow corridor, and the *media* from
the *ima* by a line of large marble slabs (Corzo Sánchez 1993; Rodríguez
Gutiérrez 2004). At Italica, there is also evidence for the differentiation
of the spectators within the seating (fig. 5.7): the *orchestra* was marked out
through the use of marble and decorative carving (Rodríguez Gutiérrez
2004: 109, fig. 43), and there is evidence from the *ima cavea* for a marble
lining to the *gradus*, and for dividers separating individual seats, which
may also have served as arm rests (ibid. 82, 87–8). These give a seat width
of 80 cm, which presumably was not repeated throughout the theatre
(the more usual seat width seems to have been about 40 cm), again producing a more comfortable experience for the elite at the front. At both
the theatre and the amphitheatre at Italica, inscriptions have been found
reserving seats in the elite areas (ibid. 563–4, 134–5; CIL 2.5102–16).
Through their knowledge of what to do and where to sit, the audience
recreated the group identities and hierarchies within the community.
These divisions would have been reinforced by the visual distinctiveness
of their clothing: for example, the magistrates and augurs in the *toga
praetexta*, and the public slaves with their own costumes (magistrates: *lex
col.* 63, 66; *limocincti*: *lex Flav.* 19).

A further social division reinforced through the spatial configuration
of these buildings was the division between the performers and the
audience. Catherine Edwards has argued that actors and gladiators, as
well as prostitutes, were considered *infames* (Edwards 1997). Yet it was
more complicated than these sections of society simply lacking honour,
as they were used to define what was honourable, and so the correct
modes of behaviour for the rest of the community:

> But so conspicuously did [these professions] lack honor that they played
> a vital part in the processes by which honor was constructed. Actors,
> gladiators, and prostitutes were paraded as examples of what those who
> sought officially sanctioned *dignitas* ("social standing") should at all costs
> avoid. Paradigms of the antithesis of honour, they occupied a crucial
> place in the symbolic order. (ibid. 67)

The disgraceful nature of these professions was enforced through a spatial
segregation within the buildings. In the theatres, the actors occupied the

Figure 5.4. Italica: amphitheatre arena and tiers of seating.

stage during the performance, whilst the side rooms evident at Italica, Clunia and Bilbilis provided them with an area separate from the rest of the audience. Similarly, at the amphitheatre at Italica the attendants, slaves and gladiators had a completely separate set of entrances and passages to the service areas. Whilst the gladiators themselves used the main entrances during the performance, the temporal sequence of the display would have maintained their segregation from the elite. However, the fact that those with most honour and those with least both used this area reinforces the ambiguous and dangerous nature of the gladiator, as a figure of both shame and glamour. This spatial separation of the two extremes was further reinforced through legal sanction, as appearing on stage meant exclusion from a seat amongst the equites (Rawson 1987: 106). Although elite discourse stressed the absolute shame of the gladiator, there was in fact a certain ambiguity over their status. For a gladiator himself, his profession could be a powerful source of his own self-identity, as Valerie Hope has demonstrated from the study of their tombstones (Hope 1998), and there are literary accounts of emperors entering the arena (most notably Caligula and Commodus, although this was made problematic by the way in which Roman historians used such activities as a topos of what made a bad emperor). At Pompeii there are examples of graffiti referring to the sexual magnetism of leading gladiators (CIL 4.4353, 4356; also, Juvenal 6.103–13), and they were a common iconographic image.

The gladiator serves as a cautionary tale that the textual evidence can at times only provide a partial insight into how the varying social groups might attach different values to social experience, and something which was considered shameful by one section of society might not be viewed in the same way by others.

Again, we have seen how activities based in the public spaces of the town were adopted to express local identities. Again, access to specific areas was governed by hierarchies of power, privileging those with power above those without. However, it should not be merely seen in terms of 'power over', as these hierarchies were reproduced by the actions of every member of the community as they negotiated their own position according to their rank, gender, age and wealth. Throughout, we are faced with the problem of actual allocation of space. As I have demonstrated, certain areas are differentiated from others, and the relative wealth of their decoration suggests that some were more prestigious. The allocation and occupation of these areas then allowed the people of the community to reproduce the inequalities within the society as well as the ideology underlying those inequalities.

5.5 BUILDINGS FOR BATHING

Thus far, I have dealt with the formalised spaces and rituals connected to political and religious activity, but within the urban setting, there were also a series of less formal ways in which status was displayed. Bathing, as a social event, had connotations within Roman society which are completely foreign to the modern viewer. More than an exercise in hygiene or part of the daily fitness regime, for some a visit to the baths was a significant social or political event. It was an integral part of Roman life and of the temporal rhythm of the day. The activities on offer were myriad: as well as cleaning the body, a Roman might exercise, meet some friends or political allies, listen to a concert, or have something to eat or drink. In writing about Roman baths and bathing, it is tempting to adopt an empathic approach, ignoring the fact that such an activity, even the body itself, was a culturally generated experience, and can only be understood within the specific cultural matrix. The fact that bathing was without doubt an important practice in the reproduction of a Roman ethnic identity makes it too easy to ignore the multiple experiences it encompassed. That the Roman male visited the bathing suite in a naked (or near naked) condition has led some to assume that social hierarchies were stripped off at the same time as the togas (for example,

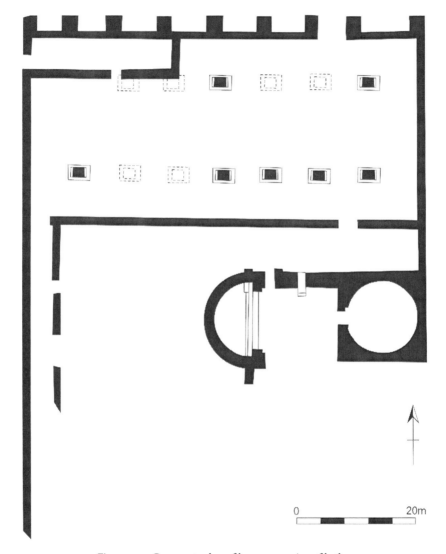

Figure 5.5. Caerwent: plan of known remains of baths.

Yegül 1992: 5). In representing it as an egalitarian occupation, part of the Roman experience, we ignore the fact that our envisaged Roman is often adult, male, and probably wealthy. However, this is contradicted by the literary evidence, which suggests that during the late Republican and early imperial period at least, bathing was a hierarchical activity, with an important part to play in the construction and affirmation of social and political influence.

Each of the towns studied here had at least one set of public baths by the early second century and some, such as Italica and Clunia, more than one. Clearly bathing was perceived to be an important part of urban living: in Caerwent, for example, where there was a very limited collection of public buildings, the large baths complex was constructed by the end of the first century AD, and completely rebuilt in the early second century (Nash-Williams 1930; see Figure 5.5). Even if this was due to the influence of the army or the patronage of provincial officials, the later phases of rebuilding testify that the routines of public bathing and exercise were adopted by the inhabitants as an important part of their social routine. Conceptually, although not always physically, the baths were usually at the heart of the public areas of the town. At Italica, the Termas Mayores were positioned near the Traianeum and *macellum*, connecting them with the public spaces of the Nova Urbs. Furthermore, their location within the network of streets places them at a major connective position: the complex fronted onto a wide street which ran parallel to the main route through the town from the amphitheatre to the Traianeum. These were connected by a further broad road which led straight to the main entrance of the complex. Thus the Termas Mayores were set at a pivotal point within the street grid, at the crossing point of two of the major routes through the town. The relationship between large bathing complexes and public space can also be seen elsewhere: at both Caerwent and Wroxeter, they lay opposite the forum, on the major route through each town, and at Bilbilis they were positioned near the theatre. In all these examples, the baths were conceived as an important element of the public spaces of the town and the inhabitants' mental landscapes.

Bathing was a communal event, where various groups came together to interact. Recent work on the distribution of sculpture within the buildings suggests that within the imperial *thermae*, there was an emphasis on the *palaestra*, bathing halls and *frigidarium* as the primary areas for people to mingle and interact (DeLaine 1988: 27; Marvin 1983: 377–8). In the Baths of Caracalla, the sculpture clustered in and around the *palaestra* and the swimming pools, with none found in the passageways, service areas and hot rooms (Marvin 1983: 350–3). In addition, whilst popularly called 'baths', the term is really something of a misnomer as the buildings often included exercise areas, areas for concerts and poetry recitals, and even libraries (Nielsen 1990: 144–5). The baths formed an important part of the elite day at Rome: it was a place where political allegiances might be formed and social relationships negotiated (ibid. 146). Where and when a man bathed dictated whom he met and with whom he dined, and it was as much through these two institutions as through activities in the forum that the political system of Rome functioned. Thus the concern voiced in Martial's epigrams over not securing a dinner invitation at the baths is not merely at missing out on a good meal, but at being excluded from behind-the-scenes political machinations (Martial *Epigrams* 1.23). The baths were an area for interaction, both social and political, and visiting them was an important part in the creation and maintenance of socio-political networks.

Whilst most of the baths are not as ostentatious as the imperial *thermae* at Rome, we can still see this public aspect of bathing in operation. Janet DeLaine has argued that the increasing size and scale of bath-houses from the Republic to the Imperial period marked a transition from bathing for bodily cleanliness to bathing for sensual pleasure (DeLaine 1992). She argues that this symbolic change can be detected through an increase in heated spaces, in cold pools, in non-essential space such as the *palaestra*, and in choice of routes and activities. This new idea of the bathing experience is visible in the provincial examples. The investment in the size and the decoration of these facilities bears witness to their importance in the urban fabric. The Huggin Hill baths in London was elaborately decorated as demonstrated by the painted plaster and fragments of marble wall lining found in the destruction layers (Marsden 1976: 59, nos. 35–41, 45–56, 59). Likewise, at Los Arcos I at Clunia, *opus sectile* floors in polychrome marble were found in situ in the *apodyterium*, *frigidarium*, *tepidarium* and *caldarium* (Palol 1991d: 371–2). The size of the rooms suggests that bathing was a group activity rather than private event, with sufficient space to accommodate large numbers of people at once: at Huggin Hill for example the size of the *caldaria* range from approximately 90 m^2 to 140 m^2 (Marsden 1976). Finally, the presence of non-bathing facilities suggests that a visit to the baths was something more than an exercise in hygiene. Many of these establishments have spaces for non-bathing activities: large covered basilicas were built at both Wroxeter and Caerwent, presumably used by the bathers for exercise, and substantial open-air *palastrae* formed part of the Termas Mayores at Italica and Los Arcos I at Clunia. The former has only been detected through geophysics, but appears to form a large rectangular complex, 16,800 m^2, consisting of an open central area surrounded by porticoes (Rodríguez Hidalgo et al. 1999: 80). At Los Arcos I, the two symmetrical wings of the complex each contained a basilica with an inner courtyard, and were separated by a large, central courtyard (see Figure 5.6). In all these examples, we can see these urban bath-houses sharing characteristics with the imperial *thermae* at Rome of monumentality, choice, and multiple facilities.

As suggested earlier, there is an underlying impression that bathing was an egalitarian experience: that in such an intimate experience all men were equal (and in this scenario, the bathers usually are all male). However, it is clear from the textual evidence that a visit to the baths was in fact an opportunity to show off personal wealth, as satirised by Petronius: Trimalcio, his nouveau riche epitome of bad taste, adopts to excess the methods through which wealth and social position were displayed (Petronius *Satyricon* 17–18). He exercises in an excessively pampered manner, and when he enters the bathing suite, his towels are of the highest quality, he is surrounded by three masseurs, and he and his attendants drink the most expensive wine. In a similar vein, Martial makes fun of the change in Aper's bathing routines once he has gained a substantial inheritance: when he was poor, he was attended by a single slave with a one-eyed crone guarding his clothes, now he is rich, he is attended by five slaves, and drinks copiously from expensive drinking vessels (Martial *Epigrams* 12.70). The manner in which one visited the baths, the level of wealth demonstrated through the number of attendants, the quality of oil used in anointing the body, and the amount of wine drunk were all indicators of wealth. Furthermore, Ray Laurence has argued that at Pompeii, this was reinforced through a temporal division in bathing (Laurence 2007: 157–66). He has demonstrated how the elite visited the baths between the sixth and the tenth hours, whilst the majority of the population would not have gone until after the tenth hour, effectively segregating the elite and their entourage from the rest of the population.

Whilst we cannot build up such a detailed account for the provinces as for the city of Rome, it is possible to trace some of the ways in which wealth and rank were displayed through a visit to the baths. The first decision was where to bathe as some towns had multiple bathhouses: Clunia had three of varying sizes, Italica two, and the choice of which to visit may not have been as innocent as we might suppose. We cannot be certain of the exact criteria: there may have been separate baths for men and women or alternatively the divisions may have been based upon rank or profession. Even the decision not to bathe in public was a significant choice; at Italica there was both a bathing suite and a gymnasium within the Casa de la Exedra. It has been argued that this was a semi-public building, such as the base for a *collegium* or association of *iuvenes* (Rodríguez Hidalgo 1991: 229). If this was the case, then the act

Figure 5.6. Clunia: Los Arcos I baths.

of bathing there rather than at the two public baths became a way to establish membership of a particular social club. If, on the other hand, this was a private house, the decision to bath at home, presumably with a select group of friends, was a mark of exclusivity.

The well-attested prohibition on mixed bathing suggests how baths became part of a wider discourse of gender identities (Nielsen 1990:

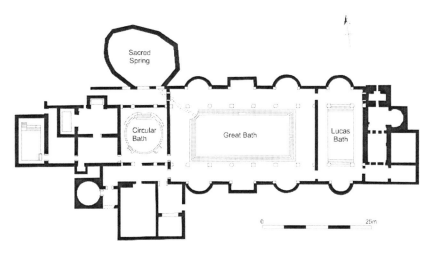

Figure 5.7. Bath: plan of period 2 baths dating to second century AD.

177

135). We have already seen how this segregation might have occurred at towns with more than one baths; in other places, with only a single bathing establishment, there were two other possibilities. The first was for men and women to bathe at separate times. The contract for the baths at Vipasca required the lease-holder to open the baths for women from the first to the seventh hour, and for men from the eighth hour of the day to the second hour of the night (CIL 2.5181), and this might have been the procedure at Bilbilis, for example, which had a single suite of rooms. The other possibility was to have two separate suites within the same baths, one reserved for each gender, as can be seen at London and Bath (see Figure 5.7; also Figure 2.5). In both cases, the main bathing rooms (*frigidarium*, *tepidarium* and *caldarium*) were repeated: at London the second suite added in the early second century may have marked a change from temporal to physical segregation, whilst at Bath, there appear to have been multiple facilities from the outset. There was less importance attached to female bathing, and the Vipasca inscription stipulates that women were to bathe early in the day, before the baths are fully up to temperature, and that they were to pay double the entrance fee of men (CIL 2.5181).

A different form of segregation was used to differentiate between those of free and unfree rank. A number of service personnel were required to keep the baths functioning, usually either slaves considered part of the property of the baths or criminals: Trajan, in a letter to Pliny, advises that cleaning the public baths was a suitable occupation for elderly criminals (Pliny *Epistulae* 10.32.2). These service areas would have been less elaborately decorated than the public suites, without the architectural marbles, wall paintings and mosaics. Spatially they were marginalised, such as at Los Arcos I at Clunia, where the furnace was fed from outside the building effectively removing them from sight. Whilst this undoubtedly has a functional explanation, it also reinforced the social inequality between the users of the baths and the (servile) stokers. Other slaves carried out functions within the baths, perhaps as an *apodyterium* attendant or a masseur, which allowed them to occupy the same spaces as the bathers, but instead they were segregated through their activities.

The social display and segregation inherent in the act of visiting the baths served to reinforce the power hierarchies within the local communities. Bathing was implicated in the maintenance of social identities and the inequalities between them and it formed a technology through which the elite male could demonstrate the superior wealth which formed the basis of his social rank. It further provided a means for the rest of the population to negotiate their own standing in relation to the elite and to each other in a variable scale of social and economic rank. Bathing also allowed the expression of other aspects of identity, and the inequalities between them, such as the hierarchies between male and female, free and unfree. These were not necessarily identical mechanisms between the different communities, and variability in the number and precise layout of the bath-houses meant that these social differences might be expressed in different ways, for example through spatial segregation as opposed to temporal segregation. Nevertheless, even with these differences in detail, a visit to the bath-house proved a potent marker of social identity.

5.6 WRITING ON STONE

One element of public space which is often overlooked is the inscriptions: these were a physical part of political and religious spaces, and an extension of elite display. Throughout this discussion of elite power, inscriptions have been used as evidence for various aspects of social relations; in this section, I want to look at the practice of inscribing on stone as a phenomenon in its own right. The adoption of the epigraphic habit was more than learning to write on stone: it was the adoption of permanently memorialising very specific activities in stone. Such markers became a way of solidifying shifting social relations, legitimating social inequalities and making ephemeral acts everlasting (Barrett 1993). They can be examined within the same framework as other forms of material culture: they are more than the text, but have a physicality and a context which represents a conscious decision on the part of the person setting up the inscription. The text also represents a series of choices: who should be named, and which actions commemorated. Furthermore, their permanence made them part of a social discourse concerning appropriate behaviour and the negotiation of who has authority to act. They served to fix social norms and to turn a momentary act into established tradition. In discussing the idea of inscriptions as part of a technology of power, we need to see the inscription within its social context. They communicated a message, but that message existed on two levels: the text itself represents one level of meaning, but they also had an embedded social meaning.

What is an inscription? Whilst this might seem a basic question, it is one which has often been overlooked, in part exacerbated by the conventions of their publication. Inscriptions are a three dimensional mass of long-lasting material, usually stone or bronze, although this does not exclude the possibility of other materials such as wood being used.

These are fashioned into a fairly limited range of possible forms (such as a statue base or architrave), and a text is then carved onto them. Finally, they are placed within a landscape, the precise location dictating who will read them. The repetitive nature of the wording and the epigraphic abbreviations mean that it was not necessary to be fully literate to read the average inscription. Whilst the majority of inscriptions from any town are usually antiquarian finds, with no secure context, those which we can recontextualize show a preference for public and highly visible locations (Revell in press; a similar pattern can be seen with statues, as argued in Stewart 2003: 136–40). They were positioned where they were easily accessible, and could be seen by the entire community. At Wroxeter, the dedication for the forum was set above the main entrance, the size of the inscription (approximately 370 cm long by 123 cm high) and the height of the letters (between 14 cm and 24 cm) making it highly visible to those entering the building (RIB 288). Similarly at Munigua the forum was used by the elite as a particularly prestigious place for their inscriptions. Two marble pedestals were set up in niches along the west wall naming Lucius Quintius Rufus, with other inscriptions from Lucius Valerius Aelius Severus and Lucius Aelius Fronto in the north portico (CILA 2.1074, 1075, 1054 and 1056, respectively). A further two, probably identical, inscriptions have been found recording the donation of money for the construction of the forum by Lucius Valerius Firmus (CILA 2.1076–7). The lettering, ranging from 5.8 cm to 9 cm, is highlighted with red paint, increasing the visibility and legibility. These inscriptions formed an epigraphic landscape, and as I shall demonstrate, their role in the reproduction of certain local power relations made this a landscape of power.

As social position and political power rested in the urban magistracies, the reiteration of the *cursus honorum* on an inscription formed a way of signifying status in a society where it was bound up in ideas of public service and the ideology of urbanism. Such magistracies were part of the unequal hierarchies of age, gender, wealth and rank, and to serve as a magistrate formed a means of negotiating and reproducing power. As we have already seen, this not only included the political magistracies, but also the local priesthoods which provided an opportunity for wealthy women and *liberti* to legitimate their own positions. Through the reiteration of their magisterial titles, they publicly proclaimed their right to superior rank within the society and reaffirmed the justification for that power. As many of these offices were for a single year, the inscriptions provided a permanent reminder of the prestige due to individual in the longer term.

The motivation behind creating such inscriptions was a desire for recognition and prestige within the community, in the context of a society where the elite fulfilled their obligations to that community through the act of munificence (Mackie 1990; Wallace-Hadrill 1995). They formed part of an ideology mystifying the unequal position of the urban magistrates, with their superior power legitimised through their acts of generosity. It also functioned as a display of wealth in a society where social rank and political office were dependant upon financial criteria. The inscription itself, a permanent marker to be seen by all, played an active part in these strategies. At Italica, Lucius Herius, Lucius Blatius Traianus Pollio and Gaius Traius Pollio, all *duoviri* and priests of the imperial cult, built substantial structures within the theatre and set up inscriptions to record the fact, stressing that they had used their own money for the good of the community (CILA 2.382–3). Such inscriptions could also be used to record donations which left no other permanent memorial, such as the donation of corn by Caius Calvisius Sabinus at Clunia (Clunia II 28). Whilst these inscriptions were set up by the person themselves, dedications were also set up by others in recognition of leading citizens, whether by the whole community or a select group of associates. Inscriptions from the whole community served as a way of honouring selected individuals according to criteria of political power and wealth. The people of Munigua set up inscriptions to an unknown man, who may have served as *duovir* (the text is badly corrupted) and to Aelia Procula (CILA 2.1070, 1079, respectively). However, inscriptions could also be used as a means of recognising and reinforcing other social groups and relationships, such as a tombstone from Clunia to Martialis from his fellow slaves (Clunia II 66).

Inscriptions were also used by those whose political position was more ambiguous: who possessed the wealth to give them a certain level of power, but were excluded from the political magistracies by their gender or former servile status. We have already seen the example of the *libertus* Lucius Caelius Saturninus who produced *ludi scaenici* at Italica to mark his election as *sevir* (CILA 2.345), and the inscription he set up to commemorate it made his act of munificence part of the collective memory of the community, and his name a fixed part of the urban landscape. Valerie Hope has argued that *liberti*, and in particular *seviri* used inscriptions as a way of making an impact, making them more visible epigraphically than the free-born elite (Hope 2001: 29–36; see also Ross Taylor 1961: 129–30). Similarly, in donating an exedra, an *aedes* and a banquet, Quintia Flaccina stressed the ambiguity of her position (CILA 2.1058; cf. 1055). As a woman, she had no authority through political office; however her wealth and her membership of one of the most influential families in the town gave her a certain standing within the community, expressed through the gift and made permanent by the inscription.

However, it was not only the wealthy elite who used inscriptions in these ways: inscriptions were used by other groups of people to express allegiance or obligation to social groups. Military rank was an important part of self-definition even in urban contexts, forming an alternative series of power hierarchies, and there are multiple examples from towns in Britain, mainly of tombstones, such as those from Bath (RIB 156–60) and Wroxeter (RIB 291–4, 296). For these men, their identity and status was constructed around their military profession, their rank and their membership of a particular unit (Haynes 1999; James 1999). For some, to mention that they served as a *miles* was enough, such as Gaius Murrius Modestus who describes himself as a soldier of Legio II Adiutrix (RIB 157), but others used them to express membership of a specific century, or a guild (RIB 157; *collegium fabricensium*, RIB 156). For those whose rank as officer made them part of the military elite, an inscription could be a permanent marker of their superior position, as in the case of the tombstone of the centurion Marcianus from London (RIB 15): whilst it is not stated in the text that he held this position, his depiction with the costume and accoutrements of his rank make it clear to the viewer that this was not an ordinary soldier. Whilst this might seem unsurprising in a military context, it is clear that within these urban contexts, military identity and military hierarchies were still used as an appropriate means of self-definition. As there are more examples of this from urban contexts in Britain than in Spain, it demonstrates that in provinces with a permanent military presence, the two social systems and hierarchies existed side by side, whether complementary or in competition. For slaves and freed slaves, inscriptions formed one way to memorialise their lives, but the conventions of naming proved a permanent reminder of their current or former owner and this relationship of inequality and power. Thus when Lucius Valerius Aelius Severus set up a dedication in the forum at Munigua, he described himself as the freedman of Lucius Valerius Celerinus and Aelia Thallusa (CILA 2.1055). He would have remained within his former owners' *clientela*, and legally had certain duties towards them. The very form of his name fixed his social position and obligations in spite of his obvious wealth.

As we have seen throughout, inscriptions can be approached on two separate levels. Firstly, they provide evidence for the power hierarchies themselves, but secondly, as material culture, they played an active role in the reproduction and negotiation of these hierarchies. To write on stone was to make something permanent and visible to the rest of the population. They reinforced the dominance of the adult, wealthy male at the pinnacle of the social hierarchy and the factors implicated in the ideology underpinning that power. They also provide the means for those excluded through that ideology (for example women and *liberti*) to challenge this and claim their own place within these hierarchies. It might explain the frequency with which *liberti* are attested in inscriptions: it was one of the few resources available to them to establish a position within the dominant hierarchies, whereas for the elite, free-born male, it formed one of many.

There are numerous examples from Spain, many of which have been discussed already. However, the evidence from Britain has long been seen as problematic, as there are relatively few inscriptions, and of these, the majority are from military contexts. Although there is a very uneven distribution between towns, none have produced the sheer numbers which are found in other parts of the empire. There are also noticeable lacunae when compared to other epigraphic assemblages: there are very few dedications to the emperor (excluding those from the military areas), and the majority of these are building dedications. Similarly, there are no examples of honorific dedications, which can be seen as an extension of the lack of individual benefactions noted by Blagg (1990). These could take the form of someone providing some form of benefaction to the community (for example, building work or a donation of money or food to individual citizens), recording this on stone, and then the community setting up an inscription in thanks, sometimes with a statue of the individual (see Revell in press for examples from Italy). We have limited evidence from Britain for either side of this relationship, which can be accounted to one of two explanations: either these acts were taking place, but were not being memorialised in stone, or relationship between the urban elites and the rest of the community did not incorporate this pattern of donation and obligation, probably indicating the absence of competition amongst the urban elites. This is echoed by the lack of statues from the province, which Stewart has attributed to the fact that "such honours lost

their force in a society where urban *celebritas* was not at a premium"
(Stewart 2003: 177). A second characteristic is the type of people responsible for those inscriptions we do have. Mann (1985) has demonstrated
that in urban contexts such as Colchester and Lincoln, a high proportion
of the tombstones commemorated soldiers (30% and 57%, respectively).
Even in the Cotswolds (i.e., the area around Gloucestershire, Cirencester
and Bath), where military occupation was short-lived, 27% commemorated soldiers. More recently, Mattingly has argued that the majority
of inscriptions from towns were set up by soldiers, officials and others
from outside the province (Mattingly 2006). He argues that there is some
adoption of tombstones by the local elites, but the lack of attested magistracies overall suggests that this is limited. Overall, the picture from
Britain suggests that in contrast to Spain and elsewhere in the empire,
the relationship between individual status and inscriptions was complex.

5.7 A MONTAGE OF EXPERIENCES

So far in this chapter, I have discussed how public buildings and inscriptions were implicated in the various forms of social identity as expressed
through the routines of everyday life. These routines of urban living in
reality came together in a cumulative way to reinforce these social hierarchies, with the experiences from one building carried over into others. There were different opportunities available for the different social
groups, and the picture should be seen as one of complexity, ambiguity and negotiation rather than a straightforward duality between elite
and non-elite. The aim of this section is to build up an idea of these
cumulative urban lives based on a single town to demonstrate how the
daily routines which placed Roman power within the local communities
also formed of the expression of local-based hierarchies and identities.
However, as already noted, it is easy to write a narrative of the powerful
as they are usually the most visible archaeologically; to write the narrative
of the less powerful and the marginalised is more difficult. In a sense, it
becomes the narrative of the gaps: as the material record represents the
resources through which they were excluded, so any analysis inevitably
becomes a narrative of absence (Bender 1992). Therefore, in this section
I shall attempt to unpick the different stories of being Roman. This is not
meant to be all-encompassing, covering all possible experiences; instead
I mainly concentrate on how a privileged range of experiences was built
up, demonstrating how the urban setting was bound up in the cumulative
expression of local hierarchies. This narrative is set in Italica and some

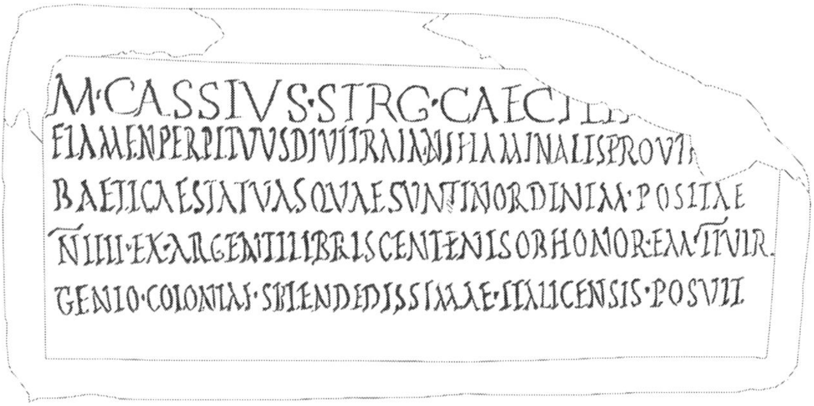

Figure 5.8. Dedication to Genius Coloniae, Italica.

of the accounts are based upon inscriptions from the site; however, in a sense this is merely a way to build up these experiences. I make no claims to be accurately reconstructing the past lives of a named individual, but rather but rather to explore how the individual elements of their identity which we can identify allowed them a particular experience of the urban setting (see also Revell 2000).

As we have seen throughout, public space privileged a specific identity: the adult, free-born, wealthy male. To take the case of Marcus Cassius Caecilianus, he would have enjoyed a particular experience of urban space: he was a member of the political and social elite and exercised his authority through the posts of *duovir* and priest of the imperial cult at both local and provincial level (CILA 2.342). Presumably he would have played a prominent role in activities held in the forum, possibly delivering judgments from a tribunal in the basilica and attending council meetings in a *curia*. As magistrate and priest, he would have acted out his religious authority and specialised knowledge through the rituals such as sacrifice. On such occasions, his distinctive costume of *toga praetexta* with the *fasces* set him apart from the rest of the community. As a demonstration of his personal *pietas*, and in thanks for his elections is *duovir*, he set up an inscription to the Genius Coloniae in the Traianeum recording his dedication of four statues each worth 100 pounds of silver (see Figure 5.8), underlining his right to his privileged position, and at the same time making his name and status a permanent part of the urban landscape. At spectacles held in the theatre and the amphitheatre, he would have had a seat amongst the most privileged, possibly in the front row of the amphitheatre with his place marked by an inscription. Sometimes he would have acted as presiding magistrate, with access to the vestibule and the tribunal in the amphitheatre. When the baths were at their hottest, he would go to socialise there with the rest of the elite men. As he moved through the streets of the town, he was accompanied by his public slaves and possibly his personal clients, signalling his authority and his importance.

For a woman from an elite family, her experience would have been somewhat different due to her inability to formally participate in political activity. Like Maurianus, Vibia Modesta also set up an inscription in the Traianeum recording her *pietas* towards the divine (CILA 2.358) through the dedication of offerings. She was publicly celebrating her election as *flaminica* of the province of Baetica for a second time, and she used the text of the inscription to emphasize her public position by recording that she was also *sacerdos coloniae*. However, in spite of her wealth and her religious offices, certain activities were barred to her due to her gender (Gardner 1993: 85–109). She was excluded from the most prestigious areas of the forum as she was ineligible to serve as political magistrate. Furthermore, as a woman she was could not officiate at a sacrifice; whatever her duties as priestess, they did not give her the same central role Maurianus enjoyed. Nevertheless, she was entitled to a distinctive costume, including the crown she dedicated in the temple, and she could contribute to the sacrifice by donating the sacrificial victim. She could not mix with the influential (male) magistrates at the baths: she either bathed at a different time or frequented a different set of baths. At the theatre and the amphitheatre, she was banished to the inferior seats, where she could neither see the action nor be seen by the rest of the community. Her wealth gave her a certain standing within the community, setting her apart from the majority of the women of Italica, but her gender excluded her from the most privileged position in Italican society.

The former slave, Lucius Caelius Saturninus also offered a statue to the divine to celebrate a priesthood, in his case in honour of becoming *sevir* (CILA 2.345). Instead of family links, he defines himself in relation to his former master and patron, describing himself as *L(uci) Caeli Parthenopaei lib(ertus)*. His social position lay somewhere above that of the majority of the population, but his servile origins prevented him from reaching the top of the social hierarchy; thus, his use of the public buildings reaffirmed his identity as somewhere in between. In spite of his wealth, he was unable to serve as a magistrate, and during political activities he was one of the crowd in the nave of the basilica, watching the more powerful on the tribunal. However, his wealth would have given him a somewhat ambiguous position within the other public buildings. As a priest of the imperial cult, he may have played a conspicuous role in certain religious ceremonies, and similarly in the baths he had the opportunity to show off his wealth with more expensive paraphernalia and more numerous attendants. This ambiguity can further be seen in the theatre and amphitheatre: he produced *ludi scaenici* at the theatre, and on that occasion would have enjoyed all the privileges of the sponsor. However, on other occasions, his position is more uncertain, as he would not have been eligible to sit in the areas reserved for the decurions, unless he were granted the *ornamenta* of a decurion which may have included a more prestigious seat (Curchin 1990: 81). Thus, like Vibia Modesta, as a wealthy *libertus* his social position was ambiguous, and his use of the various public buildings structured that experience of ambiguity.

The three examples discussed so far can broadly be described as the more powerful members of society at Italica. However, in order to reconstruct further experiences, we begin to deal with hypothetical possibilities. An ordinary male citizen of the town may well have used all the buildings and his membership of the citizen body would have been confirmed by taking part in the annual elections in the forum for example. At the same his lack of social rank was marked out by being denied access to the *curia* and the *tribunal* in the forum, or through the area he sat in in the amphitheatre and the theatre. The urban fabric also became a way to maintain gender and age distinctions, and so for women and children, their use of the public buildings was again different. For women and girls, the world of politics was one from which they were formally excluded, setting them apart from the men of the town, and this was further enforced by their different roles within public sacrifices. In a society dominated by an ideology of public participation and ritualised ceremonies of *salutatio* and more informal allegiances formed during bathing and dining, the way in which they were set apart or excluded entirely, whether spatially or temporally, all served to mark out their social inferiority and lack of authority. For boys, their exclusion through age would have been mitigated through the idea that they would eventually join the body of local citizens, and that they would learn how to act in public occasions through watching their male relatives (Laurence 2007: 167–181).

To reconstruct the experience of a slave is more difficult: in part because they have been written out of the material record in both the past and the present (Morris 1998), but also because the range of social experience encompassed within the term makes generalities impossible.

For example, a slave who was a member of the imperial service (the *familia Caesaris*) would have had a different experience to a slave running a workshop, who again would have had a different experience to a slave considered part of the fixtures and fitting of the bath-house. However, in general, slaves had no political rights: they were not entitled to serve as magistrates and had no vote in the urban elections, effectively rendering them invisible in any political context (although a slave of the emperor involved in the administration of the empire would prove an exception here). A more privileged town slave might have been chosen as the attendant a magistrate, possibly to carry his *fasces*, giving him a certain level of visibility, but this would have been a rare exception and the menial activities he carried out would have maintained his servile status. At the baths, the lowliest of the slaves were banished from sight into the service areas to stoke the furnaces. Others were allowed into the communal areas, but to serve as anointers and cloakroom attendants (Nielsen 1990: 125–131). Some of the slaves carrying out these tasks would belong to the baths, classed as part of the inventory, others would be personal slaves serving their masters. Similarly, at the theatre and amphitheatre, the slaves were banished to the service areas, out of sight, or to the upper tiers of the seating if they were watching the performance. In religious rituals their status becomes slightly more problematic: they were barred from presiding over the sacrifice, but a select few acted as religious specialists, the *victimarii* and the *popae* who were the experts in the actual techniques of sacrifice (North 1990: 53). This diffusion of religious roles and ritual knowledge problematises their status in sacrifice: some played a visible and authoritative role in the proceedings. Nevertheless, their clothing distinguished them from the actual priests: in iconographic representations they are depicted semi-clothed, thus separating them from the togate priests and other attendants. For most, their experience of being Roman was being continually denied authority and visibility, and the urban setting served to reinforce this lack of social position.

Public buildings structured the multiple experiences of being Roman: differential use of space, access to different areas and at different times, all combined to produce the numerous social experiences and local power hierarchies. However, this did not rest upon one building alone, nor did it create a simple dichotomy of powerful/powerless. As we have seen in this section, the use of space could at times be complementary, at others contradictory. The simple categories of male/female, child/adult, free/unfree, wealthy/poor combined to form a myriad of individual experiences. However, all formed part of a single discourse creating local hierarchies based upon elite wealth and magisterial office through the public buildings and spaces of the town.

5.8 CONCLUSIONS

The traditional paradigm of Roman identity within models of Romanization is that of the wealthy, adult, free-born male. However, the adoption of Roman material culture became part of the expression of other aspects of identity, and the public spaces of the town became an area where local power hierarchies were articulated. The routinised practices of urban living, with preferential experience of the architectural setting, created positions of authority for those of magisterial class. At the same time, the different roles played by others constructed their identities as female, child, slave, and the expression of their relative lack of power. In delineating social hierarchies, the material culture not only created the elite male, it created the rest of the community. The magistrate's privileged access to certain areas during specified times set him apart from the rest of the community: it constituted his position of power and was understood through the ideology underlying that power. His role within one building fed into the next, so the cumulative effect of the urban landscape was to place him at the pinnacle of the local hierarchies. His identity was not a fixed given, but rather a discourse which was created through practice, and negotiated through his difference to other members of the community. This difference gave rise to other experiences, and to the ways in which others internalized and negotiated their position with these hierarchies.

This fragmentation of being Roman undermines the notion of a normative experience of being Roman. 'Roman' is a discourse, a project which each person understands in a different way. The same material which was used to create an elite Roman experience was also used to construct the experience of a Roman woman, a Roman child or a Roman slave. Their understanding of being Roman was different from that of the local magistrate, but it was not necessarily less Roman. It was formed at a local level, and so was mediated through other elements of their individual experience: as Roman material culture became implicated in the expression of age and gender and the inequalities within them, so people's understanding of their roles within the imperial context would have differed. It is not that the magistrate's experience was any more authentically Roman than that of his wife, his children or his slaves, but that Roman identity could encompass these differences. Just as the structures of imperialism were understood slightly differently between communities, as has been demonstrated in previous chapters, so it was understood and experienced in different ways within each of these communities.

SIX

BEING ROMAN...

The question of Roman-ness lies at the heart of this book: the ways in which meaning was created for the term in the past, and how any uniformity in meaning was constantly slipping, to create a multiplicity of possible meanings. Certain structures reproduced Roman power, Roman society and Roman culture, and these provided a common understanding of what it was to be Roman. Yet at the same time, they were the means through which any unified experience broke down, producing a paradox of similarity and diversity, both within individual communities and throughout the empire as a whole. The structures of Roman imperialism, such as religion or urbanism, were located within the everyday routines of the people of the provinces, and through these activities, they shared in an empirewide discourse of how a Roman life should be lived. They expressed this discourse through the material they used and the spaces they inhabited. This has a profound implication for our understanding of the power relations at play. Part of the authority of Rome rested on its superior military force and its ability to suppress discontent when it occurred in the forms of uprisings, such as the Jewish revolts of AD 66–70 and AD 132–5. However, whilst the significance of the threat of military might should not be downplayed, by the second century AD some areas, such as southern Iberia, had no permanent military garrisons. Military force was not the only means through which the imperial authorities held sway. Instead, imperial power was exercised through allying the interests of the conquered with those of their conquerors. In this way, imperialism was a dialectic in which both sides played a part: for example, the administrative authorities through their promotion of urbanism or their suppression of unacceptable forms of religious practice, and the inhabitants of the provinces through their participation in urban lifestyles or the imperial cult. Nevertheless this relationship was still one of unequals, as these aspects such as urbanism and religion promoted Roman cultural norms to the expense of the indigenous practise.

In this way, one aspect of Roman imperialism was the process of cultural change evident within the archaeological record, as increasingly people shared in a common ethnic identity. This Roman identity was constructed through a series of social structures, from which people took their knowledge of what was appropriate within any given situation. They used these structures as a way to present, consciously or subconsciously, certain messages about themselves: their position within social hierarchies and how they expected to be treated by other people. The public buildings of the towns were implicated in these performances: their meaning was generated through these structures, and was called upon to convey aspects of identity. I have argued that we can trace three structures, or ideologies, which were bound up in a global, ethnic identity: urbanism, the emperor, and religion. People encountered these through the public spaces of the town, as they moved through the town, carrying out specific activities. In this way, a shared Roman identity became more than an elite phenomenon, but rather something within which the urban community in wider sense could participate. Some of these events were formal, large-scale activities, such as gladiatorial games; others were more informal, for example a visit to the baths. This is not to argue that the entire community was experiencing these activities in an identical way: the spatial divisions of the amphitheatre created a privileged role for the wealthy elite, women may have bathed at different times to men. Nevertheless, all the participants, through their knowledge of how to act within these contexts, were recreating their particular experience of a shared identity. This broad discourse of Roman-ness moves the question of an ethnic identity beyond the model of elite-driven Romanization and problematic non-elite emulation. For the people of the provinces, their Roman identity resided within their practical knowledge of how to act within a changing social context, and to enact roles appropriate for them. In part, this was learning how to respond to the new imperial authorities, with its administrative demands, but it was also learning new ways of expressing their place in the local community.

Running through this analysis has been the theme of variability: that the urban settings were different, the routines enacted were experienced in different ways, and so ultimately there was no paradigm of Roman identity. It is clear that this variability does not fall into simple blocks, dictated by a single factor such as geography, administrative category, moment of conquest or notions of assimilation/resistance. It was a consequence of a series of factors coming together: differences in pre-conquest culture, between the Baetica and the Celtiberian regions in Spain for example, or between south-eastern and western Britain. It may also have been the product the historical trajectories of individual communities, such as Hadrian's patronage of Italica or Wroxeter's possible military origins, or their role within the administrative structures of ruling, for example London's role as a provincial capital, or Clunia's as a *conventus* capital. But this went beyond variability between communities: it extended to different understandings of Roman-ness within any single urban community. This draws in two fundamental ideas: the multiple aspects of any single person's identity, and the multiple readings of any form of material culture. The result is that such local differences should not be seen in opposition to a shared ethnic identity. During a public event such as a sacrifice, it was possible for the group to express their common Roman-ness, and at the same time express their social rank through their specific role as priest, flute-player or onlooker. In this way, Roman ideologies and Roman material culture became bound up in the negotiation of local hierarchies, with the privileging of the wealthy, adult, free-born male through the idea of the urban magistrate, whilst rendering the less powerful participants less visible. This raises the question of whether as we concentrate on the issue of Romanization and ethnicity, we risk losing sight of the ongoing concerns of Roman discourse about social rank and display of wealth.

So the final picture is one of complexity and variability. There was no single Roman identity in the past, but instead a discourse of Roman-ness within which a multitude of experiences could be created. Nor was this discourse rooted in a single social structure, nor expressed through a single form of material culture. Roman imperialism was multi-faceted, with its power located within numerous forms of ideology and multiple situations. These were not independent, but interweaved to form a complex web of attitudes and relationships, with different ones coming to the fore in different contexts. As such, we cannot hope to write an account of every individual variable within this. Instead, we have to write of how that experience of being Roman was recreated within specific situations, and through this, to explore which were the elements of commonality, and conversely, the extent of the 'give' within them. Through this we can go beyond descriptions of Roman identity, to explore how shared experiences and different experiences were created.

REFERENCES

Abbreviations

Brit.   Annual summary of new inscriptions published in *Britannia*. Refer-
            ence by volume and entry number.
CIL   *Corpus Inscriptionum Latinarum*
CILA   *Corpus de Inscripciones Latinas de Andalucía*
Clunia II   Palol, P. de and Vilella, J. 1987. *Clunia II. La epigrafía de Clunia.*
            Excavaciones Arqueológicas en España 150. Madrid: Ministerio de
            Cultura. Reference by entry number.
CSIR   *Corpus Signorum Imperii Romani*
ILN   *Inscriptions Latines de Narbonnaise*
ILS   *Inscriptiones Latinae Selectae*
JRS   Annual summary of new inscriptions published in *Journal of Roman
            Studies*. Reference by volume number and entry number.
RIB   *Roman Inscriptions in Britain*
RIT   Alföldy, G. 1975. *Die römischen Inschriften von Tarraco*. Berlin: de
            Gruyter
Tab. Sulis Tomlin, R.S.O. 1988. 'The curse tablets'. In B. Cunliffe (ed.)
            *The temple of Sulis Minerva at Bath. Volume 2: the finds from the sacred
            spring*. Oxford University Committee for Archaeology Monograph
            16. 59–277

Alcock, S. E. 1993. *Graecia capta: the landscapes of Roman Greece*. Cambridge:
    Cambridge University Press.
Alcock, S. E. 2002. *Archaeologies of the Greek past: landscape, monuments and
    memories*. Cambridge: Cambridge University Press.
Alföldy, G. 1976. 'Consuls and consulars under the Antonines: prosopography
    and history', *Ancient Society*, 7: 263–99.

Alföldy, G. 1996. 'Subject and ruler, subjects and methods: an attempt at a conclusion'. In A. Small (ed.) *Subject and ruler: the cult of the ruling power in Classical Antiquity*. Journal of Roman Archaeology Supplementary Series 17. 254–261.

Allason-Jones, L. 1997. 'Visions and dreams in Roman Britain', *Archaeologia Aeliana*, series 5, 25: 21–5.

Allason-Jones, L. and McKay, B. 1985. *Coventina's Well: a shrine on Hadrian's Wall*. Hexham: Trustees of the Clayton Collection, Chesters Museum.

Arnold, D. 2002. *Reading architectural history*. London: Routledge.

Asad, T. 1979. 'Anthropology and the analysis of ideology', *Man* (N.S.), 14: 607–627.

Asad, T. 1983. 'Anthropological conceptions of religion: reflections on Geertz', *Man* (N.S.), 18: 237–259.

Ashby, T. 1906. 'Excavations at Caerwent, Monmouthshire, on the site of the Romano-British city of Venta Silurum, in the year 1905', *Archaeologia*, 60: 111–130.

Ashby, T., Hudd, A. E. and King, F. 1909. 'Excavations at Caerwent, Monmouthshire, on the site of the Romano-British city of Venta Silurum, in the years 1907 and 1909', *Archaeologia*, 61: 565–582.

Atkinson, D. 1942. *Report on excavations at Wroxeter, (the Roman city of Viroconium) in the county of Salop 1923–1927*. Oxford: Oxford University Press.

Badian, E. 1958. Foreign clientelae (264–70BC). Oxford: Clarendon Press.

Balil, A. 1982. 'Un retrato del emperador Tiberio procedente de Bilbilis', *Papeles Bilbilitanos I. Encuentro de estudios Bilbilitanos*. 43–46.

Balty, J. C. 1991. *Curia ordinis. Recherches d'architecture et d'urbanisme antiques sur les curies provinciales du monde romain*. Brussels: Académie Royale de Belgique.

Baker, P. A. 2003. 'A brief comment on the TRAC session dedicated to the interdisciplinary approaches to the study of Roman women'. In G. Carr, E. Swift and J. Weekes (eds.) *TRAC2002. Proceedings of the twelfth annual Theoretical Roman Archaeology Conference, Canterbury 2002*. Oxford: Oxbow Books. 140–6.

Barrett, J. C. 1988. 'Fields of discourse: reconstructing a social archaeology', *Critique of Anthropology*, 7: 5–16.

Barrett, J. C. 1989. 'Afterword: render unto Caesar . . . '. In J. C.Barrett, A. P. Fitzpatrick and L. Macinnes (eds.) *Barbarians and Roman in north-west Europe from the later Republic to late Antiquity*. British Archaeological Reports International Series 471. 235–241.

Barrett, J. C. 1993. 'Chronologies of remembrance: the interpretation of some Roman inscriptions', *World Archaeology*, 25.2, 236–247.

Barrett, J. C. 1994. *Fragments from Antiquity: an archaeology of social life in Britain, 2900–1200BC*. Oxford: Blackwell.

Barrett, J. C. 1997. 'Romanization: a critical comment'. In D. J. Mattingly (ed.) *Dialogues in Roman imperialism. Power, discourse, and discrepant experience in the Roman empire*. Journal of Roman Archaeology Supplementary Series 23. 51–64.

Bateman, N. C. W. 1997. 'The London amphitheatre: excavations 1987–1996', *Britannia*, 28: 51–85.

Bateman, N. C. W. 1998. 'Public buildings in Roman London: some contrasts'. In B. Watson (ed.) *Roman London: recent archaeological work*. Journal of Roman Archaeology Supplementary Series 24. 47–57.

Bayliss, R. 1999. 'Usurping the urban image: the experience of ritual topography in late antique cities of the Near East'. In P. Baker, C. Forcey, S. Jundi and R. Witcher (eds.) *TRAC98. Proceedings of the eighth annual Theoretical Roman Archaeology Conference, Leicester 1998*. Oxford: Oxbow Books. 59–71.

Beard, M. 1991. 'Ancient literacy and the function of the written word in Roman religion'. In J. H. Humphrey (ed.) *Literacy in the Roman world*. Journal of Roman Archaeology Supplementary Series 3. 35–58.

Beard, M. and Crawford, M. H 1985. *Rome in the late Republic: problems and interpretations*. London: Duckworth.

Beard, M and Henderson, J. 2001. *Classical art: from Greece to Rome*. Oxford: Oxford University Press.

Beard, M., North, J. and Price, S. 1998. *Religions of Rome. Volume 1: a history*. Cambridge: Cambridge University Press.

Beltrán Lloris, F. 2003. 'Una variante provincial del *hospitium*: pactos de hospitalidad y concesión de la ciudadanía local en la Hispania Tarraconense'. In S. Armani, B. Hurlet-Martineau and A.U. Stylow (eds.) *Epigrafía y sociedad en Hispania durante el alto imperio: estructuras y relaciones sociales*. Alcalá: Universidad de Alcalá. 33–56.

Beltrán Lloris, M. 1981. 'Nuevo aspecto del emperador Claudio del Museo de Zaragoza', *Caesaraugusta*, 53–4: 255–275.

Bendala Galán, M. 1973. 'Tablas de juego en Itálica', *Habis*, 4: 263–272.

Bendala Galán, M. 1982. 'Excavaciones en el Cerro de los Palacios'. In AA.VV. *Itálica (Santiponce, Sevilla): actas de las primeras jornadas sobre excavaciones arqueológicas en Itálica*. Excavaciones Arqueológicas en España 121. 29–74.

Bender, B. 1992. 'Theorising landscapes, and the prehistoric landscapes of Stonehenge', *Man* (N.S.), 27: 735–755.

Berry, J. 1997. 'Household artefacts: towards a re-interpretation of Roman domestic space'. In R. Laurence and A. Wallace-Hadrill (eds.) *Domestic space in the Roman world: Pompeii and beyond*. Journal of Roman Archaeology Supplementary Series 22. 183–195.

Birley, A. R. 1997. *Hadrian: the restless emperor*. London: Routledge.

Birley, A. R. 2005. *The Roman government of Britain*. Oxford: Oxford University Press.

Birley, E. 1986. 'The deities of Roman Britain'. In H. Temporini and W. Haase (eds.) *Aufstieg und Niedergang der römischen Welt*, II.18.1. Berlin: Walter de Gruyter. 3–112.

Blagg, T. F. C. 1990. 'Architectural munificence in Britain: the evidence of inscriptions', *Britannia*, 21: 13–31.

Blagg, T. F. C. 2002. *Roman architectural ornament in Britain*. British Archaeological Reports British Series 329.

Boatwright, M. T. 2000. *Hadrian and the cities of the Roman empire*. Princeton: Princeton University Press.

Boschung, D. 1990. 'Die Präsenz des Kaiserhauses im öffentlichen Bereich'. In W. Trillmich and P. Zanker (eds.) *Stadtbild und Ideologie: die Monumentalisierung hispanischer Städte zwischen Republik und Kaiserzeit*. Munich: Verlag der Bayerischen Akademie der Wissenschaften. 391–400.

Bowman, A. K. and Thomas, J. D. 1994. *The Vindolanda writing-tablets (Tabulae Vindolandenses II)*. London: British Museum Press.

Bowman, A. K. and Woolf, G. (eds.) 1994. *Literacy and power in the ancient world*. Cambridge: Cambridge University Press. 1–16.

Braund, D. 1996. *Ruling Roman Britain: kings, queens, governors and emperors from Julius Caesar to Agricola*. London: Routledge.

Braund, S. H. 1989. 'City and country in Roman satire'. In S. H. Braund (ed.) *Satire and society in ancient Rome*. Exeter: University of Exeter Press. 23–47.

Brewer, R. J. 1993. 'Venta Silurum: a civitas capital'. In S. J. Greep (ed.) *Roman towns: the Wheeler inheritance. A review of fifty years research*. London: Council for British Archaeology Research Report 93. 56–65.

Brigham, T. 1992. 'Civic centre redevelopment. Forum and basilica reassessed'. In G. Milne (ed.) *From Roman basilica to medieval market. Archaeology in action in the city of London*. London: HMSO. 81–95.

Brigham, T. and Crowley, N. 1992. 'Reconstructing the basilica'. In G. Milne (ed.) *From Roman basilica to medieval market. Archaeology in action in the city of London*. London: HMSO. 96–105.

Brown, F. 1961. *Roman architecture*. London: Prentice-Hall International.

Brown, F. 1980. *Cosa: the making of a Roman town*. Ann Arbor: University of Michigan Press.

Burnham, B. C., Hunter, F. and Fitzpatrick, A. 2003. 'Roman Britain in 2002. 1. Sites explored', *Britannia*, 34: 293–359.

Burnham, B. C., Keppie, L. J. F. and Esmonde Cleary, A. S. 1994. 'Roman Britain in 1993. 1. Sites explored', *Britainnia*, 25: 246–291.

Caballos Rufino, A. 1998. 'Cities as a basis of supraprovincial promotion. The *equites* of Baetica'. In S. Keay (ed.) *The archaeology of early Roman Baetica*. Journal of Roman Archaeology Supplementary Series 29. 123–146.

Canto, A. M. 1981. 'Notas sobre los pontíficados coloniales y el origen del culto imperial en la Bética'. In AA.VV. *La religión Romana en Hispania*. Madrid: Subdirección General de Arqueología del Ministerio de Cultura. 141–53.

Canto, A. M. 1984. 'Les plaques votives avec *plantae pedum* d'Italica: un essai d'interprétation', *Zeitschrift für Papyrologie und Epigraphik*, 54: 183–194.

REFERENCES

Carroll, M. 2002. 'Measuring time and inventing histories in the early empire: Roman and Germanic perspectives'. In M. Carruthers, C. van Driel-Murray, A. Gardner, J. Lucas, L. Revell and E. Swift (eds.) *TRAC2001. Proceedings of the eleventh annual Theoretical Roman Archaeology Conference, Glasgow 2001.* Oxford: Oxbow Books. 104–112.

Cepas, A. 1989. *The north of Britannia and the north-west of Hispania: an epigraphic comparison.* British Archaeological Reports International Series 470.

Ciaraldi, M. and Richardson, J. 2000. 'Food, ritual and rubbish in the making of Pompeii'. In G. Fincham, G. Harrison, R. Holland and L. Revell (eds.) *TRAC99. Proceedings of the ninth annual Theoretical Roman Archaeology Conference, Durham 1999.* Oxford: Oxbow Books. 74–82.

Clarke, M. L. 1953. *Rhetoric at Rome: a historical survey.* London: Cohen and West.

Clarke, S. 2000. 'In search of a different Roman period: the finds assemblage at the Newstead military complex'. In G. Fincham, G. Harrison, R. Holland and L. Revell (eds.) *TRAC99. Proceedings of the ninth annual Theoretical Roman Archaeology Conference, Durham 1999.* Oxford: Oxbow Books. 22–29.

Coarelli, F. 1987. 'Munigua, Praeneste e Tibur. I modelli laziali di un municipio della Baetica', *Lucentum* 6, 91–100.

Cooley, A. E. (ed.) 2000. *The epigraphic landscape of Roman Italy.* Bulletin of the Institute of Classical Studies Supplement 73.

Cooley, A. E. (ed.) 2002. *Becoming Roman, writing Latin? Literacy and epigraphy in the Roman west.* Journal of Roman Archaeology Supplementary Series 48.

Corzo Sánchez, R. 1982. 'Organización del territorio y evolución urbana en Itálica'. In AA.VV. *Itálica (Santiponce, Sevilla): actas de las primeras jornadas sobre excavaciones arqueológicas en Itálica.* Excavaciones Arqueológicas en España 121. Madrid: Ministerio de Cultura. 299–319.

Corzo Sánchez, R. 1993. 'El teatro de Itálica'. In AA.VV. *Teatros Romanos de Hispania.* Cuadernos de Arquitectura Romana 2. 157–171.

Corzo Sánchez, R. 1994. 'El anfiteatro de Itálica'. In J. M. Álvarez Martínez and J. J. Enríquez Navascués (eds.) *Bimilenario del anfiteatro Romano de Mérida. El anfiteatro en la Hispania Romana.* Badajoz: Junta de Extremadura. 187–211.

Crawford, M. (ed.) 1996. *Roman statutes.* Bulletin of the Institute of Classical Studies Supplement 64.

Creighton, J. 2000. *Coins and power in late Iron Age Britain.* Cambridge: Cambridge University Press.

Creighton, J. 2006. *Britannia: the creation of a Roman province.* London: Routledge.

Cunliffe, B. 1969. *Roman Bath.* Reports of the Research Committee of the Society of Antiquaries of London 24.

Cunliffe, B. 1988. 'Summary and discussion'. In B. Cunliffe (ed.) *The temple of Sulis Minerva at Bath. Volume 2: the finds from the sacred spring.* Oxford University Committee for Archaeology Monograph 16. 359–362.

Cunliffe, B. 1989. 'The Roman tholos from the sanctuary of Sulis Minerva at Bath, England'. In R. I. Curtis (ed.) *Studia Pompeiana et Classica in honor of Wilhelmina F. Jashemski. Volume II. Classica.* New Rochelle: Orpheus Publishing. 59–86.

Cunliffe, B. and Davenport, P. 1985. *The temple of Sulis Minerva at Bath. Volume 1: the site.* Oxford University Committee for Archaeology Monograph 7.

Curchin, L. A. 1990 *The local magistrates of Roman Spain.* Toronto: University of Toronto Press.

Curchin, L. A. 1996. 'Cult and Celt: indigenous participation in emperor worship in central Spain'. In A. Small (ed.) *Subject and ruler: the cult of the ruling power in Classical Antiquity.* Journal of Roman Archaeology Supplementary Series 17. 143–152.

Davenport, J., Poole, C. and Jordan, D. 2007. *Archaeology at Bath. Excavations at the New Royal Baths (the Spa), and Bellott's Hospital 1998–1999.* Oxford: Oxford Archaeology.

DeLaine, J. 1988. 'Recent research on Roman baths', *Journal of Roman Archaeology*, 1: 11–32.

DeLaine, J. 1992. 'New models, old modes: continuity and change in the design of public baths'. In H. J. Schalles and P. Zanker (eds.) *Die römische Stadt im 2. Jahrhundert n. Chr.: der Funktionswandel des öffentlichen Raumes.* Cologne: Reinland-Verlag. 257–275.

Delgado y Delgado, J. A. 1998. *Elites y organización de la religión en las provincias Romanas de la Bética y las Mauritanias: sacerdotes y sacerdocios.* British Archaeological Reports International Series 724.

Derks, T. 1995. 'The ritual of the vow in Gallo-Roman religion'. In J. Metzler, M. Millett, N. Roymans and J. Slofstra (eds.) *Integration in the early Roman west. The role of culture and ideology.* Luxembourg: Dossiers d'Archéologie du Musée National d'Histoire et d'Art IV. 111–127.

Díaz-Andreu, M. and Lucy, S. 2005. 'Introduction'. In M. Díaz-Andreu, S. Lucy, S. Babić and D. Edwards (eds.) *The archaeology of identity: approaches to gender, age, status, ethnicity and religion.* London: Routledge. 1–12.

Dobres, M-A. and Robb, J. E. 2000. 'Agency in archaeology: paradigm or platitude?'. In M-A. Dobres and J. Robb (eds.) *Agency in archaeology.* London: Routledge. 3–17.

Dunbabin, K. M. D. 1990. '*Ipsae deae vestigia* . . . Footprints divine and human on Graeco-Roman monuments', *Journal of Roman Archaeology*, 3: 85–109.

Dupré I Raventós, X. 1995. 'New evidence for the study of the urbanism of Tarraco'. In B. Cunliffe and S. J. Keay (eds.) *Social complexity and the development of towns in Iberia: from the Copper Age to the second century AD.* Proceedings of the British Academy 86. 355–369.

Eck, W. 1997a. 'Itálica, las ciudades de la Bética y su aportación a la aristocracia imperial romana'. In A. Caballos and P. León (eds.) *Itálica MMCC: actas de las jornadas del 2.200 aniversario de la fundación de Itálica*. Seville: Consejería de Cultura. 206–19.

Eck, W. 1997b. 'Rome and the outside world: senatorial families and the world they lived in'. In B. Rawson and P. Weaver (eds.) *The Roman family in Italy: status, sentiment and space*. Oxford: Oxford University Press. 73–99.

Eckardt, H. and Crummy, N. 2006. '"Roman' or 'native' bodies in Britain: the evidence of Late Roman nail-cleaner strap-ends', *Oxford Journal of Archaeology*, 25.1: 83–103.

Edwards, C. 1997. 'Unspeakable professions: public performance and prostitution in ancient Rome'. In J. P. Hallett and M. B. Skinner (eds.) *Roman sexualities*. Princeton: Princeton University Press. 66–95.

Elsner, J. 1995. *Art and the Roman viewer: the transformation of art from the pagan world to Christianity*. Cambridge: Cambridge University Press.

Elsner, J. 1998. *Imperial Rome and Christian triumph: the art of the Roman empire AD100–450*. Oxford: Oxford University Press.

Elsner, J. 2007. *Roman eyes: visuality and subjectivity in art and text*. Princeton: Princeton University Press.

Etienne, R. 1958. *Le culte impérial dans la péninsule ibérique d'Auguste à Dioclétien*. Paris: de Boccard.

Favro, D. 1994. 'The street triumphant: the urban impact of Roman triumphal parades'. In Z. Çelik, D. Favro and R. Ingersoll (eds.) *Streets: critical perspectives on public space*. Berkeley: University of California Press. 151–164.

Favro, D. 1996. *The urban image of Augustan Rome*. Cambridge: Cambridge University Press.

Fear, A. T. 1996. *Rome and Baetica: urbanization in southern Spain c.50BC–AD150*. Oxford: Clarendon Press.

Feeney, D. 1998. *Literature and religion at Rome: cultures, contexts, and beliefs*. Cambridge: Cambridge University Press.

Fink, R. O., Hoey, A. S. and Snyder, W. F. 1940. 'The *Feriale Duranum*', *Yale Classical Studies*, 7: 1–222.

Finley, M. I. 1973. *The ancient economy*. London: Chatto and Windus.

Fishwick, D. 1969. 'The imperial *numen* in Roman Britain', *Journal of Roman Studies*, 59: 76–91.

Fishwick, D. 1972. '*Templum divo Claudio constitutum*', *Britannia*, 3: 164–181.

Fishwick, D. 1987–2005. *The imperial cult in the Latin West: studies in the ruler cult of the western provinces of the Roman empire*. Leiden: Brill.

Fishwick, D. 1995. 'The temple of *divus* Claudius at *Camulodunum*', *Britannia*, 26: 11–27.

Flower, H. I. 1996. *Ancestor masks and aristocratic power in Roman culture*. Oxford: Clarendon Press.

Fowler, C. 2004. *The archaeology of personhood: an anthropological approach*. London: Routledge.

Foxhall, L. 1998. 'Introduction'. In L. Foxhall and J. Salmon (eds.) *Thinking men: masculinity and its self representation in the Classical tradition*. London: Routledge. 1–5.

Freeman, P. W. M. 1993. '"Romanisation' and Roman material culture', *Journal of Roman Archaeology*, 6:438–445.

Freeman, P. W. M. 1997. 'Mommsen to Haverfield: the origins of studies of Romanization in the late 19th-c. Britain'. In D. J. Mattingly (ed.) *Dialogues in Roman imperialism. Power, discourse, and discrepant experience in the Roman empire*. Journal of Roman Archaeology Supplementary Series 23. 27–50.

Frere, S. S. 1971. 'The forum and baths at Caistor by Norwich', *Britannia*, 2: 1–26.

Frere, S. S. 1987. *Britannia: a history of Roman Britain*. 3rd edition. London: Routledge and Kegan Paul.

Frere, S. S. 1988. 'Roman Britain in 1987. 1. Sites explored', *Britainnia*, 19: 416–484.

Frere, S. S. 1989. 'Roman Britain in 1988. 1. Sites explored', *Britainnia*, 20: 258–326.

Frere, S. S. 1991. 'Roman Britain in 1990. 1. Sites explored', *Britainnia*, 22: 222–292.

Fulford, M. G. and Timby, J. 2000. *Late Iron Age and Roman Silchester: excavations on the site of the forum-basilica, 1977, 1980–6*. Britannia Monograph Series 15.

Gager, J. G. 1992. *Curse tablets and binding spells from the ancient world*. Oxford: Oxford University Press.

García y Bellido, A. 1960. *Colonia Aelia Augusta Italica*. Madrid: Instituto Español de Arqueología.

Gardner, J. 1993. *Being a Roman citizen*. London: Routledge.

Gardner, A. 2002. 'Social identity and the duality of structure in late Roman-period Britain', *Journal of Social Archaeology*, 2.3: 323–351.

Gardner, J. 1993. *Being a Roman citizen*. London: Routledge.

Garnsey, P. and Saller, R. 1987. *The Roman empire: economy, society and culture*. London: Duckworth.

Garriguet, J. A. 2004. 'Grupos estatuarios imperiales de la Bética: la evidencia escultórica y epigráfica'. In T. N. Basarrate and L. J. Gonçalves (eds.) *Actas de la IV reunión sobre escultura Romana en Hispania*: Madrid: Ministerio de Cultura. 67–101.

Gazda, E. K. 1991a. 'Introduction'. In E. K. Gazda (ed.) *Roman art in the private sphere: new perspectives on the architecture and decor of the domus, villa and insula*. Ann Arbor: University of Michigan Press. 1–24.

Gazda, E. K. (ed.) 1991b. *Roman art in the private sphere: new perspectives on the architecture and decor of the domus, villa and insula*. Ann Arbor: University of Michigan Press.

Gazda, E. K. (ed.) 2002. *The ancient art of emulation: studies in artistic originality and tradition from the present to Classical Antiquity.* Memoirs of the American Academy in Rome. Supplementary Volume 1.

Geary, P. J. 1994. *Phantoms of remembrance: memory and oblivion at the end of the first millennium.* Princeton: Princeton University Press.

Geertz, C. 1977. 'Centres, kings, and charisma: reflections on the symbolics of power'. In J. Ben-David and T. N. Clark (eds.) *Culture and its creators: essays in honour of Edward Shils.* Chicago: University of Chicago Press. 150–71.

Giddens, A. 1984. *The constitution of society. Outline of the theory of structuration.* Cambridge: Polity.

Gil, J. and Luzón, J. M. 1975. '*Tabella defixionis* de Itálica', *Habis*, 6: 117–133.

Gilchrist, R. 1994. *Gender and material culture: the archaeology of religious women.* London: Routledge.

Gimeno Pascual, H. 2003. 'La sociedad de Munigua a través de sus inscripciones'. In S. Armani, B. Hurlet-Martineau and A. U. Stylow (eds.) *Epigrafía y sociedad en Hispania durante el alto imperio: estructuras y relaciones sociales.* Alcala: Universidad de Alcalá. 177–192.

Goffmann, E. 1956. *The presentation of the self in everyday life.* University of Edinburgh Social Sciences Research Centre Monograph 2.

Gombrich, E. H. 1995. *The story of art.* 16th edition. London: Phaidon Press.

González, J. 1986 'The lex Irnitana: a new copy of the Flavian municipal law', *Journal of Roman Studies*, 76: 147–243.

Gowing, A. M. 2005. *Empire and memory: the representation of the Roman republic in imperial culture.* Cambridge: Cambridge University Press.

Gowland, R. 2001. 'Playing dead: implications of mortuary evidence for the social construction of childhood in Roman Britain'. In G. Davies. A. Gardner and K. Lockyer (eds.) *TRAC2000. Proceedings of the tenth annual Theoretical Roman Archaeology Conference, London 2000.* Oxford: Oxbow Books. 152–168.

Grant, M. 1995. *Art in the Roman empire.* London: Routledge.

Graves, C. P. 1989. 'Social space in the English medieval parish church', *Economy and Society*, 18: 297–322.

Graves, C. P. 2000. *The form and fabric of belief: an archaeology of the lay experience of religion in medieval Norfolk and Devon.* British Archaeological Reports British Series 311.

Green, M. J. 1976. *A corpus of religious material from the civilian areas of Roman Britain.* British Archaeological Reports British Series 24.

Grimes, W. F. 1968. *The excavation of Roman and mediaeval London.* London: Routledge.

Gros, P. 1990. 'Théâtre et culte impérial en Gaule Narbonnaise et dans la Péninsule ibérique'. In W. Trillmich and P. Zanker (eds.) *Stadtbild und Ideologie: die Monumentalisierung hispanischer Städte zwischen Republik und Kaiserzeit.* Munich: Verlag der Bayerischen Akademie der Wissenschaften. 381–390.

Gros, P. 1994. 'L'amphithéâtre dans la ville. Politique "culturelle" et urbanisme aux deux premiers siècles de l'Empire'. In J. M. Álvarez Martínez and J. J. Enríquez Navascués (eds.) *Bimilenario del anfiteatro Romano de Mérida. El anfiteatro en la Hispania Romana.* Badajoz: Junta de Extremadura. 13–29.

Grünhagen, W. 1959. 'Excavaciones del Santuario de Terrazas de Munigua', *Congreso Arqueológico Nacional*, 5: 275–82.

Guest, P. 2002. 'Manning the defences: the development of Romano-British urban boundaries'. In M. Aldhouse-Green and P. Webster (eds.) *Artefacts and archaeology: aspects of the Celtic and Roman world.* Cardiff: University of Wales Press. 76–89.

Guiral Pelegrín, C. and Martín-Bueno, M. 1996. *Bilbilis 1. Decoración pictórico y estucos ornamentales.* Zaragoza: Institución Fernando el Católico.

Hammond, M. 1957. 'Composition of the senate, AD68–235', *Journal of Roman Studies*, 47: 74–81.

Hannestad, N. 1986. *Roman art and imperial policy.* Aarhus: Aarhus University Press.

Hanson, W. S. 1997. 'Forces of change and methods of control'. In D. J. Mattingly (ed.) *Dialogues in Roman imperialism. Power, discourse, and discrepant experience in the Roman empire.* Journal of Roman Archaeology Supplementary Series 23. 67–80.

Hanson, W. S. and Conolly, R. 2002. 'Language and literacy in Roman Britain: some archaeological considerations'. In A. E. Cooley (ed.) *Becoming Roman, writing Latin? Literacy and epigraphy in the Roman west.* Journal of Roman Archaeology Supplementary Series 48. 151–164.

Harris, W. V. 1979. *War and imperialism in republican Rome, 327–70BC.* Oxford: Clarendon Press.

Haskell, F. and Penny, N. 1981. *Taste and the antique: the lure of classical sculpture.* New Haven: Yale University Press.

Hassall, M. W. C. 1973. 'Roman soldiers in Roman London'. In D. E. Strong (ed.) *Archaeological theory and practice.* London: Seminar Press. 231–7.

Hassall, M. W. C. 2003. 'The tabularium in provincial cities'. In P. Wilson (ed.) *The archaeology of Roman towns: studies in honour of John S. Wacher.* Oxford: Oxbow Books. 105–110.

Hauschild, T. 1991a. 'Los templos Romanos de Munigua (Sevilla)'. In AA.VV. *Templos Romanos de Hispania.* Cuadernos de Arquitectura Romana 1. 133–143.

Hauschild, T. 1991b. 'Munigua. Excavaciones en el muro de contención del foro, 1985', *Anuario Arqueológico de Andalucía 1989. Vol II. Actividades Sistemáticas*: 171–184.

Haynes, I. 1999. 'Military service and cultural identity in the auxilia'. In A. Goldsworthy and I. Haynes (eds.) *The Roman army as a community.* Journal of Roman Archaeology Supplementary Series 34. 165–174.

Haynes, I. P. and Hanson, W. S. 2004. 'An introduction to Roman Dacia'. In W. S. Hanson and I. P. Haynes (eds.) *Roman Dacia: the making of a provincial society*. Journal of Roman Archaeology Supplementary Series 56. 11–31.

Henig, M. 1995. *Religion in Roman Britain*. 2nd edition. London: Batsford.

Henig, M. 1999. 'A new star shining over Bath', *Oxford Journal of Archaeology*, 18.4: 419–425.

Henig, M., Brown, D., Baatz, D., Sunter, N. and Allason-Jones, L. 1988. 'Objects from the sacred spring'. In B. Cunliffe (ed.) *The temple of Sulis Minerva at Bath. Volume 2: the finds from the sacred spring*. Oxford University Committee for Archaeology Monograph 16. 5–53.

Hennecke, E. and Schneemelcher, W. 1965. *New Testament Apocrypha. Volume 2: Apostolic and early Church writings*. London: Lutterworth.

Hill, J. D. 1995. *Ritual and rubbish in the Iron Age of Wessex: a study on the formation of a specific archaeological record*. British Archaeological Reports British Series 242.

Hill, J. D. 2001. 'Romanisation, gender and class: recent approaches to identity in Britain and their possible consequences'. In S. James and M. Millett (eds.) *Britons and Romans: advancing an archaeological agenda*. Council for British Archaeology Research Report 125. 12–18.

Hingley, R. 1991. 'Past, present and future: the study of the Roman period in Britain', *Scottish Archaeological Revue*, 8: 90–101.

Hingley, R. 1997. 'Resistance and domination: social change in Roman Britain'. In D. J. Mattingly (ed.) *Dialogues in Roman imperialism. Power, discourse, and discrepant experience in the Roman empire*. Journal of Roman Archaeology Supplementary Series 23. 81–100.

Hingley, R. 2000. *Roman officers and English gentlemen: the imperial origins of Roman archaeology*. London: Routledge.

Hingley, R. (ed.) 2001. *Images of Rome: perceptions of ancient Rome in Europe and the United States in the modern age*. Journal of Roman Archaeology Supplementary Series 44.

Hingley, R. 2005. *Globalizing Roman culture: unity, diversity and empire*. London: Routledge.

Hobsbawm, E. 1993. 'Introduction: inventing traditions'. In E. Hobsbawm and T. Ranger (eds.) *The invention of tradition*. Cambridge: Cambridge University Press. 1–14.

Hobsbawm, E. with A. Polito. 1999. *On the edge of the new century*. Translated by Allan Cameron. New York: The New York Press.

Hope, V. 1998. 'Negotiating identity and status: the gladiators of Roman Nîmes'. In R. Laurence and J. Berry (eds.) *Cultural identity in the Roman empire*. London: Routledge. 179–195.

Hope, V. 2001. *Constructing identity: the Roman funerary monuments of Aquileia, Mainz and Nîmes*. British Archaeological Reports International Series 960.

REFERENCES

Hopkins, K. 1978. *Conquerors and slaves.* Cambridge: Cambridge University Press.

Hopkins, K. 1983. *Death and renewal.* Cambridge: Cambridge University Press.

Howe, E. and Lakin, D. 2004. *Roman and medieval Cripplegate, City of London: archaeological excavations 1992–8.* MoLAS Monograph 21. London: Museum of London Archaeology Service.

Hornum, M. B. 1993. *Nemesis, the Roman state and the games.* Leiden: Brill.

Isserlin, R. M. J. 1998. 'A spirit of improvement? Marble and the culture of Roman Britain'. In R. Laurence and J. Berrry (eds.) *Cultural identity in the Roman empire.* London: Routledge. 125–155.

James, S. 1999. 'The community of soldiers: a major identity and centre of power in the Roman empire'. In P. Baker, C. Forcey, S. Jundi and R. Witcher (eds.) *TRAC98. Proceedings of the eighth annual Theoretical Roman Archaeology Conference, Leicester 1998.* Oxford: Oxbow Books. 14–25.

Johnson, M. 1989. 'Conceptions of agency in archaeological interpretation', *Journal of Anthropological Archaeology,* 8.2: 189–211.

Johnson, M. 1997. 'Vernacular architecture: the loss of innocence', *Vernacular Architecture,* 28: 13–19.

Johnson, M. 2002. *Behind the castle gate: from medieval to renaissance.* London: Routledge.

Jones, S. 1997. *The archaeology of ethnicity: constructing identities in the past and present.* London: Routledge.

Keay, S. J. 1995. 'Innovation and adaptation: the contribution of Rome to urbanism in Iberia'. In B. Cunliffe and S. J. Keay (eds.) *Social complexity and the development of towns in Iberia: from the Copper Age to the second century AD.* Proceedings of the British Academy 86. 291–337.

Keay, S. J. 1997a. 'Early Roman Italica and the Romanization of western Baetica'. In A. Caballos and P. León (eds.) *Itálica MMCC: actas de las jornadas del 2.200 aniversario de la fundación de Itálica.* Seville: Consejería de Cultura. 21–47.

Keay, S. J. 1997b. 'Urban transformation and cultural change'. In M. Diaz-Andreu and S. J. Keay (eds.) *The archaeology of Iberia: the dynamics of change.* London: Routledge. 192–210.

Keay, S. J. 1998. 'The development of towns in early Roman Baetica'. In S. J. Keay (ed.) *The archaeology of early Roman Baetica.* Journal of Roman Archaeology Supplementary Series 29. 55–86.

Keay, S. and Terrenato, N. 2001. *Italy and the west: comparative issues in Romanization.* Oxford: Oxbow Books..

Keppie, L. 1991. *Understanding Roman inscriptions.* London: Batsford.

Krautheimer, R. 1986. *Early Christian and Byzantine architecture.* 4th edition. New Haven: Yale University Press.

Laurence, R. 1999a. 'Theoretical Roman archaeology', *Britannia,* 30: 387–390.

Laurence, R. 1999b. *The roads of Roman Italy: mobility and cultural change.* London: Routledge.

Laurence, R. 2001. 'Roman narratives. The writing of archaeological discourse – a view from Britain?', *Archaeological Dialogues*, 8.2: 90–122.

Laurence, R. 2007. *Roman Pompeii: space and society*. 2nd edition. London: Routledge.

Lefebvre, S. 2004. 'Espace et pouvoir local dans les provinces occidentales: quelques remarques'. In C. Auliard and L. Bodiou (eds.) *Au jardin des Hespérides: histoire, société et épigraphie des mondes anciens. Mélanges offerts à Alain Tranoy*. Rennes: Presses Universitaires de Rennes. 379–406.

Lefkowitz, M. R. and Fant, M. B. 1992. *Women's life in Greece and Rome: a sourcebook in translation*. 2nd edition. London: Duckworth.

León, P. 1988. *Traianeum de Itálica*. Seville: Monte de Piedad y Caja de Ahorros de Sevilla.

León, P. 1995. *Escultura de Itálica*. Seville: Consejería de Cultura, Junta de Andalucía.

Lewis, M. J. T. 1966. *Temples in Roman Britain*. Cambridge: Cambridge University Press.

Linderski, J. 1986. 'The augural law'. In H. Temporini and W. Haase (eds.) *Aufstieg und Niedergang der römischen Welt, II.16.3*. Berlin: Walter de Gruyter. 2146–2312.

Lintott,1993. *Imperium Romanum: politics and administration*. London: Routledge.

Lomas, K. 1997. 'The idea of a city: élite ideology and the evolution of urban form in Italy, 200 BC-AD 100'. In H. M. Parkins (ed.) *Roman urbanism: beyond the consumer city*. London: Routledge. 21–41.

MacDonald, W. L. 1982. *The architecture of the Roman empire. Volume I: an introductory study*. Revised edition. New Haven: Yale University Press.

MacDonald, W. L. 1986. *The architecture of the Roman empire. Volume II: an urban appraisal*. New Haven: Yale University Press.

Mackie, N. 1983. *Local administration in Roman Spain AD14–212*. British Archaeological Reports International Series 172.

Mackie, N. 1990. 'Urban munificence and the growth of urban consciousness in Roman Spain'. In T. F. C. Blagg and M. Millett (eds.) *The early Roman empire in the west*. Oxford: Oxbow Books. 179–192.

MacMullen, R. 1981. *Paganism in the Roman empire*. New Haven: Yale University Press.

MacMullen, R. 1982. 'The epigraphic habit in the Roman empire', *American Journal of Philology*, 103: 233–46.

Mann, J. C. 1965. 'City foundations in Gaul and Britain'. In M. G. Jarrett and B. Dobson (eds.) *Britain and Rome: essays presented to Eric Birley*. Kendal: Wilson. 109–13.

Mann, J. C. 1983. *Legionary recruitment and veteran settlement during the Principate*. London: Institute of Archaeology Occasional Publications 7.

Mann, J. C. 1985. 'Epigraphic consciousness', *Journal of Roman Studies*, 75: 204–6.

REFERENCES

Marsden, P. 1975. 'The excavation of a Roman palace site in London, 1961–1972', *Transactions of the London and Middlesex Archaeological Society*, 28: 1–102.
Marsden, P. 1976. 'Two Roman public baths in London', *Transactions of the London and Middlesex Archaeological Society*, 27: 1–70.
Marsden, P. 1987. *The Roman forum site in London: discoveries before 1985*. London: HMSO.
Martín-Bueno, M. 1975. *Bilbilis: estudios histórico-arqueológico*. Zaragoza: Universidad de Zaragoza.
Martín-Bueno, M. 1981. 'La inscripción a Tiberio y el centro religioso de Bilbilis (Calatayud, Zaragoza)', *Madrider Mitteilungen*, 22: 244–54.
Martín-Bueno, M. 1982a. 'Bilbilis, municipio de la Celtiberia', *Revista de Arqueología*, 20: 6–15.
Martín-Bueno M. 1982b. 'Teatro Romano de Bilbilis (Calatayud, Zaragoza)', in AA.VV. *El teatro en la Hispania Romana*. Badajoz: Institución Cultural "Pedro de Valencia". 79–93.
Martín-Bueno, M. 1987. 'El foro de Bilbilis (Calatayud, Zaragoza)'. In AA.VV. *Los foros Romanos de las provincias occidentales*. Madrid: Ministerio de Cultura, Dirección General de Bellas Artes y Archivos. 99–111.
Martín-Bueno, M., Cancela Ramírez de Arellano M. L. and Jiménez Salvador, J. L. 1985. 'Municipium Augusta Bilbilis, Calatayud, Zaragoza' In AA.VV. *Arqueología de las ciudades modernas superpuestas a las antiguas*. Madrid: Ministerio de Cultura, Dirección General de Bellas Artes y Archivos. 253–270.
Marvin, M. 1983. 'Freestanding sculptures from the Baths of Caracalla', *American Journal of Archaeology*, 87.3: 347–84.
Mattingly, D. J. 2002. 'Vulgar and weak 'Romanization', or time for a paradigm shift?', *Journal of Roman Archaeology*, 15: 536–540.
Mattingly, D. J. 2004. 'Being Roman: expressing identity in a provincial setting', *Journal of Roman Archaeology*, 17: 5–25.
Mattingly, D. J. 2006. *An imperial possession: Britain in the Roman empire 54BC–AD409*. London: Allen Lane.
Meyer, E. A. 1990. 'Explaining the epigraphic habit in the Roman empire: the evidence of epitaphs', *Journal of Roman Studies*, 80: 74–96.
Mierse, W. E. 1999. *Temples and towns in Roman Iberia: the social and architectural dynamics of sanctuary designs from the third century BC to the third century AD*. Berkeley: University of California Press.
Millar, F. 1977. *The emperor in the Roman world*. London: Duckworth.
Miller, D. and Tilley, C. 1984. 'Ideology, power and prehistory: an introduction'. In D. Miller and C. Tilley (eds.) *Ideology, power and prehistory*. Cambridge: Cambridge University Press. 1–15.
Millett, M. 1990a. 'Romanization: historical issues and archaeological interpretation'. In T. Blagg and M. Millett (eds.) *The early Roman empire in the west*. Oxford: Oxbow Books. 35–41.

REFERENCES

Millett, M. 1990b. *The Romanization of Britain: an essay in archaeological interpretation*. Cambridge: Cambridge University Press.

Millett, M. 1995. 'Re-thinking religion in Romanization'. In J. Metzler, M. Millett, N. Roymans and J. Slofstra (eds.) *Integration in the early Roman west. The role of culture and ideology*. Luxembourg: Dossiers d'Archéologie du Musée National d'Histoire et d'Art IV. 93–100.

Millett, M. 1996. 'Characterizing Roman London'. In J. Bird, M. Hassall and H. Sheldon (eds.) *Interpreting Roman London. Papers in memory of Hugh Chapman*. Oxford: Oxbow Monograph 58. 33–37.

Millett, M. 1998. 'Introduction: London as capital?'. In B. Watson (ed.) *Roman London: recent archaeological work*. Journal of Roman Archaeology Supplementary Series 24. 7–12.

Millett. M. 1999. '*Coloniae* and Romano-British studies'. In H. Hurst (ed.) *The coloniae of Roman Britain: new studies and a review*. Journal of Roman Archaeology Supplementary Series 36. 191–196.

Milne, G. 1996. 'A palace disproved: reassessing the provincial governor's presence in 1st century London'. In J. Bird, M. Hassall and H. Sheldon (eds.) *Interpreting Roman London. Papers in memory of Hugh Chapman*. Oxford: Oxbow Monograph 58. 49–55.

Morley, N. 1996. *Metropolis and hinterland: the city of Rome and the Italian economy, 200BC–AD200*. Cambridge: Cambridge University Press.

Morris, I. 1998. 'Remaining invisible: the archaeology of the excluded in Classical Athens'. In S. Joshel and S. Murnaghan (eds.) *Women and slaves in Greco-Roman culture: different equations*. London: Routledge. 193–220.

Nash-Williams, V. E. 1930. 'Further excavations at Caerwent, Monmouthshire, 1923–5', *Archaeologia*, 80: 229–288.

Nicolet, C. 1991. *Space, geography and politics in the early Roman empire*. Ann Arbor: University of Michigan Press.

Nicols, J. 2001. '*Hospitium* and political friendship in the late Republic'. In M Peachin (ed.) *Aspects of friendship in the Graeco-Roman world*. Journal of Roman Archaeology Supplementary Series 43. 99–108.

Nielsen, I. 1990. *Thermae et balnea: the architectural and cultural history of Roman public baths*. Aarhus: Aarhus University Press.

North, J. 1981. 'The development of Roman imperialism', *Journal of Roman Studies*, 71: 1–9.

North, J. 1990. 'Diviners and divination at Rome'. In M. Beard and J. North (eds.) *Pagan priests*. London: Duckworth. 49–71.

Ortiz de Urbina Álava, E. 2000. *Las comunidades hispanas y el derecho latino: observaciones sobre los procesos de integración local en la práctica político-administrativa al modo romano*. Vitoria Gasteiz: Universidad de País Vasco.

Orton, C. 1989. 'A tale of two sites', *London Archaeologist*, 6.3:59–65.

Osborne, R. 1996. *Greece in the making, 1200–479BC*. London: Routledge.

REFERENCES

Palol, P. de 1991a. 'Cabeza feminina hallada en el foro de Clunia' in Palol, P. de et al. (eds.) *Clunia o. Studia varia Cluniensia.* Burgos: Servicio de Investigaciones Arqueológicas. 101–7.

Palol, P. de. 1991b. 'Clunia Sulpicia, ciudad romana. Su historia y su presente'. In P. de Palol et al. (eds.) *Clunia o. Studia varia Cluniensia.* Burgos: Servicio de Investigaciones Arqueológicas. 9–74.

Palol, P. de. 1991c. 'Clunia, cabeza de un convento jurídico de la Hispania Citerior o Tarraconense'. In P. de Palol et al. (eds.) *Clunia o. Studia varia Cluniensia.* Burgos: Servicio de Investigaciones Arqueológicas. 355–374.

Palol, P. de. 1991d. 'El foro romano de Clunia'. In P. de Palol et al. (eds.) *Clunia o. Studia varia Cluniensia.* Burgos: Servicio de Investigaciones Arqueológicas. 383–397.

Palol, P. de. 1991e. 'El teatro romano de Clunia'. In P. de Palol et al. (eds.) *Clunia o. Studia varia Cluniensia.* Burgos: Servicio de Investigaciones Arqueológicas. 325–339.

Palol, P. de. 1991f. 'Excavaciones en el foro romano de Clunia'. In P. de Palol et al. (eds.) *Clunia o. Studia varia Cluniensia.* Burgos: Servicio de Investigaciones Arqueológicas. 165–173.

Palol, P. de. 1991g. 'Perduración de las ciudades augústeas. La zona norte y la meseta'. In P. de Palol et al. (eds.) *Clunia o. Studia varia Cluniensia.* Burgos: Servicio de Investigaciones Arqueológicas. 277–294.

Palol, P. de and Arias Bonet, J. A. 1991. 'Tres fragmentos de bronces con textos jurídicos, hallados en Clunia'. In P. de Palol et al. (eds.) *Clunia o. Studia varia Cluniensia.* Burgos: Servicio de Investigaciones Arqueológicas. 185–191.

Palol. P. de and Guitart, J. 2000. *Los grandes conjuntos públicos: el foro colonial de Clunia.* Clunia VIII.1. Burgos: Excma. Diputación Provincial de Burgos.

Parker Pearson, M. and Richards, C. (eds.) 1994a. *Architecture and order: approaches to social space.* London: Routledge.

Parker Pearson, M. and Richards, C. 1994b. 'Ordering the world: perceptions of architecture, space and time'. In M. Parker Pearson and C. Richards (eds.) *Architecture and order: approaches to social space.* London: Routledge. 1–37.

Perring, D. 1991. *Roman London.* London: Seaby.

Potter, T. W. 1985. 'A republican healing-sanctuary at Ponte di Nona near Rome and the classical tradition of votive medicine', *Journal of the British Archaeological Association*, 138: 23–47.

Potter, T. W. and Johns, C. 1992. *Roman Britain.* London: British Museum Publications.

Prag, J. R. W. 2002. 'Epigraphy by numbers: Latin and the epigraphic culture in Sicily'. In A. E. Cooley (ed.) *Becoming Roman, writing Latin? Literacy and epigraphy in the Roman west.* Journal of Roman Archaeology Supplementary Series 48. 15–31.

Price, S. R. F. 1980. 'Between man and god: sacrifice in the Roman imperial cult', *Journal of Roman Studies*, 70: 28–43.

Price, S. R. F. 1984. *Rituals and power: the Roman imperial cult in Asia Minor.* Cambridge: Cambridge University Press.

Purcell, N. 1995. 'The Roman *villa* and the landscape of production'. In T. J. Cornell and K. Lomas (eds.) *Urban society in Roman Italy.* London: UCL Press. 151–179.

Rankov, B. 1999. 'The governor's men: the *officium consularis* in provincial administration'. In A. K. Goldsworthy and I. Haynes (eds.) *The Roman army as a community.* Journal of Roman Archaeology Supplementary Series 34. 15–34.

Rawson, E. 1987. '*Discrimina ordinum*: the *lex Julia theatralis*', *Papers of the British School at Rome*, 55: 83–114.

Raybould, M. E. 1999. *A study of inscribed material from Roman Britain: an inquiry into some aspects of literacy in Romano-British society.* British Archaeological Reports British Series 281.

Reece, R. 1999. *The later Roman empire: an archaeology AD150–600.* Stroud: Tempus.

Revell, L. 1999. 'Constructing *Romanitas*: Roman public architecture and the archaeology of practice'. In P. Baker, C. Forcey, S. Jundi, R. Witcher (eds.) *TRAC98. Proceedings of the eighth annual Theoretical Roman Archaeology Conference, Leicester 1998.* Oxford: Oxbow Books. 52–58.

Revell, L. 2000. 'The creation of multiple identities in Roman Italica'. In G. Fincham, G. Harrison, R. Holland and L. Revell (eds.) *TRAC99. Proceedings of the ninth annual Theoretical Roman Archaeology Conference.* Oxford: Oxbow Books. 1–7.

Revell, L. 2002. 'Story-telling in Roman archaeology', *Archaeological Dialogues*, 9.1: 44–7.

Revell, L. 2005. 'The Roman life course: a view from the inscriptions', *European Journal of Archaeology*, 8.1: 43–63.

Revell, L. 2007. 'Architecture, power and politics: the forum-basilica in Roman Britain'. In J. Sofaer (ed.) *Material identities.* Oxford: Blackwell. 127–151.

Revell, L. in press 'Inscriptions and the ideology of urbanism'. In R. W. B. Salway (ed.) *Epigraphy and Public Space from the Severans to the Theodosian Era. Actes de la XIIe Rencontre sur l'épigraphie du monde romain, Rome, 16–18 septembre 2004.* Bulletin of the Institute of Classical Studies Supplement.

Rich, J. 1993. 'Fear, greed and glory: the causes of Roman war-making in the middle republic'. In J. Rich and G. Shipley (eds.) *War and society in the Roman world.* London: Routledge. 38–68.

Richardson, J. S. 1995. '*neque elegantem, ut arbitror, neque urbanum*: reflections on Iberian urbanism'. In B. Cunliffe and S. J. Keay (eds.) *Social complexity and the development of towns in Iberia: from the Copper Age to the second century AD.* Proceedings of the British Academy 86. 339–354.

Richardson, J. S. 1996. *The Romans in Spain.* Oxford: Blackwell.

REFERENCES

Richlin, A. 1997. 'Gender and rhetoric: producing manhood in the schools'. In W. J. Dominik (ed.) *Roman eloquence: rhetoric in society and literature*. London: Routledge. 90–110.

Rodá, I. 1997. 'Los mármoles de Itálica. Su comercio y origen'. In A. Caballos and P. León (eds.) *Itálica MMCC: actas de las jornadas del 2.200 aniversario de la fundación de Itálica*. Seville: Consejería de Cultura. 155–180.

Rodríguez Gutiérrez, O. 2004. *El teatro romano de Itálica: estudio arqueoarquitectónico*. Monografías de Arquitectura Romana 6. Madrid: Servicio de Publicaciones de la Universidad Autónoma de Madrid, Fundación Pastor de Estudios Clásicos, Diputación de Sevilla.

Rodríguez Hidalgo, J. M. 1991. 'Dos ejemplos domésticos en Traianopolis (Itálica): las Casas de los Párajos y de la Exedra'. In AA.VV. *La casa urbana Hispanorromana: ponencias y comunicaciones*. Zaragoza: Institución Fernando el Católico. 291–302.

Rodríguez Hidalgo, J. M. 1997. 'La nueva imagen de la Itálica de Adriano'. In A. Caballos and P. León (eds.) *Itálica MMCC: actas de las jornadas del 2.200 aniversario de la fundación de Itálica*. Seville: Consejería de Cultura. 87–113.

Rodríguez Hidalgo, J. M. and Keay, S. J. 1995. 'Recent work at Italica'. In B. Cunliffe and S. J. Keay (eds.) *Social complexity and the development of towns in Iberia: from the Copper Age to the second century AD*. Proceedings of the British Academy 86. 395–420.

Rodríguez Hidalgo, J. M., Keay, S. J., Jordan, D. and Creighton, J. 1999. 'La Itálica de Adriano. Resultados de las prospecciones arqueológicas de 1991 y 1993', *Archivo Español de Arqueología*, 72: 73–97.

Roldán Gómez, L. 1993. *Técnicas constructivas Romanas en Itálica (Santiponce, Sevilla)*. Monografías de Arquitectura Romana 2. Madrid: Universidad Autónoma de Madrid.

Roldán Gómez, L. 1994. 'El anfiteatro de Itálica. Técnicas y materiales de construcción'. In J. M. Álvarez Martínez and J. J. Enríquez Navascués (eds.) *Bimilenario del anfiteatro Romano de Mérida. El anfiteatro en la Hispania Romana*. Badajoz: Junta de Extremadura. 213–238.

Rose, C. B. 1997. *Dynastic commemoration and imperial portraiture in the Julio-Claudian period*. Cambridge: Cambridge University Press.

Ross Taylor, L. 1961. 'Freedmen and freeborn in the epitaphs of Imperial Rome', *American Journal of Philology*, 82.2: 113–32.

Ryberg, I. S. 1955. *Rites of state religion in Roman art*. Memoirs of the American Academy in Rome 22.

Rykwert, J. 1988. *The idea of a town: the anthropology of urban form in Rome, Italy and the ancient world*. Cambridge, Mass.: MIT Press.

Said, E. W. 1995. *Orientalism*. Harmondsworth: Penguin.

Saller, R. P. 1982. *Personal patronage under the early empire*. Cambridge: Cambridge University Press.

Saller, R. P. 1989. 'Patronage and friendship in early Imperial Rome: drawing the distinction'. In A. Wallace-Hadrill (ed.) *Patronage in ancient society*. London: Routledge. 49–62.

Salmon, E. T. 1969. *Roman colonization under the Republic*. London: Thames and Hudson.

Salway, R. W. B. (ed.) *Epigraphy and Public Space from the Severans to the Theodosian Era. Actes de la XIIe Rencontre sur l'épigraphie du monde romain, Rome, 16–18 septembre 2004*. Bulletin of the Institute of Classical Studies Supplement.

Schattner, T. G. 2003. *Munigua: cuarenta años de investigaciones*. Seville: Junta de Andalucía, Consejería de Cultura.

Scheid, J. 1992. 'The religious roles of women'. In P. Schmitt Pantel (ed.) *A history of women in the west. Volume 1: from ancient goddesses to Christian saints*. Cambridge, Mass.: Harvard University Press. 377–408.

Scheid, J. 1995. 'Les temples de l'Altbachtal à Trèves: un "sanctuaire national"?', *Cahiers du Centre Glos*, 6: 227–43.

Scheid, J. 2003. *An introduction to Roman religion*. Translated by Janet Lloyd. Bloomington and Indianapolis: Indiana University Press.

Scott, E. 1993. 'Introduction: TRAC (Theoretical Roman Archaeology Conference) 1991'. In E. Scott (ed.) *Theoretical Roman archaeology: first conference proceedings*. Aldershot: Avebury. 1–4.

Scott, E. 1995. 'Women and gender relations in the roman empire'. In P. Rush (ed.) *Theoretical Roman Archaeology: second conference proceedings*. Aldershot: Avebury. 174–89.

Scott, E. 1996. 'Locating women: space and gender', *Cambridge Archaeological Journal*, 6.1: 124–126.

Scott, S. 1995. 'Symbols of power and nature: the Orpheus mosaics of fourth century Britain and their architectural contexts'. In P. Rush (ed.) *Theoretical Roman Archaeology: second conference proceedings*. Aldershot: Avebury. 105–123.

Scott, S. 2000. *Art and society in fourth century Britain: villa mosaics in context*. Oxford: Oxford University School of Archaeology.

Sear, F. 1982. *Roman architecture*. London: Batsford.

Sellwood, L. 1988. 'The Celtic coins'. In B. Cunliffe (ed.) *The temple of Sulis Minerva at Bath. Volume 2: the finds from the sacred spring*. Oxford University Committee for Archaeology Monograph 16. 279–280.

Shanks, M. and Tilley, C. 1982. 'Ideology, symbolic power and ritual communication: a reinterpretation of Neolithic mortuary practices'. In I. Hodder (ed.) *Symbolic and structural archaeology*. Cambridge: Cambridge University Press. 129–154.

Shanks, M. and Tilley, C. 1992. *Re-constructing archaeology: theory and practice*. 2nd edition. London: Routledge.

Simpson, C. J. 1993. 'Once again Claudius and the temple at Colchester', *Britannia*, 24: 1–6.

Smith, A. 2001. *The differential use of constructed sacred space in southern Britain, from the late Iron Age to the fourth century AD*. British Archaeological Reports British Series 318.

Stamper, J. W. 2004. *The architecture of the Roman temples: the Republic to the Middle Empire*. Cambridge: Cambridge University Press.

Stewart, P. 1995. 'Inventing Britain: the Roman creation and adaptation of an image', *Britannia*, 26: 1–10.

Stewart, P. 2003. *Statues in Roman society: representation and response*. Oxford: Oxford University Press.

Strong, D. E. 1953. 'Late Hadrianic architectural ornament in Rome', *Papers of the British School at Rome*, 21: 118–151.

Swan, V. G. 1997. 'Vexillations and the garrisons of Britannia in the second and early third centuries: a ceramic viewpoint'. In W. Groenman-van Waateringe, B. L. van Beek, W. J. H. Willems and S. L. Wynia (eds.) *Roman Frontier Studies 1995. Proceedings of the XVIth International Congress of Roman Frontier Studies*. Oxford: Oxbow Books. 289–294.

Syme, R. 1964. 'Hadrian and Italica', *Journal of Roman Studies*, 54: 142–9.

Szemler, G. J. 1986. 'Priesthoods and priestly careers in ancient Rome'. In H. Temporini and W. Haase (eds.) *Aufstieg und Niedergang der romischen Welt, II.16.3*. Berlin: Walter de Gruyter. 2314–2331.

Taylor, L. R. 1931. *The divinity of the Roman emperor*. American Philological Association Philological Monographs 1.

TED'A. 1989. 'El foro provincial de Tarraco, un complejo arquitectónico de época Flavia', *Archivo Español de Arqueología*, 62: 141–191.

Thomas, J. 1996. *Time, culture, and identity: an interpretive archaeology*. London: Routledge.

Tilley, C. 1994. *A phenomenology of landscape: paths, places and monuments*. Oxford: Berg.

Tomlin, R. S. O. 1988. 'The curse tablets'. In B. Cunliffe (ed.) *The temple of Sulis Minerva at Bath. Volume 2: the finds from the sacred spring*. Oxford University Committee for Archaeology Monograph 16. 59–277.

Tomlin, R. S. O. 2002. 'Writing to the gods in Britain'. In A. E. Cooley (ed.) *Becoming Roman, writing Latin? Literacy and epigraphy in the Roman west*. Journal of Roman Archaeology Supplementary Series 48. 165–179.

Tomlin, R. S. O. 2003. ''The girl in question': a new text from Roman London', *Britannia*, 34: 41–51.

Toynbee, J. M. C. 1965. *The art of the Romans*. London: Thames and Hudson.

Trillmich, W. and Zanker, P. (eds.) 1990. *Stadtbild und Ideologi: die Monumentalisierung hispanischer Städte zwischen Republik und Kaiserzeit*. Munich: Verlag der Bayerischen Akademie der Wissenschaften.

Wallace-Hadrill, A. 1994. *Houses and society in Pompeii and Herculaneum*. Princeton: Princeton University Press.

REFERENCES

Wallace-Hadrill, A. 1995. 'Public honour and private shame: the urban texture of Pompeii'. In T. J. Cornell and K. Lomas (eds.) *Urban society in Roman Italy.* London: UCL Press. 39–62.

Wallace-Hadrill, A. 1998. 'The villa as cultural symbol'. In A. Frazer (ed.) *The Roman villa: villa urbana.* Philadelphia: University of Pennsylvania Museum. 43–53.

Ward-Perkins, J. B. 1970. 'From Republic to Empire: reflections on the early provincial architecture of the Roman west', *Journal of Roman Studies,* 60: 1–19.

Webster, G. 1988. 'Wroxeter (Viroconium)'. In G. Webster (ed.) *Fortress into city: the consolidation of Roman Britain, first century AD.* London: Batsford. 120–144.

Webster, G. 1993. 'The city of Viroconium (Wroxeter): its military origins and expansion under Hadrian'. In S. J. Greep (ed.) *Roman towns: the Wheeler inheritance. A review of fifty years research.* London: Council for British Archaeology Research Report 93. 50–55.

Webster, J. 1995a. '*Interpretatio*: Roman word power and Celtic gods', *Britannia,* 26: 153–161.

Webster, J. 1995b. 'Translation and subjection: *interpretatio* and the Celtic gods'. In J. D. Hill and C. G. Cumberpatch (eds.) *Different Iron Ages. Studies on the Iron Age in temperate Europe.* British Archaeological Reports International Series 602. 175–181.

Webster, J. 1997a. 'A negotiated syncretism: readings on the development of Romano-Celtic religion'. In D. J. Mattingly (ed.) *Dialogues in Roman imperialism: power, discourse, and discrepant experience in the Roman empire.* Journal of Roman Archaeology Supplementary Series 23. 165–84.

Webster, J. 1997b. 'Necessary comparisons: a post-colonial approach to religious syncretism in the Roman provinces', *World Archaeology,* 28.3: 324–338.

Webster, J. 1999. 'At the end of the world: Druidic and other revitalization movements in post-conquest Gaul and Britain', *Britannia,* 30: 1–20.

Webster, J. 2001. 'Creolizing the Roman provinces', *America Journal of Archaeology,* 105.2: 209–225.

Webster, J. 2003, 'Art as resistance and negotiation'. In S. Scott and J. Webster (eds.) *Roman Imperialism and provincial art.* Cambridge: Cambridge University Press. 24–51.

Whittaker, C. R. 1994. *Frontiers of the Roman empire: a social and economic study.* Baltimore: Johns Hopkins University Press.

Whittaker, C. R. 1995. 'Integration of the early Roman west: the example of Africa'. In J. Metzler, M. Millett, N. Roymans and J. Slofstra (eds.) *Integration in the early Roman west. The role of culture and ideology.* Luxembourg: Dossiers d'Archéologie du Musée National d'Histoire et d'Art IV. 19–32.

Whittaker, C. R. 1997. 'Imperialism and culture: the Roman initiative'. In D. J. Mattingly (ed.) *Dialogues in Roman imperialism: power, discourse, and discrepant experience in the Roman empire.* Journal of Roman Archaeology Supplementary Series 23. 143–63.

Wiedemann, T. 1992. *Emperors and gladiators.* London: Routledge.

Williams, T. 1993. *Public buildings in the south-west quarter of Roman London. The archaeology of Roman London, volume 3.* Council for British Archaeology Research Report 88.

Williamson, C. 1987. 'Monuments of bronze: Roman legal documents on bronze tablets', *Classical Antiquity*, 6: 160–83.

Willis, S. 1997. 'Samian: beyond dating'. In K. Meadows, C. Lemke and J. Heron (eds.) *TRAC96. Proceedings of the sixth annual Theoretical Roman Archaeology Conference, Sheffield 1996.* Oxford: Oxbow Books. 38–54.

Wilkes, J. 1996 'The status of Londinium'. In J. Bird, M. Hassall and H. Sheldon (eds.) *Interpreting Roman London. Papers in memory of Hugh Chapman.* Oxford: Oxbow Monograph 58. 27–31.

Wilson Jones, M. 1989. 'Designing the Roman Corinthian order', *Journal of Roman Archaeology*, 2: 35–69.

Wilson Jones, M. 2000. *Principles of Roman architecture.* New Haven: Yale University Press.

Wood, S. E. 1999. *Imperial women: a study in public images, 40BC-AD68.* Leiden: Brill.

Woodward, A. 1992. *Shrines and sacrifice.* London: Batsford/English Heritage.

Woodward, P. and Woodward, A. 2004. 'Dedicating the town: urban foundation deposits in Roman Britain', *World Archaeology*, 36.1: 68–86.

Woolf, G. 1994. 'Power and the spread of writing in the West'. In A. K. Bowman and G. Woolf (eds.) *Literacy and power in the ancient world.* Cambridge: Cambridge University Press. 84–98.

Woolf. G. 1995. 'The formation of Roman provincial cultures'. In J. Metzler, M. Millett, N. Roymans and J. Slofstra (eds.) *Integration in the early Roman west. The role of culture and ideology.* Luxembourg: Dossiers d'Archéologie du Musée National d'Histoire et d'Art IV. 9–18.

Woolf, G. 1997. 'Beyond Romans and natives', *World Archaeology*, 28.3: 339–350.

Woolf, G. 1998. *Becoming Roman: the origins of provincial civilization in Gaul.* Cambridge: Cambridge University Press.

Woolf, G. 2000. 'The religious history of the northwest provinces', *Journal of Roman Archaeology*, 13: 615–630.

Yegül, F. 1992. *Baths and bathing in Classical Antiquity.* Cambridge, Mass.: MIT Press.

Yule, B. 2005. *A prestigious Roman building complex on the Southwark waterfront: excavations at Winchester Palace, London, 1983–90.* Museum of London Monograph 23. Museum of London Archaeology Service and English Heritage.

Yule, B. and Rankov, B. 1998. 'Legionary soldiers in third century Southwark'. In B. Watson (ed.) *Roman London: recent archaeological work.* Journal of Roman Archaeology Supplementary Series 24. 67–77.

Zanker, P. 1988. *The power of the images in the age of Augustus*. Translated by Alan Shapiro. Ann Arbor: University of Michigan Press.

Zanker, P. 1998. *Pompeii: public and private life*. Translated by Deborah Lucas Schneider. Cambridge, Mass.: Harvard University Press.

Zanker, P. 2000. 'The city as symbol: Rome and the creation of an urban image'. In E. Fentress (ed.) *Romanization and the city: creation, transformations, and failures*. Journal of Roman Archaeology Supplementary Series 38. 25–41.

Zoll, A. L. 1995. 'A view through inscriptions: the epigraphic evidence for religion at Hadrian's Wall'. In J. Metzler, M. Millett, N. Roymans and J. Slofstra (eds.) *Integration in the early Roman west. The role of culture and ideology*. Luxembourg: Dossiers d'Archéologie du Musée National d'Histoire et d'Art IV. 129–137.

INDEX

CPSIA information can be obtained
at www.ICGtesting.com
Printed in the USA
LVOW10s1806141117
556264LV00014B/289/P